COOKING MEAT

A BUTCHER'S GUIDE
TO CHOOSING, BUYING,
CUTTING, COOKING,
AND EATING MEAT

PETER SANAGAN

appetite
by RANDOM HOUSE

Appetite by Random House® and colophon are registered trademarks
of Penguin Random House LLC.

Library and Archives Canada Cataloguing in Publication is available
upon request.
ISBN: 978-0-525-61034-2
eBook ISBN: 978-0-525-61035-9

Photography by Peter Chou
Book and cover design by Leah Springate
Illustrations by Doras Creative
Images on pages 260, 280, 318, 340, and 358 are in the public domain
Printed and bound in China

Published in Canada by Appetite by Random House®,
a division of Penguin Random House Canada Limited.

www.penguinrandomhouse.ca

10   9   8   7   6   5   4   3   2   1

appetite
by RANDOM HOUSE | Penguin
Random House
Canada

For Alia and Desmond.
I am the luckiest.

Contents

INTRODUCTION

I NEVER INTENDED TO OWN A BUTCHER SHOP. Neither did I imagine that becoming a vegetarian would launch my food career. But that's exactly what happened. When I was 16, I listened to The Smiths and thought Meat really *was* Murder, so I told my parents I was done with consuming flesh. My mother, like any good parent, acknowledged my right to choose but would not make me special food. Instead, she gave me a copy of a Moosewood Restaurant cookbook and free rein in the kitchen to make my own dinner. I ate a lot of sauerkraut and cheddar sandwiches. After six months of iron deficiency and exhaustion, I finally succumbed to the pleasures of a Toronto hot dog. And the rest is history.

While the vegetarianism didn't last, my enjoyment of working in a kitchen did. I was fascinated to discover that I could take an ingredient that just happened to be in the fridge (this was before I really understood grocery shopping) and turn it into something that people thanked me for—all in the time it takes to watch two episodes of *The Simpsons*. Something about that really spoke to me in a way that nothing I was learning in high school did. Cooking was new, exciting, painful, thrilling, and *gratifying*.

Around this time my father got a contract to work in Hong Kong for two years. The family packed up, got on a plane (the first in my life), and flew for about 8,000 hours. Hong Kong is an enormous, populous, loud, bright, beautiful city. It is intense and magical, the perfect place for a 17-year-old to develop an affinity for food and cooking. What struck me most was the obvious foreignness: not only did we take ferries a lot to get around but there were also entire markets dedicated to dried seafood and tiny fishing villages that boasted seaside fish restaurants. There were fruits and vegetables I had never seen before. And there were people and foods from all over the world. If my time as a vegetarian sparked my interest in cooking, my time in Hong Kong kindled my passion for food.

By the time I returned to Toronto I knew that I wanted to try cooking professionally, and I got a job with Mövenpick, an international marketplace-style restaurant where I learned the importance of consistency, service, and building flavor. I made many dishes, but my favorite was Rösti (page 345), a fried potato cake made with parcooked potatoes that are grated and pan-fried in clarified butter until golden. Served with sour cream alongside a grilled steak, it is probably one of the most delicious potato side dishes I've ever eaten. But while I enjoyed learning how to make pastas, sauces, and rösti, and to set up and prepare their garnishes, I often looked longingly at the grill and rotisserie cooks. They were the lumberjacks of the kitchen—burly and weathered—who cooked steaks to whatever color you wanted; seasoned pork chops with special spice mixes they blended in the back kitchen and then grilled them until they were just pink around the bone; and loaded the rotisserie with ducks, quails, and pork roasts and basted them with juices that collected in the drip tray. Although I never worked that station at Mövenpick, I knew that I wanted to end up there.

I attended culinary school to learn the foundational aspects of my trade. Proper knife skills. Internationally observed terminology. Mother sauces. Pastry work. Many things I would never learn in a restaurant setting. Five days a week I went to school and five nights a week I made simple everyday European dishes such as Cassoulet (page 321), steak au poivre, and Duck Confit (page 304) at Le Sélect Bistro, an old-school French bistro. I learned how to make a sausage, using parchment paper as a "skin," and how to make a Brandy Peppercorn Sauce (page 366) consistently. I learned colors (industry speak for cooking steaks to their desired internal temperatures). I drank good beer and wine after each shift, ate a lot of frites, and slept very little. But Le Sélect Bistro was where I knew I wanted to be a chef. The food was delicious but not fussy, and everyone could enjoy it. Bistro food is happiness on a plate.

From Le Sélect I made my way to Mistura to work with Massimo Capra (affectionately known as Mass), then one of the best Italian chefs in the city. I remember watching him taste a chicken stock that was slowly simmering on the stovetop and proclaim it "fucking delicious." Seeing how obviously passionate he was about the food his kitchen was producing, especially the chicken stock—the back-bone of the kitchen and the foundation for as many as 40 dishes—I knew I wanted to work with him. I spent the next four years immersed in Italian food. I learned a lot at Mistura, but it wasn't until I traveled and worked in Italy that I truly understood how closely food is related to culture, family, and the land. Slowing down, eating with friends and family, appreciating the time you are given on this planet—these are the important things in life.

I returned to Canada with a renewed sense of why I was cooking. I changed gears and went to work at Auberge du Pommier, a fine-dining restaurant just north of Toronto. The kitchen brigade there was intense and fanatical, and I learned that food, and meat in particular, could be not only cooked wonderfully but also plated so artistically that the "wow" factor stayed with guests long after their meal was finished. The chance to take charge of a kitchen for the first time then drew me back to Mistura, where I became Chef de Cuisine. I loved creating menu items, like Flat Iron Steak with Bread Sauce and Roasted Cippolini (page 205), and executing the tried-and-true recipes Massimo had cultivated over the years. And then I had the opportunity to be the Chef at The Falls Inn in Walter's Falls. My menu was French country–influenced, and I made dishes like Pork Tenderloin Stuffed with Radicchio and Gorgonzola Cheese (page 120), Pork and Dried Fruit Terrine (page 312), and Ballotines of Chicken with Apple and Sage (page 84). I worked exclusively with the farmers in the area, and I soon realized that Torontonians were largely missing out on the remarkable quality and variety of food being produced by these small Ontario producers.

By that time, meat cooking—more than any other type of cooking—had become part of my soul. I thought about it daily, sometimes hourly. I knew I wanted to continue working closely with meat and growing my career, but I wasn't quite sure how to do it, as I didn't want to open my own restaurant. I returned to Toronto to teach culinary classes at George Brown College, all the while thinking about how to express my love of the farmland in the city. While walking through Kensington Market one day, I finally figured out my next step. Max & Son Meat Market had been serving the community for more than 50 years, but owner Solly Stern was ready for a break. And I was ready for mine. I saw the For Sale sign in the window, and within a week my decision was made: I was going to open a small butcher shop in the heart of one of the world's greatest markets and showcase exceptional Ontario meats and poultry. Easy-peasy, right?

Opening a butcher shop has taught me many things. I have learned how to butcher whole pigs, lambs, cows, and poultry properly and efficiently. I have learned how to make yield tests to determine the correct selling price of a steak. And most importantly, I have learned how necessary it is to talk to customers. By listening to them I have been able to adapt and grow my business from one store to two plus a wholesale division, and to make delicious prepared foods alongside our meats. I cook differently now because of advice and recommendations from people who have been with me since Day One. And in turn, my customers ask for advice and allow my staff and me to help them make their meals. This is a magical connection, and this book has grown out of those experiences.

But this is not just a book for my customers. Every summer my parents host a "fam-jam" at their house in a small town on Lake Huron, a.k.a. the Greatest Lake. My two sisters, one brother, various in-laws and children, aunts, uncles, and cousins descend on a three-bedroom house to talk loudly over each other, play trivia games, drink, and feast. At the last fam-jam, I had a conversation with my brother, Chris, that has stuck with me. He and his wife both have long commutes to work outside the city, and my sister-in-law doesn't always get home in time to have dinner ready for their two kids. My brother told me that at those times he wished he knew how to cook.

> **Me:** What do you mean you don't know how to cook?
> **Chris:** Yeah, I can't cook. I can make a sandwich, but cooking just eludes me.
> **Me:** What?! You're 36 years old. You don't know how to cook anything?
> **Chris:** I *want* to know how to cook. I would take classes if I could find good ones. It's just that Danielle is such a good cook and she takes care of that stuff . . .
> **Me:** And if she's not home in time for dinner you make the kids sandwiches?
> **Chris:** Yeah, they eat a lot of peanut butter sandwiches.
> **Me (shaking my head):** You really need to learn how to cook, man.

I'd been ruminating on the kind of cookbook I wanted to write for some time. I'd spent 15 years working in restaurant kitchens and working my way up from Garde Manger to Chef de Cuisine. So, as a chef, I had a bit of a desire to write an ego-driven look-how-awesome-my-food-is–type of cheffy book. However, as I've transitioned to being a butcher and owning my own butcher shop, I've developed an understanding of what my customers want in a cookbook, which is how to buy and cook different types of meats.

As a supplier of exceptional meat and poultry from small family farms in Ontario, my company has a culture of supplying excellent cuts, classic charcuterie, and delicious prepared foods to restaurants and home cooks. We also strive to provide an attentive and customized service experience. Many of my customers ask: "How do I roast a chicken?" or "What do you do with oxtail?" Others ask: "How was this chicken raised?" or "Is this meat organic?" Still others ask: "If I buy a whole chicken, can you cut it up for me?" These are the kind of questions that have driven my desire to write this cookbook. I want people to feel more comfortable choosing, buying, cooking, and eating meat—whether they're preparing basic recipes (the best hamburger recipe, page 222) or more challenging ones (Beef Eye of Round Roast with Mustard Sauce, page 230). Above all, this book is designed to be approachable: it is a cookbook about meat, written for my brother who can't cook. Yet.

HOW TO USE THIS BOOK

CONSIDER THIS BOOK a guide to buying, handling, cutting, and cooking meat, one that focuses on butchery you can do at *home*, followed by recipes that everyone can enjoy. My dream would be that if you are a meat eater, you will become a meat cook after reading this book. Maybe you already know how to cook, but you want to know a good way to break down a whole chicken. That's here (page 23). Maybe you don't eat meat, but you eat fish and you're looking for a spot-on Herb Pesto to go with a roasted sea bass. That's definitely here too (page 371). Maybe you don't eat any meat products at all and think this book is terrible. That's ok, just use it to hold up your box spring because your bedframe is broken—but remember, meat eaters helped you get a good night's sleep.

Whole animal butchery, except for poultry, is something that most people will never have the means or desire to do at home. So I'm not going to be detailing how to break down a whole steer, especially if you just want to use the sirloin. Instead, this book will show you where the muscles are on a carcass, and in some cases explain step by step how to break them down to recipe-sized cuts. I find the best way to describe where muscles are on an animal is by actually comparing them to the muscles on our bodies (i.e., shoulder to shoulder, belly to belly). Humans (a.k.a. long pigs) share a similar musculature to pigs, steers, lambs, and goats. Once you understand where the muscle is, you can sort out the best method of cooking it. Meat cooking is a language many of us have forgotten how to speak and, in most cases, never even learned in the first place. Even in restaurants where butchery was once commonly practiced, most of the steaks, chops, cutlets, and sausages you order are now purchased already portioned. I know of only a handful of restaurants that bring in whole animals and butcher them, and they're only able to do it because they have ever-changing menus, which means they can create dishes to use all parts of the animal. Having said that, you shouldn't have to go to a restaurant to get a great meat dish. Use this book to learn a bit about how to buy meat, locate a knowledge-able butcher, and you can create your own delicious meat dishes at home.

BUYING MEAT

WHEN I FIRST OPENED SANAGAN'S MEAT LOCKER, I was on a serious budget. Instead of finding a good interior designer to decorate the store, I went to the City of Toronto Archives and purchased old photos of butcher shops in Ontario, framed and hung them. These photos showed the types of shops that I imagined my grandmother went to. I'm sure she had a guy for everything she needed. The fishmonger would have helped her select a nice snapper. (She probably looked for clear eyes and, when seeing a bit of cloudiness, refused. The fishmonger would have pleaded with her, but to no gain—her family had standards!). At the produce store, she would have picked up a potato, inspected it for eyes and bruises, then reamed the grocery clerk out because they were way too expensive, before relenting and getting them anyway. And then she went to the butcher.

Knowing my grandmother, I imagine the conversation at the butcher shop was less of a discussion, and more of an interrogation. She would want to know where the beef came from, and why prices had increased. She would direct the butcher on how she wanted her chicken cleaned, and she would have wanted to smell her stewing beef for freshness. All of this was important to make sure her high standards were met. And once the butcher earned her trust, going forward there would be (slightly) less interrogation.

This back-and-forth conversation occurred every couple of days, sometimes daily, because she always cooked meat the day she bought it. Obviously most of us don't shop like that anymore, but it certainly doesn't hurt to take shopping lessons from the matriarchs of times past.

You may have watched your parents or grandparents pick up packages of meat from the grocery store, mix them with premade spices and sauces, and throw them in the oven or on the barbecue without thinking too much about it. But today there's a new generation of people rediscovering and revitalizing the arts of farming and butchery. It's a great time to build relationships with your local growers and suppliers so you can ask questions, much like my grandmother did.

TALK TO YOUR BUTCHER

I cannot stress how important it is to buy meat and poultry from someone who knows what they're selling. Meat is often the most expensive part of a meal (and for many, the focus of the entire menu); therefore, you should be able to ask a simple question like "Where is the meat from?" and get a clear answer. This doesn't mean that your butcher needs to have a PhD in butchery, but knowing the answer shows they're interested in and proud of the product they're selling.

Ask for Recommendations

"If I really wanted to make money," I sometimes joke with my staff, "I would just sell burgers, sausages, ground beef, and boneless, skinless chicken breasts." While there's nothing wrong with these top sellers, I like to have a good variety of other cuts on hand. Not all grocers or butcher shops can carry as large a selection as we do, though, so do ask for a good substitute if the item you're looking for isn't available. They don't have blade roast? Try the brisket. No bavette, you say? Why not have a flank steak? Be flexible and work with what the butcher has in their shop. You might just discover a new favorite cut.

Ask for Special Items

A good butcher will be able to accommodate almost any request, subject to the season and local availability. Let's say that for your birthday you got a copy of *Odd Bits* by Jennifer McLagan and, while flipping through it, you come across a sweetbreads recipe you want to try. Butchers don't usually showcase these organ meats in their display case, because their shelf-life is notoriously short, but they should be able to source some for you—or at the very least ask their supplier.

LOOK FOR A CLEAN, WELL-ORGANIZED CASE

Good butchers are very proud of their display cases. They should be neat and easy to navigate, with the names of the cuts as well as the prices prominently displayed. A case where pork chops spill onto the sausages and striploin steaks are butted closely against rib eyes makes it both difficult for customers to find what they're looking for and, worse, increases the risk of cross-contamination among the various cuts.

USE YOUR EYES AND NOSE

Sight and smell are the best tools to use to test if meat is fresh. In general, meat and poultry should have an attractive and appetizing look. They should also have a clean smell. So should the shop. Meat, and the shops in which meat is sold, should smell clean and slightly minerally, if indeed they smell at all. What you're *looking* for depends on the meat:

Meat	Signs of freshness
Chicken	Pinkish-white skin, and either pink meat in the breast or deeper rose in the leg. Avoid sour-smelling poultry, which indicates that it's past its prime.
Pork	Light pink flesh. Avoid gray pork, which can indicate oldness.
Lamb	Rosy with a slight smell of damp grass. Avoid gray-green lamb and a strong gamey smell, which indicates the cuts have been sitting around too long. Lamb also tends to get quite tacky when it is old.
Beef (not dry aged)	Bright red flesh (just cut) or slightly gray (lightly oxidized). If the meat has oxidized, ask to smell it for freshness. If it's wrapped in plastic and you're unsure/unable to assess its quality, pass.
Dry-aged Beef	More of a burgundy color than fresh meat, perhaps with a bit of gray around the edges, and a smell like a good cheese. Any shop that ages its own beef should have no problem with you wanting to "smell the funk."

DEFINITIONS

Navigating the numerous claims and statements you see on meat labels can be super challenging. Here are simple explanations of the most commonly used terms, so you can break through the rhetoric and understand what you're buying.

100% Grass-Fed Beef

100% grass-fed beef has been raised exclusively on fresh grass, hay (dried grass), and silage (fermented grass). True 100% grass-fed beef has never had grains, potatoes, fruit, vegetables, or anything else introduced into its diet. Grass-fed beef is generally leaner meat that provides greater health benefits, in particular for the cardiovascular system. It is much higher in omega-3 fatty acids and conjugated linoleic acid than grain-fed beef, and much lower in monounsaturated fat. Also, it has an almost herbaceous flavor, which is a nice change from the sweetness of corn- and grain-fed beef.

Certified Organic

Meat that has been approved and certified by the organic body where you are shopping: in Canada, this means the Canadian Food Inspection Agency (CFIA), and in the U.S., the United States Department of Agriculture (USDA). While organic standards can vary internationally, generally speaking any food products labeled organic have been raised according to farming practices that promote ecological balance and conserve biodiversity. Certification adds to the cost of doing business for farmers, which in turn means a higher price point for consumers. However, certification ensures that the meat you're buying meets the regulatory standards, and the associated high level of scrutiny and accountability that accompany them.

Free-Run, Free-Range, and Pastured

These three terms are regularly applied to chicken and egg products, but they describe quite different husbandry methods. *Free-run* chickens are raised in barns, but are not caged or penned. They're free to run around. *Free-range* chickens are also raised in barns, but they must have free access to the outdoors, via a door or gate, and spaces to roost in the barns. Egg-laying hens tend to stay inside, near their roosts, but they have the option to go outside if they so desire. *Pastured* chickens, on the other hand, are raised in large moveable cage-like structures typically made from chicken wire, or a similar material, to protect the birds. These pens are rotated throughout a farmer's pasture to ensure the birds have access to new areas to forage for delicious worms, bugs, and the like. If your chicken is not labeled with any of these three categories, you're more than likely getting a conventional product, which can mean birds raised in battery cages and feed that may be laced with antibiotics. This meat may be the cheapest option, but it is a terrible life for the animal and a terrible "food" to put into your body.

Grade A, AA, AAA, or Prime

Beef is graded based on the marbling visible on the carcass, and AAA and prime beef are the most prized because they have the most marbling. However, the beef in all these categories has a bright red rib-eye muscle with at least 2 mm ($\frac{1}{10}$ inch) of fat. Note that 100% grass-fed beef is rarely graded, to avoid confusing consumers.

Meats highly marbled with fat are prized for their flavor. However, lean beef does not equal bad beef, and some recipes require a lean cut. A lean piece of AA beef could very well be ideal for making beef tartare, for example. Additionally, most beef from Italy and France, two of the most iconic food countries in the world, is also the leanest in the world. Which explains the heavy use of sauces when serving steaks over there . . .

Grain-Fed/Corn-Fed/Grain-Finished Beef

Grain-fed beef has been raised mainly on pasture, but has been fed a mix of grains, soy, and corn in the last three or more months of its life to promote fattening and marbling. Grain (and particularly corn) are high-energy carbohydrates that animals love to eat and that make them deliciously fatty. Grain-fed beef fat has a sweet flavor and a velvety texture, and it's considered the beef of choice in North America.

Kosher

Kosher meat refers to meat that conforms to Jewish dietary regulations, and must only be from the forequarters (front half of the animal, from the rib to the shoulder) of ruminant land animals that have cloven hooves such as beef, goat, sheep/lamb, oxen, and deer. Some domesticated fowl are also permitted, like chicken, turkey, goose, and quail. The meat must prepared by a person certified in kosher slaughtering and butchery, and needs to be soaked in order to remove any traces of blood before cooking.

Halal

Halal (translated as "lawful") refers to foods that Islamic followers are allowed to eat as part of their religious beliefs. This excludes pork meat and its by-products, but includes most other farmed meat as long as it has been slaughtered in Allah's name and is processed according to Islamic law. Many lamb farmers and processors are being certified halal now, given the growing market in North America.

Raised without Antibiotics (RWA)

Meat from animals raised without antibiotics literally means no antibiotics have been administered from the time the animal was born to the time it is slaughtered.

Antibiotics are used on some farms to treat illness in animals but must be administered according to strict government protocols. By law, if animals raised in Canada and the U.S. are treated with antibiotics, they must go through a withdrawal period (which varies among species) so the medications have time to be eliminated from the animal's system before slaughtering. Animals are regularly and randomly tested after they've been slaughtered to be sure they're safe for you to eat. Violators are subject to stiff fines and their products are removed from the market.

Raised without the Use of Added Hormones

All animals, including humans, have hormones (ask any 13-year-old boy how he's managing those . . .), so packagers are not legally allowed to claim that meats are hormone-free. Beef producers can claim that an animal has been "raised without the use of added hormones," as long as that statement is true.

Growth hormones are not legally allowed in pork or poultry production in Canada or the U.S., so all poultry and pork has been raised without the use of added hormones. Additionally, in Canada, growth hormones are not used in the raising of lambs. However, many conventional beef producers use bovine growth hormones to promote speedy muscle growth because, hey, faster meat equals less-expensive meat. It is up to you to decide if this is a good or bad thing for you. My personal belief is that animals need time to grow in order for them to have the best life possible—and to develop the best flavor.

Regular, Medium, Lean, and Extra Lean
Ground meats—whether beef, pork, or lamb—are classified according to how much fat they contain. Regular means a maximum of 30% fat; medium, 23%; lean, 17%; and extra lean, 10%. Generally speaking, lean ground meat will do for just about all recipes—unless you're making sausage. In that case, the fattier the better!

PREPARING MEAT

CUTTING AND COOKING MEAT has become a bit of a lost skill. Many of my friends and family don't have the foggiest clue how to roast something as basic as a whole chicken, let alone how to butcher it. Yet, knowing how to cook meat is what separates humans from other animals. That's just basic evolution.

One reason that many people are reluctant to prepare meat is that it's foreign to them. We have grown accustomed to buying processed cuts from grocery stores that require very little thought about how to cook them. We choose meat that is already tender, already seasoned, and essentially all ready for the pan, with the result that a whole pork butt might scare the average cook. Most shoppers want to know how to choose meat and then have their butchers do the dirty work, like pounding, dicing, skinning, etc. And the reality is that you aren't really going to do a lot of butchering meat at home. As a general rule, you should let the pros do the majority of your work. *However,* it is very good to know the basics of butchery so that you can do simple tasks like breaking down chicken into different cuts, boning out a lamb shoulder for a stew, or cleaning the silverskin from a beef tenderloin. Why? Price, baby, price!

You see, every time a butcher puts a knife to a piece of meat, you, the shopper, are going to pay for it. You have to pay for the butcher's time, as well as for the "waste" they are removing. So it might be a good time to step back, breathe deeply, learn a new skill that requires using your hands, and save a few bucks at the same time. Having said that, don't be discouraged if you "eff it up" the first few times. It happens. To get really comfortable at butchery, you have to get your hands familiar with the task, and that can take time. It usually takes novices about an hour to debone a 50-pound case of chicken legs; my trained butchers do it in 18 minutes, and some even faster than that. It takes a lot of practice and a lot of chicken legs to become a professional.

Luckily, when you're at home deboning four chicken legs for fried chicken, you have the luxury of time. Go slowly and make sure you're doing it properly, and there's less chance you'll eff it up. I've included some simple butchery tasks specific to the animals in each chapter to get you started. And before you begin, here are some more general points to keep in mind as you wield your cleaver.

GETTING DIRTY

If you want to get comfortable cooking meat, touching it is important. I'm not saying you need to work in an abattoir for a day (although visiting one should be on the bucket list of any meat eater), but you do need to be comfortable and confident about touching raw meat. I know many people are squeamish about this, but you can get over that pretty quickly, especially if you follow a few guidelines:

- **Get a few pairs of latex gloves** (or non-latex, if you're allergic) from the drugstore. I commonly wear tight-fitting gloves when butchering. I find it's the easiest and fastest way to keep my hands clean and dry while handling meat.
- **Wash your hands regularly** with soap and hot water if you are not wearing gloves.
- **Make sure your knives are sharp**. Sharp knives prevent accidents!

GETTING CLEAN

It's also important to know how to clean up after you've touched meat. The number one cause of food-borne illness is cross-contamination. Sanitation is a huge part of butchery and cooking, and the cleaner and more organized you can keep your kitchen, the safer you will keep your friends and family. In the kitchen, a little soap and hot water go a long way. Young cooks in restaurants have the phrase "clean as you go" drilled into their heads. Keep the following tips in mind when cleaning up while you work:

- **Clean your cutting board and work bowls** with hot water and soap as soon as you've finished working with them. Hot water and soap are sufficient for cleaning, but at the butcher shop we go the extra step by creating a bleach-water solution for sanitizing. One capful (about 2 Tbsp/30 mL) of bleach in a quart of hot water is a good mix to use when wiping down your work station and equipment while you work with raw meat, especially if you're working with a lot of it.
- **Clean your tools as well!** Knives and spoons must be thoroughly cleaned between each job. I have seen bits of chicken get stuck around the handle of a knife after it's been used to cut up a bird, then go straight into chopping up lettuce for a salad. Not good, people!

A Note on Rinsing Meat

Over the years I have often been asked: "Should I rinse the meat before cooking it?" I never came across this habit while working in restaurants, but I've since learned that many people do this at home. They will buy a chicken, for example, and rinse it well under cold, running water before starting a recipe.

After doing a bit of research, I've discovered that rinsing meat, whether with water or a vinegar-based solution, is common practice in some parts of the world. In places where local butchery methods leave more bone fragments on the cut than are desired, running water is one of the easiest ways to get those fragments off your meat. In places where meat is hung in open-air markets and attracts pests, I would want to rinse that meat before cooking it as well.

However, in North America we rarely have to be concerned about these issues, so my recommendation is that you don't need to rinse or wash the meat. *Ever.* In fact, when you rinse, you are potentially and unintentionally spreading any bacteria that may have been on the meat. Washing meat does not get rid of bacteria, but the heat from cooking will.

GETTING ORGANIZED

In cooking school, there are a few things you have to learn in your first week or two. You need to learn how to hold a knife and tie an apron and look professional, and you need to understand the importance of prepping your station. You don't even get to *look* at a stove until you've practiced these core elements of professional cooking. And really, all these skills are equally useful for the home cook. Even tying an apron. (The key is to wrap the strings around your back and tie the knot around your belly. It turns your apron strings into a "belt" through which you can tuck a kitchen towel. Pro move on a first date.)

Every time I cook, I think about setup—or mise en place—first. *Mise en place* is French for "in its place" and just like the Radiohead song "Everything in Its Right Place," it means having everything for a recipe—from the right cooking pot to a finely chopped onion—set up and ready to go at your fingertips. It's a habit that will lead to faster meal prep times, a cleaner kitchen, and less stress. To put it very simply, if you learn to set up your station, every meal you make going forward will be better than it is now: it might taste the same, but you will be more relaxed, able to interact with people while cooking, and confident about not screwing up a recipe ever again.

Almost every ingredients list has a preparation method for the ingredients. For example, it might say "1 onion, finely chopped," or "2 pounds boneless, skinless pork shoulder, cut in 2-inch cubes." If you already prepare all your ingredients before you start cooking, you know how to do mise en place. What most recipes don't tell you is that you should also always do a few other things before you start.

Set Up Your Kitchen Like a Pro

- **Make sure your kitchen is clean and tidy before you start cooking.** That will make it easier to find everything you need.
- **Secure your cutting board.** To prevent the board from sliding on the counter, dampen a tea towel and set it under the cutting board.
- **Place a work bowl nearby for "trim,"** such as vegetable peelings, unwanted skin and fat from the meat, or even foil wrappers from butter.
- **Keep a couple of clean and dry folded kitchen towels handy.** Use these towels to wipe up spills, hold a hot tray, dry off meat before searing it . . . Their uses are endless.
- **Set a baking tray beside you.** Use it to hold prepared cuts of meat while you prepare other ingredients or get ready to cook them.
- **Chop, prepare, and gather all of your ingredients before you start cooking.** If you have everything ready to go, there will be less scrambling while you're cooking.

If you choose to ignore this advice, you can still cook every recipe in the book. However, following this advice will prevent you from having to exclaim: "DAMMIT, I FORGOT TO CHOP THE CARROTS AND THE ONIONS ARE ALREADY BURNING AND WHY IS THE OVEN OFF AND THE BEEF IS STILL IN THE FREEZER AND WHY IS MY SON CRYING AND WHERE'S MY DRINK?"

GETTING KNIFE SKILLS

Knife skills may sound like a cool indie rock band, but it means the ability to cut anything properly, efficiently, and cleanly, without slicing off a digit. Here are a few pointers for acquiring both cooking knife skills and butchery knife skills.

Know Your Tools

Like many chefs and butchers, I have a fondness for knives. I see them not only as useful tools for getting dinner on the table but also true works of art. The best knives are made by craftspeople who have spent their lives dedicated to creating the strongest and sharpest tools, but you don't need a collection of super-expensive, elite knives to make any of the recipes in this book. Restaurant supply stores sell reasonably priced knives designed to take a beating in the kitchen while retaining their sharp edge (restaurateurs are cheap!). I recommend having the following knives on hand:

- **Chef's knife** (also called a French knife): The standard large kitchen knife that does the lion's share of the work. I prefer an 8-inch blade.
- **Boning knife:** A knife with a flexible blade that's essential if you're doing butchery at home. I prefer a blade with medium flexibility for best control. To test the flexibility, turn the blade on its side and press down lightly on a tabletop or counter while holding the handle of the knife. It should give a little bit.
- **Paring knife:** The best knife for small work, like coring a tomato or peeling garlic.
- **Serrated knife:** The knife for cutting bread. Remember, it only cuts bread.
- **Slicer knife:** The best tool for carving roasts, from a roasted turkey to a top sirloin, because it makes long, clean cuts. If you don't have one, a chef's knife makes a fine substitute.
- **Honing steel** (also called a sharpening steel): The long, stick-like rod of steel, ceramic, or diamond-coated steel used to realign the knife's edge. Learn the best way to use one by watching videos online, and get comfortable enough with it to maintain your knife's edge.

Keep Your Knives Sharp

A sharp knife is your friend. A dull knife will slip on whatever you are cutting and cut you instead. To keep your knife sharp, either sharpen it yourself using a whetstone and an online tutorial or call a hardware store or kitchen supply store to find a sharpening service. The second option is more expensive, but you only need to do it a few times a year. In addition, using a honing steel to maintain that sharp edge will benefit your blade and help you avoid mistakes.

Hold Your Knife with Confidence

Hold the knife as if it were an extension of your arm.

- **For a chef's knife:** tightly pinch the heel of the knife between your thumb and the second joint of your index finger, then curl your hand around the handle. This grip guards against the knife slipping out of your hand. Next, hold the knife so the meatiest part of your index finger rests on the top, dull part of the blade ("the spine"). That's how close you want to be to the action for best control.
- **If you're butchering meat from the bone:** hold a boning knife with the blade pointing downwards and facing you. Holding the knife like this is more ergonomic and gives you more control as you cut through larger cuts of meat. If you're not butchering larger cuts of meat, I don't recommend holding your knife like this—you could get arrested.
- **Learn how to "rock" the knife:** When using a chef's knife, get used to rocking the blade on the tip of the edge, where the knife curves toward the point. This is

not only ergonomic, it will also help you gain speed. You should be using the back half of the blade edge to cut.

How to Avoid the Emergency Room

- **Keep your free hands away from the blade edge.** This sounds like a no-brainer, but most kitchen and butchery accidents result from people working very quickly, with their hands in compromising positions, and slipping. A sharp knife can cut through skin and into bone in no time.

- **Use your free fingers to protect yourself.** Get used to holding the product in your free hand as if you were typing on a keyboard or playing piano. Now turn your hand toward the knife, which should be pointing down toward your cutting board. As you cut, your free fingers will both control the product and create a "wall" that your knife can't pass through.

- **When walking with a knife:** hold it down to your side, parallel to your leg. Hold it a little loosely, so that if you trip, you can quickly release the knife to the floor.

- **If you drop a knife, don't try to catch it:** While trying to catch falling babies is awesome, it's a bad idea when it comes to knives.

Here's a helpful tip: You will cut yourself if you cook regularly. Just get over it. Keep some bandages close by. You will definitely also burn yourself. Have fun out there!

BASIC BUTCHERY TECHNIQUES

TRUSSING

It is important to know how to truss a bird because this technique ensures that the bird will cook evenly and the breast won't dry out while roasting. Here is a simple method that works.

1. Place the chicken, breast side up, on a work surface with the legs facing you.

2. Cut a length of kitchen twine that loops around your elbow and just back to your hand.

3. Tuck the wings underneath the body of the bird, so it looks like it's doing the chicken dance at a wedding.

4. Loop the twine around the top of the breasts, bring each side of the twine over the wings, and then cross it over through the gap between the thigh and the breast.

5. Cross the legs so the "ankles" are on top of each other, then loop each length of twine around the ankles. Tie a tight knot—as you do so, the legs will pull in toward the breasts, and the chicken will become a uniform little football.

TEN-CUT

This essential skill allows you to buy a whole chicken and break it down yourself, which gives you more value for money than purchasing the bird in individual pieces. It also allows you to cut the chicken into evenly sized portions, which a lot of recipes require. And it allows you to quickly roast a whole chicken in individual pieces so you don't have to worry about trussing or carving. As the name implies, you will end up with 10 evenly sized pieces of chicken.

1. Place a whole chicken on a cutting board in a seated position, with the backbone facing you.

2. Using a sharp boning knife, cut down one side of the backbone, keeping your knife close to the spine. Your knife will slide through the rib cage and go through the joint that connects the thigh bone to the backbone. Repeat on the other side. Save the backbone for making soup or stock.

3. Lay the bird flat on its breast, then split it right down the center, through the breast bone.

4. Separate the leg from the breast on each half.

5. Separate the drumstick from the thigh by cutting through the joint. Repeat with the other drumstick.

6. Set a chicken breast on the cutting board in front of you. Separate the wing where it meets the breast and then cut the breast in half along its equator. Repeat with the other breast.

SPATCHCOCKING

Spatchcocking is an essential skill to have in your repertoire if you like a crispy pan-fried whole bird, or if you're grilling the meat on the barbecue under a brick, like they do in Tuscany. I like to spatchcock the bird so the breast is boneless, but you can cheat and just butterfly the chicken, leaving the breast bone in. This alternative prevents the breast from drying out during cooking; however, the eating experience is elevated with the breast bone out.

1. Place the chicken on a work surface, breast side down, legs toward you.

2. Run your knife along each side of the backbone, slowly revealing the rib cage. Separate the backbone from the thigh bone at the joint.

3. Turn the chicken around so that the legs are facing away from you. Using your fingers, locate the wishbone at the top of the breast. Use the point of your knife to loosen and remove the wishbone. Separate the backbone from the wing bone at the joint.

4. Turn the chicken around again, so the legs are facing you. Working close to the bone, slowly separate the rib cage from the breast meat. Eventually you will get to the soft cartilage at the center of the two breasts. Repeat the cutting on the other side of the breast. When you reach the soft cartilage again, gently pull the carcass away from the meat. There may be a little residual cartilage, but don't mind that.

5. Remove the wing tips and lightly score the meat on the underside of the thigh. This will help with even cooking.

DEBONING CHICKEN LEGS

An easy home butchery task, this cut is essential if you're making a ballotine (page 84). Boneless chicken legs are also a hot seller to restaurants who make fried chicken, especially if they offer sandwiches. You can easily substitute boneless leg meat in the Fried Chicken (page 71), slap it between a couple of slices of Texas toast with a few pickles, and bingo bongo—you've got yourself a tasty treat!

1. Lay the chicken leg on a work surface, skin side down.

2. Starting from the end of the thigh bone, score the meat along the bone all the way down to the end "knuckle" of the drumstick.

3. Using the point of your knife, separate the meat from either side of the thigh bone. Expose the whole bone, then use your fingers to pinch around it. Use your knife to scrape the meat away from the thigh bone, working toward the end of the thigh. Finally, release the thigh bone.

4. Use the same technique to release the drumstick bone. Afterward, you'll be left with two bones jutting awkwardly out of the meat but still attached at the joint.

5. Carefully cut around the joint to separate the bone from the meat. You want to ensure that you remove all cartilage but not cut through the skin. Sounds easy enough, but I've witnessed a ton of junior butchers screw up this part.

CARVING WHOLE POULTRY

This tried-and-true technique applies to pretty much all birds, but you'll use it most for chicken and turkey. Keep in mind that the bird will be hot when you carve it, so handle it with a folded tea towel to avoid burning your fingers.

1. Place the cooked chicken on a cutting board, with a clean baking sheet next to it. Get a platter ready for the carved bird. (If you're carving a large turkey, you can cut it while it's still in the roasting rack.)

2. Discard any trussing twine. Starting on one side of the bird, cut the breast away from the rib cage on either side of the breast bone. When the breast is fully hanging away from the carcass, remove it and place it on the baking sheet. Repeat with the opposite side of the bird.

3. Separate the thigh from the backbone at the joint. Your knife should easily slide between the bones once you find the right spot. Split the drumstick and the thigh by cutting through the joint; again, your knife will easily go through the joint once you've found it. You may need to move your knife a little to either side to find the sweet spot. Place the thigh and drumstick on the baking sheet, then repeat with the other leg. Arrange the drumsticks on the platter.

4. Separate the wings from the carcass and put them on the baking sheet. Save the carcass for soup or broth, if you like. Wipe your cutting board clean.

5. Return the breast to the cutting board and slice it from tip to tip. Arrange the meat beside the drumsticks.

6. Return the thighs to the cutting board and slice the meat on either side of the bone. Arrange the thigh meat and bones on the platter next to the drumsticks and breast meat.

7. Arrange the wings on the platter.

TYING A ROAST 101

This book contains many references to tying a roast. There is an excellent method for tying what's called a "butcher's knot," but it is almost impossible to describe in writing. Much like riding a bike, you have to be shown it to get it—I recommend searching for "tying a butcher's knot" online to find a video that will work for you. Having said that, I will share a trick for securing twine around any roast. And bonus—you can use this technique when tying presents with ribbon . . .

- Cut a length of twine long enough to create a loop around your meat.

- Place the roast, presentation side down, on your cutting board.

- Wiggle the center of the piece of twine to position it under the middle of the roast, and draw the two ends together over the meat.

- **Here's the tricky part:** Lace the twine together (as if you're tying your shoes), *but before tying tightly, repeat the step, adding an extra loop*, then pull as tightly as you can. This extra loop will give the knot stability while you double-knot the twine.

- Repeat to secure your roast.

COOKING MEAT

WHEN CHOOSING WHAT MEAT TO COOK FOR DINNER, most cooks start with one of two questions: "What type of meat or poultry do I want to cook?" or "What cooking method do I want to use?" The first question is somewhat simpler to answer, as many people will drift toward their preferences. Chicken is the most popular protein these days. It's less expensive than beef and leaner than pork. The answer to the second question is usually guided by the season. Summer often brings requests for "something good for the grill." Winter brings recommendations for "a good slow-cooked braise." In either case, you need to know the fundamentals of both meat theory and cooking methods. Once you have a good grasp on those, you will be able to confidently tackle any recipe, or even come up with your own. So here's a little meat theory.

MEAT CUTS: UNDERSTANDING MUSCLE MAPS

All four-legged mammals have the same basic muscle "map." Every muscle on a pig can also be found on a steer. And a lamb. And a goat. So, once you have a grasp on where a muscle is located on a pig, you know where to find the same muscle on a lamb, for example. This same theory applies to birds; chicken, duck, quail, and pheasant all have the same cuts: legs, wings, breast, etc. And now that you understand *that*, you will realize that similar cooking methods apply to similar cuts from different animals.

Working versus Nonworking Muscles

All muscles, whether they are on a bird or a mammal, can be categorized as "working" or "nonworking." Any muscles that are constantly in use are usually categorized as working. This means hind legs that keep the animal moving and hold up its backside. It also means shoulders, necks, and front legs that support the upper body and head. Muscles that aren't in constant use, like the back muscles and the flank, are categorized as nonworking. Working muscles tend to be darker in color and tougher than nonworking muscles, but the trade-off is a little more flavor.

The age of the animal comes into play as well: working muscles on a four-month-old lamb are going to be much more tender than working muscles on a two-year-old steer. But regardless of age, working muscles will always have a bit more chew than nonworking muscles. The same applies to birds. A leg is considered a working muscle and a breast is nonworking.

Different methods of cooking should be applied to working and nonworking muscles (see below). If you know how hard the muscle was working, you will know what cooking methods to apply to it. The harder a muscle works, the more collagen it develops. The more collagen, the denser its connective tissue. For that connective tissue to tenderize, the muscle must be cooked slowly at a low temperature, allowing the protein fibers to soften and yield. If you take the time to consider the muscle and how it worked on the animal, you can decide on the best cooking method.

THE PERFECT MATCH: PAIRING MEAT CUTS WITH COOKING METHODS

The chart of meat cuts and common cooking techniques on pages 30 to 35 is a handy reference tool. These recommended cooking methods are not hard-and-fast rules—you can apply different methods to many cuts of meat, and that's the fun part of cooking—but they'll get you started. Good butcher shops and meat counters will have all these cuts—and more—and later chapters describe them in greater detail. Familiarizing yourself with the common cooking terms I've used here is worth the effort for successful meat cookery (see page 36).

Cooking method	Fiber content of meat	Common fat content of meat
Roasting	Tender (nonworking)	Lean or fatty
Slow-roasting	Tough (working)	Fatty
Pan-frying	Tender (nonworking)	Lean or fatty
Sautéing	Tender (nonworking)	Lean
Braising (or stewing)	Tough (working)	Lean or fatty
Grilling	Tender (nonworking)	Lean
Poaching	Tender (nonworking)	Lean
Cold-smoking	Tough or tender (working or nonworking)	Fatty
Hot-smoking	Tough or tender (working or nonworking)	Lean or fatty
Sous vide	Tough or tender (working or nonworking)	Lean or fatty
Pressure cooking	Tough (working)	Lean or fatty

Meat Cuts

BEEF

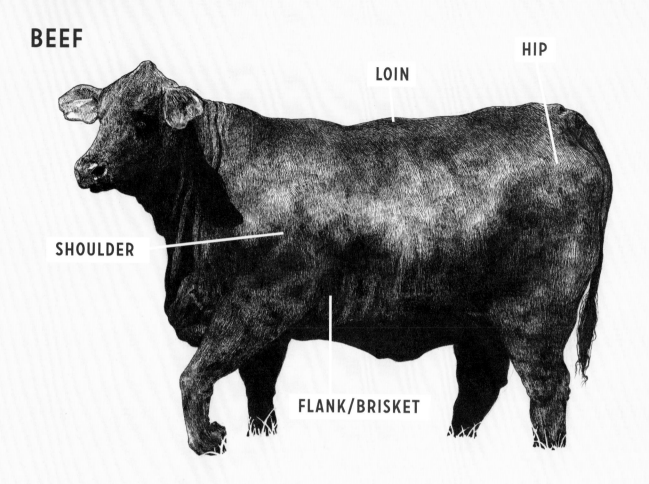

LOIN

HIP

SHOULDER

FLANK/BRISKET

PORK

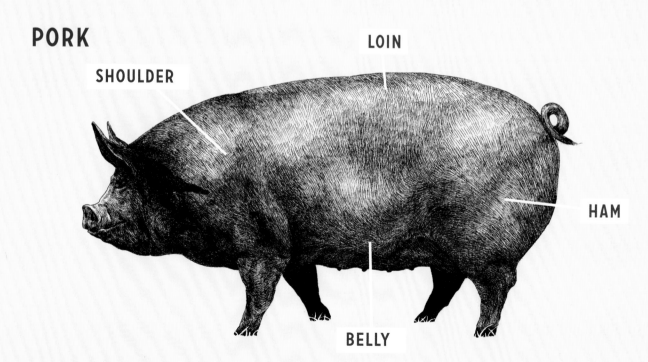

LOIN

SHOULDER

HAM

BELLY

LAMB

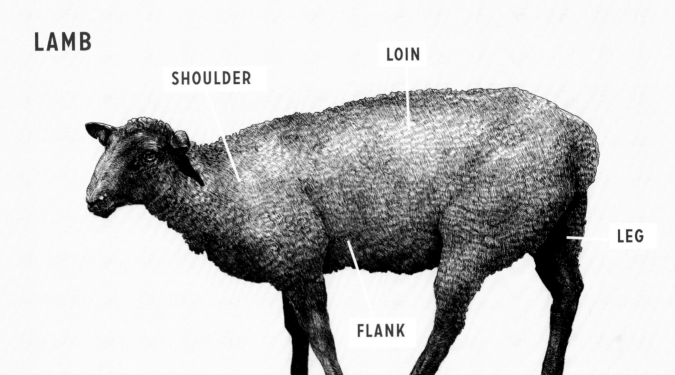

SHOULDER

LOIN

LEG

FLANK

CHICKEN

WING

BREAST

LEG

GUIDE TO PAIRING MEAT CUTS WITH COOKING TECHNIQUES

	Roast	Pan fry	Sauté	Braise	Grill	Poach	Smoke	Pressure cook	Sous vide
CHICKEN									
Whole birds	One of the essential and very versatile meats to know how to handle.								
Whole trussed	●					●	●		
Butterflied	●				●				
Spatchcocked		●							
Chicken breast	The main body of the bird, including the wing, which can be separated from the breast muscle.								
Boneless, skinless		●	●		●	●	●		
Supreme	●	●				●			
Bone-in, skin-on	●				●				
Wings	●				●		●		
Chicken leg	The well-exercised muscle that supports the bird. This flavorful meat is the preferred cut of chicken for chefs, as it lends itself to a variety of cooking methods.								
Whole leg	●			●	●	●	●	●	
Drumstick				●	●		●	●	
Bone-in thighs	●	●		●	●			●	
Boneless thighs		●	●						
PORK									
Pork shoulder	The shoulder and front leg can be sold whole. It is full of versatile muscle groups that range from tender to very tough.								
Butt	●			●	●		●	●	
Shoulder chops		●			●		●		●
Picnic shoulder	●			●			●	●	
Hock				●			●	●	
Capicollo roast	●			●			●	●	●
Pork loin	The mid-section along the backbone, these nonworking muscles are the most tender cuts.								
Rib chop		●			●		●		
Center-cut loin chops		●			●		●		
Tenderloin	●	●	●		●	●			
Rib roast	●						●		
Boneless loin roast	●						●		
Butterflied loin roast	●				●				

	Roast	Pan fry	Sauté	Braise	Grill	Poach	Smoke	Pressure cook	Sous vide
PORK continued									
Stuffed pork chops		●			●		●		
Baby back ribs	●			●	●		●		
Pork belly	The belly is tough, flavorful, and fatty.								
Belly	●			●			●		●
Bone-in belly chops			●	●			●	●	
Side ribs	●			●	●	●	●	●	
Skirt steak		●	●		●				
Thin-cut belly		●	●		●				
Ham	The whole back leg is full of lean muscles, and sold either whole-smoked, whole fresh, or cut for stew or cutlets.								
Cutlets/scaloppini		●	●						
Fresh ham roast	●			●			●	●	
Hock	●			●			●	●	●
Stew meat				●				●	
LAMB									
Lamb shoulder	Shoulder cuts are generally tough, and include the neck and foreshank.								
Boneless neck roast				●				●	
Neck medallions				●				●	
Boneless shoulder roast			●	●				●	
Stew				●				●	
Shank				●				●	
Shoulder chops				●	●			●	
Lamb loin	The nonworking muscles that run along the backbone. These cuts are the most tender and are commonly used for grilling and roasting.								
Rack	●								
Rib chops		●			●				
T-bone chops		●			●				
Sirloin roast	●		●		●				●
Lamb flank	The hardworking muscles that run from the breast to the belly. These tough bits are mostly ground or made into sausage.								
Stuffed breast roast	●			●				●	●

	Roast	Pan fry	Sauté	Braise	Grill	Poach	Smoke	Pressure cook	Sous vide
LAMB continued									
Side ribs				●				●	
Belly				●	●				
Lamb leg	The whole leg, including the back shank, which is lean and relatively tender.								
Bone-in leg roast	●				●				
Boneless leg roast	●				●				
Lamb leg steaks		●			●				
Shank				●				●	
BEEF									
Beef shoulder	Holds up the neck and head, and includes the front legs. These cuts are generally tough and well marbled.								
Blade roast				●				●	
Neck roast				●				●	
Chuck short ribs				●	●		●	●	
Shank roast/osso buco				●				●	
Ground		●	●	●				●	
Paleron				●	●			●	
Flat iron		●			●				
Petite tender		●			●				
Beef loin	The mid-section along the back bone. Loin cuts are nonworking muscles, and they are the most tender and prized for steaks, premium roasts, and dry-aged cuts.								
Rib eye		●			●				●
Bone-in rib steak					●				●
Prime rib roast	●						●		
Côtes de boeuf					●				
Striploin		●			●				●
T-bone/porterhouse		●			●				
Tenderloin		●			●	●			●
Top sirloin medallion steaks		●			●				●
Coulotte	●	●			●				●
Top sirloin roasts	●								

	Roast	Pan fry	Sauté	Braise	Grill	Poach	Smoke	Pressure cook	Sous vide
BEEF continued									
Beef flank/brisket — The mid-section from breast to lower belly. Many "butcher's steak" cuts originate from this area, which works at supporting the loin, or back. The cuts are more flavorful and less tender.									
Brisket				●			●	●	
Beef back ribs				●	●		●	●	
Skirt steak		●			●				
Bavette		●		●	●				●
Flank		●		●	●				●
Tri tip	●			●	●		●	●	
Beef hip — The whole hind leg, where the muscles are generally very lean and tough because they hold up the back of the animal.									
Eye of round	●			●	●				
Outside flat	●	●			●				
Inside round	●	●		●	●				
Sirloin tip	●	●		●	●				
Knuckle				●				●	
Shank				●				●	
Beef offal — Sometimes called variety meats, offal is organs, such as the liver and kidneys, or internal muscles, such as the heart.									
Oxtail				●				●	
Hanger steak		●			●				
Liver		●	●						
Heart		●			●		●		
Kidney		●			●				

COOKING METHODS FOR MEAT

Some of the common cooking methods below will be familiar to you, others may be less so. Each of them is fairly easy, and once you have a grasp of the basics, your cooking repertoire will suddenly surge like Uber pricing on New Year's Eve.

Braising

Braising means slow-roasting in an aromatic liquid and is commonly used on tougher, harder working cuts of meat to break down the muscle's protein fibers and make them tender. Braising smaller pieces of tough meat is known as stewing. If you've ever pot-roasted something, you know how to braise.

1. Season the meat with salt and pepper. In a large ovenproof pot, brown the meat in hot fat (e.g., olive oil). When it's brown all over, remove from the pot.

2. In the same pot, sauté some aromatic vegetables (onion, garlic, carrot, celery, etc.). Add liquid (wine, stock, water, beer, juice, etc.) and herbs to the vegetables.

3. Return the meat to the pot. Make sure it is at least three-quarters covered with liquid. Put a lid on the pot and cook it in a 300°F oven until the meat is tender.

USING HERBS AND SPICES IN BRAISES

Many braising recipes require herbs and spices to impart flavor to the dish, but rather than adding them individually and having to pick branches and seeds out of the finished dish, use one of these techniques:

HERB BUNDLE: Simply wrap a piece of kitchen twine around a few different herbs and knot it tightly to create a bundle that you can add to the cooking pot and fish out easily once the braise is done. My standard recipe is 6 sprigs thyme, 4 sprigs Italian parsley, 1 sprig rosemary, and 3 bay leaves, although you will see variations throughout the book. Used regularly in mild chicken and fish dishes.

HERB SACHET: A step above an herb bundle, a sachet also includes a few whole spices. Simply place all the ingredients in the center of a 6-inch square of cheesecloth, roll up the cheesecloth, and tie tightly with kitchen twine. My go-to recipe contains the herb bundle above plus 1 tsp whole black peppercorns and 1 whole clove, although you'll see variations throughout the book. Used regularly in most stews and braises.

SPICE BALL: When I'm making dishes that require whole spices like allspice, coriander, star anise, etc., I like to use a large tea infuser. Place the spices in the infuser, seal it, and pop it in your braise. I don't have one go-to recipe because I like to vary the spices depending on what I'm cooking. Used regularly in more heavily spiced dishes.

Grilling

Grilling means cooking on a grate over an open fire, either with "direct heat" (grilling right over the flame) or "indirect heat" (grilling away from the flame). The heat source can vary from propane, gas, or wood to my personal favorite, charcoal. Grilling is perfect for tender, leaner, nonworking cuts because fatty cuts can cause flare-ups on the grill. Any cuts that can be grilled can also be broiled, which is to say cooked under the broiler in your oven.

1. Bring the meat to room temperature. Season the meat well with salt and pepper (or marinate overnight—in which case, don't preheat the grill until ready to cook), then oil it lightly.

2. Preheat the grill—half should be high heat, half should be medium.

3. Sear the meat on the hot (direct) side of the grill, browning each side. For thicker cuts, move the meat to the indirect side of the grill and cook until the desired internal temperature is met (see page 41).

4. Rest the meat for 15 minutes before carving/serving.

Pan-Frying

Sometimes referred to as "pan-searing," cooking meat in a pan has many advantages, including preventing flare-ups, creating pan sauces, and basting the meat. It is used for lean and fatty nonworking cuts of meats; thicker cuts of meat are often transferred to the oven to finish cooking.

1. Bring the meat to room temperature. Season the meat well with salt and pepper (or marinate overnight—in which case, don't preheat the grill until ready to cook), then oil it lightly.

2. Heat an ovenproof pan over medium-high heat.

3. Sear the meat in the pan, and turn when one side is golden brown.

4. Don't overcrowd the pan, as the meat could steam and not brown.

5. For thicker cuts, transfer the pan to a 350°F oven until the desired internal temperature is met (see page 41).

6. Rest the meat for 15 minutes before carving/serving.

7. Make a quick pan sauce by deglazing the pan with a flavorful liquid (wine, beer, stock, juice, etc.), and whisking in some cold butter.

Sautéing

Sautéing means quickly cooking smaller pieces of meat in fat in a frying pan. The key to sautéing well is to keep your fat hot by not overcrowding the pan. Too much meat cools the fat down and the meat steams instead of browning. Also, flipping the meat flamboyantly while lifting the pan into the air will cool the pan down and lead to poorly sautéed meat. I like to use my wooden spoon for turning the meat and use it often.

1. Cut your meat into small pieces and season with salt and pepper.

2. Add fat (e.g., olive oil or butter) to a pan over medium-high heat.

3. Add the meat to the hot fat.

4. Stir often.

5. When the meat is golden, remove from the pan to cool before serving.

Roasting

Roasting means cooking in a hot oven without liquid and is commonly used on tender, non-working cuts of meat that are either lean or fatty. The expression "slow-roasting" generally refers to cooking at 300°F or lower, and is used for tougher, working cuts like pork shoulder. Many roasting recipes use two different temperatures: lower for the actual cooking and higher to brown the outside of the roast.

1. Note the weight of the roast. Bring the meat to room temperature. Season well with salt and pepper (or marinate overnight), then oil lightly.

2. Preheat the oven (350°F is the most common oven temperature for roasting).

3. Place the meat on an elevated rack in a roasting pan, which allows hot air to circulate around the meat and cook it more evenly. If there is no rack, elevate the roast by cooking it on top of halved onions, carrots, etc.

4. Cook the roast for an average of 20 minutes per pound, but you can play with these times based on the roast, until the desired internal temperature is met at the thickest part of the meat (see page 41). Allow to rest before carving.

Poaching

Like braising, poaching means slowly simmering meat in broth, but it's used with tender, non-working cuts of meat and requires way less cooking time. Because you aren't cooking the meat for very long, the poaching liquid needs to be flavorful. Poached meat is considered a low-calorie cooking option because it does not use additional fat.

1. Bring the meat to room temperature.

2. In a medium-sized pot, make a poaching liquid by fortifying stock or broth with added aromatics.

3. Bring the liquid to a strong simmer.

4. Gently drop your meat into the liquid and turn down the heat to a low simmer.

5. Poach the meat until the desired internal temperature is met (see page 41).

Smoking

Smoking is an old method of cooking, where the meat is "cooked" by smoke. There are two ways to smoke food: cold-smoking and hot-smoking. Cold-smoking is allowing smoke from a fire to cool off before coming in contact with the food, usually by creating the fire and smoke in one chamber and having the smoke run through a pipe or tube to a second chamber where the meat is hung or set on a rack. Most Canadian streaky bacon is prepared this way. Cold-smoking invites bacteria if it's not done safely and in a controlled environment. Hot-smoking food is safer and more common for home cooks because the fire, smoke, and meat are all in the same chamber. We refer to this method as "cooking with smoke" because you're bringing the internal temperature of the meat up to the bacteria-killing temperatures, as you do when you are roasting meat.

1. Brine your meat in a cure of 1 cup sugar, 1 cup salt, and 4 quarts water for at least 4 hours. (This will make more than enough brine for many things, such as a whole turkey or a brisket. You can store any extra brine in the freezer for up to 6 months.)

2. Start your smoker machiand then follow the manufacturer's directions. If you are using a barbecue, start by getting the temperature up to 250°F.

3. Soak some wood chips in water for 15 minutes, then place them in a smoke box or a packet of aluminum foil and place on or near the heat source.

4. When smoke starts billowing out of the box (or packet), put your brined meat into the barbecue, close the lid, and maintain the temperature at 250°F until the desired internal temperature is met.

5. Determine doneness by inserting a meat thermometer into the thickest part of the meat (see page 41). Allow to rest before carving.

Pressure Cooking

Pressure cooking is an old technique, where food is cooked in a special pot that has an air-tight lid. The steam cannot escape from the pot, and the resulting pressure increases the internal temperature of the pot, decreasing the cooking time. Recently, newer pressure-cooking appliances, like the Instant Pot, have become versatile pieces of equipment in many home kitchens, helping speedily cook everything from rice to chili.

1. Set the pressure cooker to a "sear" function. Add oil to the pot. Season the meat and brown it in the pot.

2. Add the rest of your ingredients to the pot and stir well. Turn off the sear function.

3. Add the liquid to the pot. You won't lose any liquid while cooking, so use a quarter of the amount you would normally use in a braising recipe.

4. Place the lid onto the pressure cooker and seal it as per the appliance's instructions. Set the cooker onto the pressure setting and cook for your desired time (most tough meat cut into 1- to 2-inch stewing-sized pieces will be tender in about 30 minutes).

5. Slowly release the steam (as per the appliance's instructions) before opening the lid and serving.

Sous Vide

Translated from French as "under vacuum," sous vide is a technique widely used in fancy restaurants. Meat, fish, or vegetables are sealed and vacuum packed in a food-grade bag and cooked in a water bath for an extended amount of time at a very low temperature. The benefit, especially for cooking meat, is that the finished product is very consistently cooked, and the margin of error (or "overcooking"), is extremely low. A medium-rare steak will be pink from edge to edge, and all the cook has to do is brown the outside of the steak with a blowtorch to get a golden brown, crunchy exterior. This all sounds a bit space-age, but once a cook uses this technique, they tend to fall in love with the perfectly cooked and tender results. Note that you will need both an immersion circulator and a vacuum pack machine to do this properly.

1. Insert an immersion circulator into a large pot. Fill the pot with water to 1 inch above the minimum water level line on the circulator.

2. Program the circulator to the desired temperature; the temperature of the water reflects the finished internal temperature of the meat (for a medium-rare striploin steak, for example, that would be about 130°F; see page 41). Let the water heat up (it takes about 20 to 30 minutes).

3. Season the meat and place it in a pouch/bag with some other aromatics (e.g., garlic and thyme). Vacuum seal it as per your machine's instructions; you can also use a zippered freezer bag for this: place the meat in the bag, press out as much air as you can and seal it, leaving an inch of an opening on one corner.

4. Place the bag into the water and cook for one to three hours. If using a zippered bag, leave the zipper end of the bag hanging over the container's edge and clip it onto the side so that it doesn't fall in. The pressure from the water will push the remaining air out of the bag as the meat cooks.

5. Once cooked, remove the meat from the bag and dry it off well with paper towel.

6. Sear the outside of the meat with a blowtorch or in a very hot, preheated heavy-bottomed pan over high heat. Slice and serve.

GETTING THE INTERNAL TEMPERATURE RIGHT

As a young professional cook, I had very strict beliefs about how long meat should be cooked. I have relaxed those views over the years, especially since I opened the butcher shop. Why? Because I truly believe that if you are using good-quality meat, the "doneness" of the cut is less important. I've had well-done steaks from well-marbled, dry-aged beef, and it is phenomenal. Cooking some cuts too rare can be off-putting. For example, if you have a fatty rib-eye steak and it's cooked blue-rare, any large pieces of fat probably wouldn't have time to render properly. Fat is delicious to eat, but not when it's cool in the center; that's just unpleasant. But perhaps most importantly, ask whoever you're cooking for how they want their meat cooked. If they say well-done, then cook the meat through. Don't be a jerk about it. Giving people what they want will give them the best kind of dining experience.

Restaurant cooks use the "touch" test to see if the meat they are cooking is done. Poke, poke, poke, done! I don't recommend this technique for use at home, as it isn't very reliable. Instead, get an internal probe thermometer, and test the cooked meat in its thickest part. Shell out to get a good-quality one that won't break after a few uses, and use the following chart to get the temperature you're looking for. As a rule, I will take meat off the heat a good 5 degrees before it hits the final desired temperature, as the meat will continue to cook while it's cooling. Additionally, you want to allow the meat to rest before slicing or carving. As meat cooks, the heat tenses up and contracts the muscle fibers. As meat rests, the internal temperature cools down, allowing the fibers to stretch and relax. As they stretch, the fibers are able to absorb any juices that would have spilled out onto your cutting board if you sliced the steak immediately after it left the grill. This will ensure a juicier, more flavorful steak.

Meat	Desired result	Internal temperature
Chicken and poultry	Whole chicken (well-done)	165°F
	Leg/breast (well-done)	165°F
Pork	Medium-well	145°F
	Well-done	160°F
Beef, lamb, and game	Rare	115°F to 120°F
	Medium-rare	120°F to 125°F
	Medium	130°F to 135°F
	Medium-well	145°F to 150°F
	Well-done	160°F

A FEW NOTES ON INGREDIENTS AND MEASUREMENTS

When it comes to following recipes in a cookbook, many people want specific direction, with exacting measurements, because they want to recreate the dish exactly. Others prefer to follow recipes loosely, because they have a decent understanding of the dish and are willing to play with quantities or ingredients. I fall somewhere in between: I understand the desire for perfect replication but don't mind when things are a little looser. Depending on your inclination, take the notes below with a grain of (kosher) salt:

- **Salt** = kosher
- **Pepper** = freshly ground black
- **Butter** = unsalted
- **Milk** = whole
- **Oil** = olive
- **Onions** = yellow
- **Herbs** = fresh (even bay leaves)
- **Wine, beer, or other booze** = I generally don't have a preference for which varietal or type you use. That being said, if you wouldn't drink it, don't cook with it. That's not to say you shouldn't use boxed wine; it just means don't be a snob. Drink the boxed wine already!
- **Chopped** = roughly cut, with no shape in mind
- **Cut in large dice** = pieces about 1.5 inches square
- **Cut in medium dice** = pieces about ¾ inch square
- **Cut in small dice** = pieces about ½ inch square
- **Finely diced** = pieces about ¼ inch square
- **Minced** = Food cut *very* small, almost to a purée, and almost always applies to garlic. (A *grate* way to mince garlic: use a microplane or rasp, and grate the garlic clove.)
- **Nonreactive bowls and containers** = Plastic, stainless steel, glass, or ceramic. Use these instead of aluminum for marinades, because acids such as vinegar and citrus juices react with aluminum and can leach metal into the food.

GOOD LUCK!

Finally, dear reader, I would like to ask that you throw some of your inhibitions to the wind when it comes to cooking. Start easy, with a whole chicken perhaps, and move on to something more involved. Perhaps something that forces you to connect with your food. It is so very important that we learn how to get comfortable in the kitchen and feed ourselves and our families. And especially if you are a meat eater, you must become part of the process. But most of all, have fun! Life is just too damn short to not enjoy eating.

CHICKEN

Chicken

BACK IN THE EARLY '80s, before most of my staff were born, and before the Internet and grunge and balsamic "glaze," beef reigned supreme at the dinner table. Since then, chicken has usurped beef from its Formica throne, likely because of society's obsession with fighting fat. First came exercise videos starring gurus in leggings and neon jumpsuits promoting aerobics and weight-loss regimens. Then came new government-sanctioned dietary guidelines telling people to reduce their fat intake. And then suddenly skinless, boneless chicken breast became the healthiest thing to eat since wheatgrass and bulgur.

Compared to larger animals, chickens are inexpensive to raise and slaughter, and home cooks like that it's a naturally lean meat. It also comes in conveniently sized portions—a chicken leg or breast is usually good for one person, maybe even with a few leftovers. It also makes a great Sunday roast, an even better fried chicken, or a fantastic soup! Chicken is inexpensive, versatile, easily digested, and tasty. No wonder we sell more chicken than any other meat at the shop.

RAISING CHICKENS

There are a few ways to raise chickens, some more virtuous than others. I believe that a good bird needs exercise, a grain-based diet, warmth, and a healthy amount of socialization.

Chickens definitely need space to spread their wings. Some farmers *pasture-raise* their birds, which means the birds roam in a field protected by chicken wire, usually in a movable pen, during the day and sleep in an enclosed coop overnight. Other farmers *barn-raise* their birds, which means the birds live in a building that receives a constant supply of fresh air through giant wall fans. These birds have plenty of room to run around and they aren't caged or penned, but they also don't get outside. This is the more common way of raising conventional birds, as it is cost-effective for the farmer and protects the birds against predators.

A responsible farmer wants to raise healthy birds that are consistently strong. The food the birds eat plays a big role in this. Our farmers feed their birds a vegetable and grain diet designed for optimal health. The amount of protein in the feed is monitored to restrict hormonal aggression (the chickens we get at the shop are male; when these birds reach market weight, they're fully fledged teenagers—and act like teenage boys as well, jostling and pecking at each other), and the feed is augmented with vitamins and minerals. Chickens are omnivorous by nature, and the pastured birds get to peck around the grass for bugs and worms, the poultry world's gold standard of meat, to round out their diets.

The farmer also has to maintain a secure environment for the birds to live in year-round. Responsible farmers therefore build heating units in their barns to ensure their birds don't get too cold in winter, and this is the main benefit to the consumer of barn-raising. Pastured birds are really only available from mid-summer through fall. You can buy frozen pasture-raised product throughout the year, but for a good, fresh chicken in deepest February, you're looking to get a barn-raised bird.

Some farmers raise their chickens in barns with access to the outdoors, normally via a flap or gate. These birds are known as free range because they can go outside if they want to. Not all birds are inclined to go outside, however. One of my farmers mused that due to cross-breeding over the years, the conventional chicken rarely wants to stray far from the food source. He once tried raising White Rocks (a common breed); these fat birds had to be lifted by hand out of the barn into the fresh air, and once outside, they would just run back in!

The chickens our farmers raise are social; they like to be close to each other, whether they're raised indoors or out. This socialization is necessary for the birds to feel comfortable and stress-free, which leads to great-tasting meat.

BREEDS

Like most foods, chickens have been cross-bred over the years to create an ideal breed for the market: a bird that reaches market weight quickly, with a large breast and strong legs. If you ask a conventional farmer what breed they raise, their answer will probably be "a White Rock or a Cornish."

In recent years there has been a push for farmers to raise heritage breeds of birds whose lineage dates back decades, if not centuries. Some of these heritage chickens include Rhode Island Reds, Chantecler, and Plymouth Rocks, all of which came to North America with the European explorers. While these breeds have almost died out, a dedicated group of farmers is working hard to bring them back into the public eye. Your best bet for finding them nowadays is to visit your local farmers' market.

There are a couple of main differences between heritage chickens and conventional ones. A heritage chicken is usually an older bird, as it takes longer for it to reach market weight. Depending on the breed, it will be bigger (up to 8 pounds per bird) and have more muscle strength (the meat may seem tougher than you are used to). Because these birds take longer to raise, they are more expensive to purchase. However, I do think they make excellent roasting birds, and their flavor is something special—mainly because they are generally fattier than conventional birds. Note that heritage chickens are almost always sold whole.

SHOPPING FOR CHICKEN

When buying a chicken, look for a plump, dry bird (for a detailed breakdown on what chicken cuts to buy, see Chicken Cuts from page 50 to 54). Chickens need to be well chilled soon after slaughter to prevent bacterial growth, and the main thing that sets a good chicken apart from a crummy one is how that's done. Many chicken factories cool their chickens in an ice-water bath in a machine designed to quickly lower the bird's body temperature. The customer ends up paying more for water-chilled birds because they're heavy with water, and the chicken will have an insipid flavor. An air-chilled bird, which has been hung to cool naturally in a refrigerated room soon after slaughter, has a tight muscle fabric, which means dense, flavorful meat. That's the bird for me.

Look for chicken meat that smells clean. If you can ask to smell the bird, by all means do. A fresh chicken will barely have a smell. One that has seen better days will smell sour. That is the result of bacterial growth on the surface of the bird—and it's most common around the bones. I find whole chickens, wings, and legs are the first products to develop that smell.

Chicken has about a six-day shelf-life from the time it was slaughtered. When buying fresh chicken, ask your butcher when they received the product. The slaughter day was probably the day before. Most slaughter facilities ship products the day following slaughter, after the birds have had time to go through rigor mortis. So, if your butcher received the chicken on a Thursday, it will likely be good until the following Tuesday, assuming it has been well refrigerated. If you are buying chicken to eat more than four days in advance, it is always a good practice to freeze the chicken when you purchase it, then defrost in your fridge the day before you want to cook it.

Chicken Cuts

1. Whole chicken

2. Chicken breast, whole

3. Chicken breast, boneless and skinless

4. Chicken supreme

5. Chicken leg, whole

6. Chicken thigh

7. Chicken thigh, boneless and skinless

8. Chicken drumstick

9. Chicken wing

10. Chicken carcass

11. Chicken neck

12. Chicken skin

13. Chicken feet

Whole Chicken

Whole chickens are usually sold in two weight ranges: "fryers" are 3 to 3½ pounds each and "roasters" are 4½ to 5½ pounds each. They both make great roasts, but the smaller birds tend to be more tender. Look for birds with a clean-smelling interior cavity and dry skin.

Good for: **poaching, roasting, smoking**

Chicken Breast, Whole

A whole chicken breast has the skin attached and the rib cage left in. This cut is great value, and roasting it on the bone ensures moister meat near the bone. (Home butchers looking to practice their knife skills can remove the breast bone and use it in a stock.)

Good for: **grilling, roasting**

Chicken Breast, Boneless and Skinless

The best-selling protein in the shop is breast meat with the skin and bones removed. It carries many flavors well, so is excellent for marinating. The breast can also be cut into strips for breaded chicken fingers, or cubed and skewered for souvlaki.

Good for: **grilling, pan-frying, poaching, smoking, sautéing**

Chicken Supreme

Boneless chicken breast, with the skin left on and the wing tip left attached, is a popular cut in restaurants, hence its inclusion in my window, and it looks very attractive on the plate. A supreme gives diners the extra fun of eating a wing and getting some crispy skin.

Good for: **pan-frying, poaching, roasting**

Chicken Leg, Whole

A chicken leg is the whole leg—including the thigh and the drumstick—attached at the joint. A whole leg can be sold with the backbone on or off. While the "back on" version is generally cheaper per pound, you're paying for the backbone, which doesn't make for great eating.

Good for: **braising, grilling, poaching, pressure cooking, roasting, smoking**

Chicken Thigh

The meatiest part of the leg, the thigh is the upper portion of the leg. It's probably the best muscle for dishes like fried chicken or stewed chicken. The leg meat is generally a little fattier and carries more flavor and moisture than the breast, so it makes any chicken dish taste better.

Good for: **braising, grilling, pan-frying, pressure cooking, roasting**

Chicken Thigh, Boneless and Skinless

The thigh meat with skin and bones removed is the cut of choice for restaurants selling fried chicken because, without the bone, the portion size is very consistent. The down side is that the thigh can dry out more easily without the bone, so be wary when using them.

Good for: **grilling, pan-frying, sautéing**

Chicken Drumstick

The drumstick is the lower leg or calf. It's considered the black sheep of the chicken cut family because it lacks the meatiness of the thigh, the healthfulness of the breast, and the bar-food-prestige of the wing. However, it is a delicious cut, and excellent when marinated.

Good for: **braising, grilling, pressure cooking, smoking**

Chicken Wing

The wing can be sold whole or in two parts: the drumette, the meatier part next to the body, and the flat, the moister middle section (often with the wing tip attached). All wing cuts are delicious. Deep-fried, they're a staple of bar menus; they're also great oven-baked.

Good for: **grilling, roasting, smoking**

Chicken Feet

Chicken feet—the very bottom of the leg and the four "toes"—can be hard to find because they take a lot of cleaning to make them salable. However, they make a great addition to stocks and broths, and they are an important part of Chinese dim sum culture. Look for them in Asian markets.

Good for: **braising, deep-frying, roasting**

Chicken Neck

The neck is a long, tubular, lightweight muscle with a ton of collagen and meat bits that make for delicious stocks. Although it can be a little pricier than the carcass, it is a surprisingly popular cut.

Good for: **boiling for stock and broth**

Chicken Skin

Once plucked and rendered (slowly cooked over low heat to draw out the fat), chicken skin makes a fantastic fat for making fried rice and roasting chickens. If it's cooked down with onions and seasoning, chicken fat becomes spreadable schmaltz, a delicious alternative to butter on bread.

Good for: **using as a cooking fat**

Chicken Carcass

The carcass is what remains when all the meat has been removed. It's crucial for making stocks and broths. Try to shop at a store that has bones available, as that usually means they are processing their own poultry and will have a wider variety of chicken cuts.

Good for: **boiling, braising, poaching for soup and broth**

Why We Don't Pluck Our Own Chickens

The main chicken farm I work with has an onsite slaughter facility. This means the birds don't travel far from barn to box, which I believe helps their stress levels. A slaughter facility is an interesting place to visit, and the most ingenious of its machines is the feather-plucker, as it quickly and efficiently does a job that takes forever to do by hand. I know this from experience.

A restaurant once asked me for aged chicken. You see, back in the day, fowl were killed and then "hung in feather"—which means hung without being eviscerated or plucked—in a cool room to tenderize. Much like the process of hanging beef, this breaks down the tough muscle tissue and produces tender meat. The practice is still popular in Europe, especially for game birds like pheasants and partridge. I was happy to source some dry-aged chicken, but I needed a farmer who was willing to try doing it. Luckily, I knew just the guy.

Mark Trealout used to raise beautiful vegetables and sell them at local farmers' markets. He was an agri-hippie and a phenomenally positive energy in the sustainable food movement. I use the past tense because he has now moved on to teaching, but at one time he was definitely one of the more inventive farmers on the scene. I called Mark to ask if he was interested in testing the hanging-in-feather technique. He said yes—on one condition. I would have to come to his farm and help pluck the birds because that part is "a huge pain in the ass." How could I resist?

One cool October morning I arrived at Mark's farm around 10:00. Hanging above the riding lawnmower and the kids' bikes in his tool shed were four beautiful chickens, their orange-red plumage lit up in the morning sun. They had been hanging for four days.

"Just in here?" I asked, wondering if the tool shed was cold enough. The overnight temperatures had only got down to about 42°F.

"Yep," Mark replied, "they don't need to be chilled when they're in feather like this. They don't spoil."

I looked around at the prep area Mark had laid out for us. There were two chairs, four big plastic buckets lined with garbage bags, and a giant stockpot full of simmering water on top of a propane burner.

"Ok, here's the drill," Mark explained. "You take the bird and dunk it in the water four or five times to scald it. After plucking, the next step is to eviscerate it, using this." He pulled out a small pocket knife that looked like a Leatherman multi-tool. "Don't worry, it's clean," he assured me.

He demonstrated his technique, dunking the bird to scald the feathers and make plucking a lot easier. I copied him. Then we went at the feathers, pulling them out one by one and throwing them in the buckets. This took a really long time. Chickens have a lot of feathers, and even with the scalding they didn't all want to come out easily. On top of their resistance to pulling, they also sometimes want to take bits of skin with them. Which was a problem, because no matter how long I spent trying to pull the feathers out perfectly, if there was even a slight tear in the skin I was going to have a chef on the other end of this transaction giving me shit for a poor product. So, slowly and carefully was the way to go.

Once all the feathers were removed, it was time for the evisceration. We cut the first bird open near its rear and pulled out its innards (not something I recommend trying at home). I'd have sworn that after four days of hanging in a barn at an average temperature of 50°F, the guts would have been putrid. But quite the opposite was true; in fact, I have never smelled a cleaner liver in my life. The aroma was similar to cultured butter's. The innards went into a small plastic bag, and the rest of the bird (head and feet included) went into a garbage bag. And then we repeated the process on the other three chickens.

At the end of the day we had four nicely cleaned, if slightly torn, chickens and a small bag of offal. It was 2:30 p.m., and we had started just after 10:00 a.m. As we were cleaning up the yard, I thanked Mark.

"No problemo! I've always wanted to do this," he said. "But you know what?"

"What?"

"I'm never plucking doing this again."

"I'm with you on that one."

So, the moral of this story is: pay the money to get someone else to do the work.

I love everything about roasting chickens. I love the way it makes your kitchen smell, the way the skin gets all crispy, the way the meat pulls away from the chicken's ankle when it's done. Most of all, I love that no matter what recipe you use to roast a bird, *it will always be fantastic.*

One recipe question is asked at the butcher shop more than any other: "How do I roast a chicken?" This book offers several options, but this simple recipe requires very little prep time and produces a juicy, flavorful chicken. A little salt, pepper, butter—a few extras perhaps—are all you need to add to accentuate the flavor of a good-quality chicken.

SIMPLE ROAST CHICKEN

Preheat the oven to 450°F. Have a roasting pan with an elevated roasting rack ready (this allows hot air to circulate around your bird and cook it more evenly).

Season the chicken quite liberally with salt and pepper, taking a healthy pinch of each and let it fall like snow all over the chicken.

Cut the lemon in half widthwise, juice one half over the chicken, and stuff the other half into the cavity. Slice the whole bulb of garlic widthwise and put both halves into the cavity. Push the bay leaves and thyme into the cavity too.

Using your hands, rub the butter all over the chicken, massaging it into the crevices and putting a healthy coating over the entire bird. Set the chicken breast side up on the roasting rack. Roast the chicken for 15 minutes, then, without opening the door, turn the oven down to 350°F and roast for another hour.

Insert a meat thermometer into the thickest part of the thigh. It should read 175°F to 180°F. (If not, return the chicken to the oven for 5 to 10 minutes more and check again.) Turn the oven off, keep the door closed, and leave the chicken inside for another 15 minutes. This will allow the chicken to rest and the internal temperature to rise to about 165°F.

Remove the chicken from the oven and carve (page 26). Arrange the meat on a serving platter. Strain the pan juices through a fine-mesh sieve into a gravy boat and pour it over your platter of carved chicken.

Serves 4

1 (3½ pounds) whole chicken
Salt and pepper
1 lemon
1 bulb garlic, unpeeled
2 bay leaves
½ bunch thyme
1 cup butter, at room temperature

NOTE: After you've drained the juices from the roasting pan, rub a slice of baguette, ciabatta, or similar good-quality crusty bread all over the bottom of the pan, making sure you collect all the bits that have settled and caramelized on the bottom. Eat while drinking Champagne.

Roasting chicken with compound butter has become a game changer for me. By using a ton (the scientifically correct amount) of butter, you get a lot of tasty roasting fat at the bottom of the pan. Add a touch of flour, chicken stock, bay leaves, and a splash of brandy and you get a killer gravy. If preparing this meal isn't the greatest thing you do all weekend, it had better be because you roasted the chicken right after Bruce Springsteen serenaded you while you got a foot massage from John Travolta.

BUTTERY ROAST CHICKEN

Preheat the oven to 450°F. Have a roasting pan with an elevated roasting rack ready.

Place the butter in a mixing bowl. Add the shallots, garlic, thyme, sage, rosemary, and lemon zest and juice and mix thoroughly with a fork until well combined. Set aside this compound butter.

Using your hands, separate the skin from the breast meat of the chicken. Don't be too forceful. You don't want the skin to break—you want to create a "pocket" for the butter. Massage the butter, 1 Tbsp at a time, inside the pocket until the entire bird has butter under its skin.

Truss the bird (page 22) to ensure even cooking, rub it all over with the oil, and season liberally with salt and pepper.

Set the bird on the roasting rack, breast side up, and place in the oven. Roast for 30 minutes. Turn the oven down to 350°F, add the white wine to the pan, and roast for another hour or so, until an internal thermometer stuck in the thickest part of the thigh reads 165°F. Remove the chicken from the oven and allow to cool in the pan for 10 minutes.

Using a pair of tongs, transfer the chicken to a serving platter. Tent the foil over it, cover with a clean kitchen towel to keep it warm, and allow it to rest for about 30 minutes while you make the gravy.

Scrape the bottom of the roasting pan with a wooden spoon to loosen the caramelized bits. Pour the cooking juices and bits of scraped-up meat into a bowl, and allow to sit for a couple of minutes to allow the fat to separate from the juice. Use a ladle to skim some of the fat from the top. (You can leave some fat, as it's delicious.) Reserve for the gravy.

Serves 4

ROAST CHICKEN

1 cup butter, at room temperature, cubed

4 large shallots, finely chopped

4 garlic cloves, finely minced

½ bunch thyme, leaves picked and finely chopped

½ bunch sage, leaves picked and finely chopped

½ bunch rosemary, leaves picked and finely chopped

1 lemon, zest and juice

1 (3½ to 4 pounds) whole chicken

Salt and cracked black pepper

1 cup white wine

GRAVY

2 Tbsp butter

2 Tbsp all-purpose flour

1 cup pan juices from roasting the chicken

1 cup Chicken Stock (page 360)

2 bay leaves

2 Tbsp brandy (optional)

recipe continues

For the gravy, melt the butter in a small saucepan over medium heat. When it starts to foam, add the flour and stir with a wooden spoon until the mixture resembles toothpaste. Keep cooking this roux for about 5 minutes. Add the roasting juices and stir well to incorporate. When it's smooth, gradually add the chicken stock and bay leaves. Bring to a simmer and cook until the sauce coats the back of a spoon. Add the brandy, if using, then strain through a fine-mesh sieve.

To serve, carve the chicken (page 26) and arrange slices on individual plates. Pour the gravy into a gravy boat and set alongside the chicken.

Now that I have a kid, I often need to get food on the table in very short order. This quick whole-chicken recipe is super delicious and ridiculously easy, and it cooks in about an hour. That means I can get it ready *and* enjoy cocktail hour at the same time! These days, I like a little vermouth on the rocks while I cook. Pour yourself a drink and sip it while you work.

LEMON AND OREGANO-ROASTED CHICKEN

Preheat the oven to 425°F and line a baking tray with parchment paper.

Place the oil in a large bowl. Season the chicken pieces with the nutmeg, and salt and pepper to taste, then toss them in the oil. Arrange the chicken, skin side down, in a single layer on the baking tray and roast for 30 minutes.

To make the dressing, place the oil and lemon juice in a bowl. Add the oregano, chili flakes, garlic, and salt and pepper to taste. Mix until well combined. Set aside.

At the 30-minute point, remove the chicken from the oven and turn up the heat to 475°F. Turn the chicken pieces so they're skin side up. Return the baking tray to the oven and roast until a meat thermometer inserted in the thickest part of the thigh reads 165°F, about 15 minutes. The meat around the thigh and drumstick pieces will be pulling away from the bone.

Add the hot cooked chicken to the dressing, mix gently to coat each piece, cover the bowl tightly with plastic wrap, and allow the chicken to sit at room temperature for 15 minutes to absorb the dressing.

To serve, arrange the chicken pieces on a large platter. Drizzle the dressing over top and serve immediately.

Serves 3 to 4

2 Tbsp olive oil

1 (3½–4 pounds) whole chicken, cut in 10 pieces (page 23)

1 tsp grated nutmeg

Salt and pepper

DRESSING

3 Tbsp olive oil

1 lemon, zest and juice

1 Tbsp dried oregano

1 tsp chili flakes

1 tsp minced garlic

Salt and pepper

I first heard about beer can chicken when I was 19 or 20 and anything to do with beer was cool—especially the idea of shoving an open can of beer up a chicken's cavity and then roasting it. Now that I'm older, cooking a chicken on a painted aluminum can just doesn't seem so great. I still use the beer, obviously, because it makes the moistest roast bird imaginable without imparting too much flavor, but these days I use a small mason jar instead of a can. A jam jar that's been thoroughly cleaned and scrubbed of all labels and glue bits also works well. I often use this recipe when cooking on the barbecue, but roasting in the oven also gives excellent results.

BEER-ROASTED CHICKEN

Preheat the oven to 375°F. Have a roasting pan with an elevated roasting rack ready.

Mix the spice rub and oil together in a small bowl. Using your hands, slather the mix all over the chicken, making sure you get it into all the little crevices.

Pour the beer into a clean mason jar just large enough to fit into the chicken's cavity. Place the jar in the roasting pan, then press the chicken, butt down, over top. The jar should fit almost entirely in the chicken's cavity, allowing the bird to balance standing up.

Roast the chicken until an internal thermometer stuck into the thickest part of the thigh reads 165°F (about 25 minutes per pound). Remove the roasting pan from the oven, tent the bird with aluminum foil, and allow it to rest in the pan for 30 minutes.

Using either tongs or a carving fork pierced far enough into the bird to lift it, and a kitchen towel (to pull off the jar), carefully pull the jar out of the chicken. A lot of hot juice may come out with it, so be careful. Discard the beer.

To serve, carve the chicken (page 26), arrange it on a platter, and pass the plates!

Serves 4

¼ cup BBQ Dry Rub (page 376)

2 Tbsp vegetable oil

1 (3½ pounds) whole chicken, trussed (page 22)

1 cup beer (a pilsner or lager is good here)

NOTE: If you don't want to use the BBQ Dry Rub, a little salt and pepper with olive oil is fine for seasoning as well.

When I worked at Mistura, I was introduced to a wet-roast method of roasting whole birds. This method works particularly well with game birds, as the liquid braises the legs while the breasts get browned by the dry heat. It also produces a particularly tasty sauce: a pool of butter-enriched red wine that the chicken swims lazily in.

RED WINE–ROASTED CHICKEN

Preheat the oven to 425°F. Have a roasting pan with an elevated roasting rack ready.

Season the chicken liberally with salt and pepper. Using your hand and a bit of pressure, roll the lemon on your work surface to "loosen" the juice by breaking up the pulp. Using a toothpick, poke a few holes in the lemon. Place the lemon in the cavity of the chicken.

Pour the oil all over the bird and, using your hands, work it into the skin, getting into all the crevices. Place the chicken on the roasting rack, roast for 20 minutes, and then remove from the oven and set aside. Turn the oven down to 350°F.

While the bird is in the oven, melt 1 Tbsp of the butter over medium-low heat in an ovenproof pot large enough to hold the bird. Add the onions and cook, stirring frequently, until translucent. Add the garlic and sweat for a few minutes until fragrant. Add the carrots and celery and turn up the heat to medium, stirring constantly until the vegetables have softened. Season with salt and pepper.

Add the thyme and bay leaves, then deglaze the pot with the wine. Bring the liquid to a simmer and reduce by half, about 5 minutes. Add the stock and bring to a simmer over medium heat.

Transfer the chicken to the pot, along with any cooking juices from the roasting pan. Bring the liquid to a simmer again, then roast, uncovered, for about 1 hour. The chicken is cooked when an instant-read thermometer inserted in the thickest part of the thigh reads 165°F. Remove from the oven and let sit, still uncovered, for 20 minutes.

Transfer the chicken to a cutting board. Strain the roasting juices into a saucepan (discard the solids) and bring to a light boil over high heat. Reduce the sauce by one-quarter, about 5 minutes, and season with more salt and pepper, if necessary.

Serves 4 to 6

1 (3½ pounds) whole chicken, trussed (page 22)

Salt and pepper

1 small lemon

2 Tbsp vegetable oil

4 Tbsp butter, cold, cubed (divided)

1 small onion, diced

4 garlic cloves, minced

1 carrot, diced

1 celery stalk, diced

4 thyme sprigs

2 dried bay leaves

1 cup dry red wine

1 cup Chicken Stock (page 360)

Turn down the heat to a simmer. Gradually add the remaining cold butter, whisking constantly to emulsify the sauce. Do not let the sauce come to a boil after adding the butter or it will split. Once the butter is incorporated, turn off the heat and set the sauce aside.

To serve, carve the chicken (page 26). Arrange the meat (including the wings) on a deep platter and pour half the sauce over the chicken. Pour the remaining sauce into a gravy boat and serve on the side.

Poached whole chicken is one of the easiest and most satisfying one-pot meals you can make, and you can vary the ingredients according to your mood. In place of bread, this recipe is equally tasty with cooked rice or pasta to soak up the broth.

SIMPLE POACHED CHICKEN

Serves 6 to 8

POACHED CHICKEN

1 (3½ pounds) whole chicken

2 onions, cut in large dice

2 carrots, cut in large dice

2 turnips, cut in large dice

1 celery stalk, cut in large dice

1 leek, washed thoroughly and cut in large dice

5 garlic cloves, halved

2 Tbsp salt

1 Tbsp whole peppercorns

1 herb bundle (see Using Herbs and Spices in Braises, page 36)

1 Tbsp butter

1 cup shredded cabbage (Savoy or green)

12 shiitake mushrooms, sliced

1 tsp finely chopped thyme

Salt and pepper

2 cups roughly torn stale French bread

MAYONNAISE SAUCE

¼ cup mayonnaise (store-bought is fine, but bonus points for homemade)

2 Tbsp finely sliced green onions or chives

Zest of 1 lemon

1 tsp lemon juice

Salt and pepper

The day before you plan to serve this dish, place the chicken, onions, carrots, turnips, celery, leeks, garlic, salt, peppercorns, and herb bundle in a deep pot and just cover with cold water. Bring the water to a low simmer over medium-low heat and poach the chicken, uncovered, for 1½ hours, skimming and discarding any fat and impurities that rise to the surface.

Insert a meat thermometer into the thickest part of the thigh. It should read 180°F. (If not, cook the chicken for 5 to 10 minutes more and check again.) The meat will be pulling away from the bone, especially around the leg knuckle. Turn off the heat and allow the chicken to cool in its own liquid before covering and refrigerating overnight.

30 minutes before you plan to serve the chicken, skim off and discard any solidified fat. Transfer the chicken to a cutting board, reserving the poaching liquid in the pot. Using a sharp knife, cut the breasts and legs away from the carcass. Using your thumb, strip off any meat clinging to the carcass and put it back into the pot with the vegetables. Discard the skin from the breasts and slice the meat before adding it to the pot. Discard the skin from the legs and strip the meat away from the bones.

Place the leg meat back in the pot and discard the bones. Discard the herb bundle, then bring the broth to a simmer over medium-low heat.

For the sauce, mix the mayonnaise with the green onions (or chives) and lemon zest and juice. Season with salt and pepper and set aside.

To finish the chicken, melt the butter in a large frying pan over medium heat. Add the cabbage and mushrooms, stir well, and cover. Steam the vegetables until fully cooked, about 10 minutes. Season with the thyme and salt and pepper to taste, and keep warm.

To serve, place a few pieces of torn-up bread at the bottom of each bowl. Add a couple of tablespoons of the cabbage and mushroom mixture, then ladle a good amount of the chicken and vegetable mixture with some broth over everything. Top with a spoonful of the mayonnaise sauce and serve.

This recipe is a great way for beginners to learn how to butcher a chicken. If you want to do this ahead of time, use the bones to make the cup of stock you'll need for this recipe. The cooking method is perfect for getting a beautifully roasted chicken skin as well, and the sauce is a pretty dynamite flavor combo.

PAN-ROASTED HALF CHICKEN WITH MADEIRA, ROSEMARY, AND LEMON

Preheat the oven to 475°F.

To butcher the chicken, place it on a cutting board with the breasts up and the legs toward you. Using a boning knife, cut through the center of the bird on either side of the breast bone. As your knife comes to the ball joint between the backbone and the thigh bone, pop the knife in between the joint to separate it. Return to the breast and cut along the ribs; as your knife gets to the backbone, separate the breast. At the top of the bird, cut between the ball joint where the drumstick of the wing meets the backbone. Separate the wing flat from the drum and reserve for another purpose (wing night!). Leave the leg attached to the breast skin. Repeat the process on the other half of the chicken.

With the tip of your boning knife, slowly and carefully remove the thigh bone. Separate the bone from the ball joint where it meets the drumstick. You will now have 2 mostly boneless half chickens, and some bones and wings that you can freeze for making stock.

To cook the bird, set a large ovenproof frying pan over high heat. Season the half chickens liberally with salt and pepper and rub them with the oil. When the pan is very hot, add the chicken, skin side up, and sear for about 1 minute. Using tongs, flip the chicken over and brown the skin side for 4 minutes.

Without turning the chicken again, place the pan in the oven and roast until an internal thermometer inserted into the thickest part of the thigh reads 180°F, about 15 minutes.

Remove the pan from the oven and return it to the stovetop over medium heat. If the skin isn't super golden and crispy, pan-fry it for a minute or so. Use tongs to transfer the chicken to a cutting board.

Serves 4

1 (3½ pounds) whole chicken
Salt and pepper
2 Tbsp olive oil
1 rosemary sprig
½ cup Madeira
½ lemon
1 cup Chicken Stock (page 360)
2 Tbsp butter, cold, cut into pieces

Add the rosemary to the pan, then deglaze the pan with the Madeira. Scrape up all the chicken bits with a wooden spoon, then squeeze the lemon over top. Allow the sauce to reduce by one-quarter, about 3 minutes, before adding the stock. Reduce by one-quarter again, then remove the sauce from the heat.

Add the cold butter all at once, stirring constantly to emulsify the sauce. It should be shiny.

To serve, cut each half chicken into 3 or 4 pieces and arrange on a platter. Strain the sauce through a fine-mesh sieve and serve it in a gravy boat or drizzled over the chicken.

There is something deeply satisfying about making your own fried chicken. It takes a bit of time and patience, but the results will be excellent. Many chefs use only thighs and drumsticks, as these muscles are the juiciest, but I like to use a whole chicken. You get the most cluck for your buck.

FRIED CHICKEN

To brine the chicken, stir together the buttermilk, hot sauce, salt, and pepper in a large bowl or a deep casserole. Submerge the chicken in the brine, cover tightly, and refrigerate for 2 hours.

Place 2 inches of oil in a deep-fryer and preheat it to 325°F (or fill a large, heavy-bottomed pot with 2 inches of oil and set it over medium heat). Arrange a layer of paper towels on a large plate.

Prepare a dredging station on your work surface. Stir together the dry dredging ingredients in a large bowl, then mix in the buttermilk to create a "wet-sand" texture. Beside this bowl, place a wire cooling rack on top of a baking tray to receive the chicken. Remove the chicken from the brine and place it in a large bowl.

Working with one piece at a time and using a bit of force, press the chicken into the dredging mixture, covering it completely and then shaking off any excess. Set the dredged chicken on the wire rack. Repeat until all the chicken is dredged.

Once the oil has reached 325°F (if you're using a pot for frying, use a deep-fat or candy thermometer to test the temperature; if using a deep-fryer, the oil has been preheated to 325°F), use tongs to lower the chicken pieces, a couple at a time, into the fryer (or pot) and cook for about 15 minutes. Start with the thicker breast pieces, then cook the thighs and drumsticks, and finish with the wings, waiting about 30 seconds between each addition. (Adding the pieces all at once will cool the oil rapidly, which could make your chicken soggy.) As the chicken cooks, you may need to flip the pieces to ensure both sides fry evenly.

At the 15-minute point, insert a thermometer into the thickest part of each piece. When the temperature reads 180°F, the chicken is fully cooked. Transfer to the prepared plate and allow to drain on the paper towels for 5 to 10 minutes. To serve, arrange the fried chicken on a large platter and serve immediately.

Serves 6 to 8

BRINED CHICKEN

4 cups buttermilk (save 2 Tbsp for the dredge)

¼ cup Frank's RedHot sauce

¼ cup salt

2 Tbsp pepper

1 (3½–4 pounds) whole chicken, cut in 10 pieces (page 23)

2–3 cups vegetable oil

DREDGE

2 cups all-purpose flour

2 Tbsp baking powder

2 Tbsp salt

2 Tbsp paprika

2 Tbsp garlic powder

1 Tbsp onion powder

2 Tbsp buttermilk

NOTE: Start this dish at least 3 hours before you plan to serve it.

This pretty, classic breaded cutlet will be a winner in any household. Breading food (page 122) is a fantastic technique to master, and Parmigiana toppings—Parmesan cheese, tomato sauce, and bread crumbs—are guaranteed to put a smile on every kid's face! Fresh mozzarella balls sold in liquid in small bags are nicer in this recipe, but the regular mozzarella cheese sold in plastic packaging is fine too. Serve with a salad or a side pasta, or on a toasted bun.

CHICKEN PARMIGIANA

Serves 4

Heat 1 Tbsp of the oil in a medium pot over medium heat. Add the onions and sweat until slightly caramelized, about 5 minutes. Stir in the garlic, turn down the heat to medium-low, and cook until fragrant, about 3 minutes. Add the passata and basil and simmer, uncovered, for about 30 minutes, until the sauce has thickened and tastes sweet. Season with salt and pepper and remove from the heat. Set aside.

While the tomato sauce is simmering, prepare the chicken. Lay each breast flat on your cutting board and slice them in half widthwise. Set aside.

Prepare a breading station on your work surface. Place the flour in a large bowl. Crack the eggs into a second bowl and whisk them well. In a third bowl, mix together the bread crumbs, oregano, 1 Tbsp salt, and 1 tsp pepper. Set a clean plate beside the bowls to receive the chicken.

One piece at a time, press the chicken into the flour, coating it on both sides and shaking off any excess. Next, dip the chicken in the egg mixture, shaking off any excess again, and then dredge it in the bread crumbs, ensuring it is well coated but shaking off any excess. Set the breaded chicken on the plate. Repeat until all the chicken is breaded.

Preheat the oven to 375°F. Line a baking tray with aluminum foil.

Heat the remaining 6 Tbsp oil in a large frying pan over medium heat. When the oil is hot, add the breaded chicken and fry until golden brown, about 5 minutes per side.

Arrange the chicken in a single layer on the baking tray. Cover each breast with a few spoonfuls of the tomato sauce, 2 Tbsp of the Parmigiano, and 2 pieces of mozzarella (or ½ cup grated mozzarella). Bake until the cheese is slightly golden and bubbly, about 10 minutes. Serve hot.

7 Tbsp olive oil (divided)

1 small onion, finely diced

2 garlic cloves, minced

1¼ cups passata (puréed tomatoes)

6 basil leaves, chopped

Salt and pepper

2 (each 9–10 ounces) boneless, skinless chicken breasts

1 cup all-purpose flour

2 eggs

1½ cups bread crumbs

1 tsp dried oregano

½ cup freshly grated Parmigiano-Reggiano cheese

8 ounces fresh mozzarella cheese, sliced in 8 rounds (or 2 cups shredded regular mozzarella)

Everyone likes Shake 'n Bake seasoned bread crumbs, but I prefer to make my own, mostly because I like *a lot* of bread crumbs on my chicken. And this cheater's breaded chicken skips the egg wash step and the frying bit, which means it's both faster and less fatty than the standard recipe—perfect for a busy Tuesday night! I like Frank's RedHot sauce best in this recipe, but you can use your own favorite or substitute ketchup or barbecue sauce if you have wussy kids. (But Frank's RedHot really is the best: in the words of the old lady in the commercial, I put that s#!t on everything.)

FAKE 'N' BAKE CHICKEN FINGERS

Preheat the oven to 350°F. Line a baking tray with a piece of aluminum foil and coat it with the oil.

Slice the chicken into long thin strips, about six per chicken breast. In a mixing bowl, combine the garlic, green onions, and hot sauce. Add the chicken strips and mix until well coated. Shake off any excess.

In a large bowl, season the bread crumbs with salt and pepper. Toss the chicken in the bread crumbs, using a little pressure to help the crumbs stick, until well coated.

Arrange the chicken in a single layer on the baking tray and bake for about 15 minutes. Turn the chicken strips and bake until a thermometer inserted in the thickest part of the breast reads 165°F, about 15 minutes.

To serve, arrange the strips on individual plates and serve with ketchup or barbecue sauce—or more hot sauce.

Serves 4

2 Tbsp vegetable oil

2 (each 10 ounces) boneless, skinless chicken breasts

3 or 4 garlic cloves, minced

3 Tbsp sliced green onions

2 dashes hot sauce

2 cups bread crumbs

Salt and pepper

One of my favorite Filipino recipes is adobo, which is Spanish for "marinade" or "seasoning." The soy-vinegar-based seasoning works well with pork, fish, vegetables, and especially chicken. My son is cared for by a woman named Annie who is from the Philippines and has been making adobo chicken for him since he could first chew. He still goes nuts for it. Once you make this recipe, you will too. Serve this dish with steamed white rice.

CHICKEN ADOBO

Place the chicken in a large pot. Add the garlic, bay leaves, pepper, vinegar, and water. Bring to a boil over high heat, then lower the heat to medium and simmer, uncovered, for 20 minutes.

Pour in the soy sauce, cover, and simmer until the meat easily pulls away from the bone, about 30 minutes.

Place your oven rack in the center of the oven (it mustn't be directly below the broiler), then preheat the oven to broil. Line a baking tray with aluminum foil. Place the chicken on the baking sheet, skin side up. Pat the skin dry with a paper towel.

Over medium heat, reduce the liquid in the pot to 1 cup. Discard the bay leaves, skim any fat from the surface, and remove from the heat. Set aside.

Broil the chicken, rotating the pieces regularly, until they're nicely caramelized, about 5 minutes.

To serve, arrange the chicken on a platter and pour the sauce over top.

Serves 6 to 8

8 chicken legs, skin-on and bone-in, split between the thigh and the drumstick

10 garlic cloves, smashed with the side of a knife

3 bay leaves

1 Tbsp cracked black pepper

1½ cups white vinegar (see note)

1 cup water

¾ cup Japanese soy sauce (shoyu)

NOTE: I like the bite of white vinegar in this recipe, but you can substitute cider vinegar, as many Filipino cooks would do, or, if you want to be super traditional, cane vinegar. You can also prepare this dish using a pressure cooker. Reduce the vinegar to 1 cup, omit the water, and cook the chicken for about 15 minutes.

Marrying a Jamaican woman changed my culinary life. Before Alia and I got together, my seasoning method consisted of adding some salt and pepper to allow the flavor of the ingredient to shine. I still primarily adhere to that philosophy, but the mix of Scotch bonnet (for flavor more than heat), green onions, garlic, thyme, and allspice that characterizes Jamaican jerk seasoning has become one of my favorite combinations. Cooks on the island use this spice mix, either dry or wet, on a variety of meats they cook slowly over a wood fire. Although you can easily purchase premade jerk marinade, there is nothing like the homemade version. Serve jerk chicken the traditional way, with Rice and Peas (page 348).

JERK CHICKEN

To make the marinade, place the garlic, Scotch bonnets, and ginger in a food processor and process at high speed until finely chopped. Transfer to a small bowl. Place the green onions in the food processor and purée. Stir this purée into the garlic mixture and pour it all into a blender. Add the soy sauce and oil, followed by the sugar, allspice, thyme leaves, salt, dried thyme, cinnamon, and nutmeg, and purée on high speed until well combined. Measure ½ cup of the marinade into a clean bowl and refrigerate the rest, reserving it for another use (see note).

Place the chicken in a nonreactive bowl, add the ½ cup marinade, and toss well. If you prefer a healthier dose of marinade, help yourself. Stir in the sliced green onions. Cover the bowl and refrigerate for at least 8 hours or up to 7 days. (The longer you marinate the meat, the more flavorful it will be.)

Preheat the barbecue to medium-high on one side and medium on the other. Place the chicken on the hotter side of the grill to sear, about 5 minutes per side. Transfer it to the cooler side to finish cooking, about 20 minutes. The chicken is done when a thermometer inserted into the thickest part of the thigh reads 165°F.

To serve, arrange the legs on a platter and serve immediately.

Serves 4

MARINADE

3 Tbsp chopped garlic

1½ Tbsp seeded and chopped Scotch bonnet pepper (see note)

1 Tbsp chopped ginger

3 cups chopped green onions

½ cup soy sauce

¼ cup vegetable oil

¼ cup packed brown sugar

2½ Tbsp ground allspice

2 Tbsp fresh thyme leaves

2 tsp salt

1 tsp dried thyme

1 tsp ground cinnamon

½ tsp ground nutmeg

CHICKEN

4 chicken legs, skin-on and bone-in, split between the thigh and the drumstick

½ cup sliced green onions

NOTE: Start this at least the day before you plan to eat it. For best results, keep the chicken in the marinade for as long as possible—at least overnight, but even up to a week! The recipe yields 2 cups of marinade, which is more than you'll need here. Refrigerate any leftovers for up to 2 weeks, and try it on pork or turkey, as well as chicken.

If you can't find fresh Scotch bonnet chilies, substitute a teaspoon or two of a hot sauce made from Scotch bonnets (the West Indian brand Grace makes a couple of dependable ones). Use gloves when handling the Scotch bonnet or wash your hands thoroughly after cutting it to get rid of the heat-producing capsaicinoids. Be warned, guys: failure to do so could result in a life-altering moment the next time you relieve yourself.

Chicken legs are definitely among my top 10 foods to grill, especially when they are marinated. The sugars in the marinade char the skin a bit, and nothing says summer eating more than that sweet char flavor. In this recipe, splitting the legs into three evenly sized pieces is a great way to get more marinade flavor throughout the meat (and it exposes the bone marrow in the thigh for you to suck out). When you eat these chicken legs, your mouth is like "Kapow! I wasn't expecting that flavor punch!" You can make this recipe on either a propane/gas barbecue or a charcoal grill. My preference is for charcoal, as it produces a more pronounced smoky flavor. Serve this dish with steamed rice, Roasted Broccoli with Soy Butter (page 354), pickled vegetables and an ice-cold lager.

"KAPOW" CHICKEN LEGS

Using a strong cleaver, separate the drumstick from the thigh in between the joint, then chop the thigh bone in half using one swift commanding motion. Repeat with the remaining legs. You will end up with 12 pieces of chicken. (Alternatively, have your butcher do this for you.)

In a large, nonreactive bowl, mix together the soy sauce and vinegar. Add the garlic, green onions, sugar, pepper, and bay leaves, and stir until well combined. Add the chicken legs to mix and coat thoroughly, cover, and refrigerate overnight.

Preheat the barbecue to a medium-high on one side and medium on the other.

Place the chicken on the hotter side of the grill to sear, about 5 minutes per side. Transfer to the cooler side to finish cooking, about 20 minutes. The chicken is done when a thermometer inserted into the thickest part of the thigh reads 165°F.

To serve, arrange on a platter and serve immediately.

Serves 4

4 (each 10–12 ounces) chicken legs, skin-on and bone-in

1 cup Japanese soy sauce (shoyu)

1 cup Chinese red rice vinegar (or cider vinegar)

3 garlic cloves, minced

1 cup sliced green onions

2 Tbsp brown sugar

1 Tbsp pepper

3 bay leaves

Coq au vin sounds super exotic but it's actually an easy chicken stew made with red wine. Traditionally this dish is made with a rooster, an older animal in need of a long bath in a hot stock, but a stewing hen is easier to find these days. Or do what I do and use regular chicken legs. They turn out tender and supple when stewed.

COQ AU VIN

Preheat the oven to 325°F. Place a heavy-bottomed ovenproof pot over medium heat.

Place the flour in a large bowl, season with salt and pepper, and stir to combine. Dredge the chicken legs in the seasoned flour, and shake gently to remove any excess. Set aside.

Melt 3 Tbsp of the butter in the pot, then add the chicken legs and brown both sides, 3 to 5 minutes per side. Transfer the chicken to a plate and set aside.

As the chicken is cooking, prepare the onions. Fill a bowl with ice water. Bring a small pot of water to a boil over high heat. Using a paring knife, cut the root ends off the pearl onions. Plunge the onions into the boiling water for 30 seconds, then drain and refresh in the ice bath. When cool, drain the onions, and slip them out of their skins.

Once the chicken is cooked, turn the heat under the heavy-bottomed oven proof pot down to medium low. Melt 1 Tbsp of the butter in the pot (no need to wipe it out first) and add the mushrooms, stirring to release their moisture and help pick up any bits of browned chicken stuck to the bottom of the pot. Continue cooking, stirring once in a while, until the mushrooms are slightly browned, about 5 minutes.

Once the mushrooms have browned, transfer them to the plate with the chicken and place the bacon and pearl onions in the pot. Turn the heat back up to medium and sweat until they are just starting to get golden, about 8 minutes. Deglaze with the brandy, then return the chicken and mushrooms to the pot. Add the herb sachet and then the wine. Bring to a simmer, cover, and transfer to the oven to braise for 1 hour, or until the chicken falls away from the bone.

Serves 4

¼ cup all-purpose flour

Salt and pepper

4 (each 8–10 ounces) chicken legs

4 Tbsp butter (divided) + 1 Tbsp butter, cold, cubed

1 cup pearl onions

1 pound button mushrooms, cleaned with a brush or towel (don't wash them)

¼ pound slab bacon, cut in medium dice

2 Tbsp brandy

1 herb sachet (page 36)

3 cups red wine

1 Tbsp minced Italian parsley

Transfer the chicken legs to a serving platter, leaving everything else in the pot. Discard the herb sachet, place the pot over medium heat, and bring to a simmer. Add more salt and pepper if needed. Add the 1 Tbsp cold butter and parsley, stirring continuously until the sauce is emulsified.

To serve, pour the sauce over the chicken legs and divide among individual plates.

Ok, it's game day and you want to recreate your favorite pub-style chicken wings at home. The only problem is, you don't have a deep-fryer. You could fill a pot with oil and deep-fry the wings on your stovetop, but not only is that solution super messy, it can also lead to serious injury—especially after a few drinks! This method allows you to make deep-fryer-crispy wings in your oven. Less mess and lots of crunch!

CRISPY BAKED CHICKEN WINGS

Preheat the oven to 250°F. Set a wire baking rack over a baking tray and rub it with a bit of vegetable oil.

Divide the wings between two medium bowls. Divide the baking powder, salt, and pepper evenly between each bowl. Toss the wings well to coat them thoroughly.

Arrange the wings on the wire rack, leaving room between them so the hot air can circulate freely. Bake for 30 minutes.

Turn up the oven to 425°F and cook the wings for another 50 minutes.

Meanwhile, make the sauce. In a small saucepan over medium heat, melt the butter with the hot sauce, stirring until emulsified. Remove from the heat and set aside.

To serve, place the wings in a large bowl, pour the sauce over top, and toss to coat. Serve immediately.

Serves 6 to 8

1 Tbsp vegetable oil

4 pounds chicken wings, split between drumettes and flats

2 Tbsp baking powder (divided)

3 tsp salt (divided)

1½ tsp pepper (divided)

½ cup butter, cold, diced

½ cup Frank's RedHot sauce (see note)

NOTE: These wings are great without sauce, of course. But a classic hot sauce is the way to go: the not-so-secret ingredient is Frank's RedHot sauce (or your favorite hot sauce, if you prefer).

A ballotine is boned poultry stuffed with meat and seasonings, and then tied and roasted or poached. It's a great way to maximize a leg of poultry and is a sophisticated dinner option. This dish is not difficult to make and allows you to practice a bit of home butchery.

BALLOTINES OF CHICKEN WITH APPLE AND SAGE

Set aside the chicken bones for the cranberry glaze. In a bowl big enough to hold the leg meat, combine ¼ cup of the cranberry juice with the salt and the whole sage leaf. Add the meat to the brine, cover, and refrigerate for 1 hour.

Set a medium frying pan over medium heat. Add 1 Tbsp of the butter and the bacon, then add the onions and sweat until translucent, about 8 minutes. Add the garlic and sauté for another few minutes, until fragrant. Stir in the apple and sliced sage leaves, and continue cooking until the apple has softened, about 5 minutes. Add the bread crumbs and cheese and stir well to create a stuffing. Remove from the heat.

Preheat the oven to 400°F. Line a baking tray with parchment paper. Have handy 10 lengths of kitchen twine, each about 6 inches long.

Remove the leg meat from the brine and lay the pieces flat on a cutting board, skin side down. Place one-quarter of the stuffing in the middle of each piece and roll the chicken around it to make a fat cigar. Tie the roll with twine to seal it then season with salt and pepper. Set the ballotines (that's what they are now), skin side up, on the baking tray. Drizzle with 1 Tbsp of the oil, place 1 Tbsp of butter on each one, and roast for 45 minutes.

To make the glaze, heat the remaining 1 Tbsp of oil in a small frying pan over medium heat. Add the reserved chicken bones and brown them. Deglaze the pan with the remaining ¾ cup cranberry juice and add the cranberries and thyme. Reduce the juice until it is syrupy, about 5 minutes, then remove the pan from the heat and stir in the remaining 1 Tbsp of butter. Discard the bones and thyme and keep the sauce warm.

The ballotines are done when the thickest part of the meat reaches 180°F. Remove from the oven and allow to rest for 5 minutes, before discarding the twine and slicing the ballotines into rounds. Arrange the slices on a serving platter, and drizzle with the cranberry glaze.

Serves 4

2 chicken legs (each about 10 ounces), butchered (page 25)

1 cup cranberry juice (divided)

2 tsp salt

9 sage leaves, 1 left whole and 8 finely sliced

6 Tbsp butter (divided)

2 slices bacon, diced

3 Tbsp finely chopped onion

1 garlic clove, minced

1 Granny Smith apple, peeled, cored, and cut in small dice

¼ cup bread crumbs

2 Tbsp grated Parmigiano-Reggiano cheese

Salt and pepper

2 Tbsp vegetable oil (divided)

3 Tbsp dried cranberries

2 thyme sprigs

PORK

Pork

PIGS GIVE US RAW CUTS, cured cuts, smoked cuts, and even crispy skin—so many delicious options. While some cultures view pork as an unclean meat, those of us who consume it have a different take on it. Pork is a butcher's best friend: the heads are used for headcheese, the skin for chicharrón (crackling), the feet for stocks, and the fat for cooking. Most of the meat gets cut up and sold as chops or turned into sausage. Butchering whole hogs is one of the most satisfying jobs in butchery because hardly anything goes in the waste bin.

RAISING PIGS

Pigs are raised in a few different environments, the most common being *hog barns*. These barns have fresh air pumped in through the side walls, but the pigs don't get time outside. This is the conventional hog-raising practice, and I don't care too much for it. Although the pigs have room to move, it's not enough to really break free on their own if they want to. The farmers I deal with raise their pigs in *open-air barns*. The pigs live in the barns, where they get fresh hay and can be warm and safe, and they have open-door access to the outdoors. Unlike chickens, these pigs make it their mission to get out and wallow in the mud.

One of the farmers I work with raises heritage breeds of pigs almost completely outdoors. The pigs have small pens they can retire in, much like doghouses, but otherwise they're outside snuffling about for food. However, not all pigs being raised for meat can be successfully raised outdoors. Among the most popular commercial breeds are white pigs—so called because their hair is white—but as I discovered when speaking with a farmer who had just started rearing these pigs, they can get sunburned. His white pigs had been roaming free in the sunshine on a beautiful summer's day and by the end of it the poor animals' skin was all red and blistered! Those pigs had to spend the rest of their days in a barn and the farmer learned a valuable lesson.

Most piglets are farrowed on the same farm they are raised on, which means they're raised on their mother's teat until around six to eight weeks, at which point they start to eat grains, fruits, and farm scraps. Pigs are omnivores and will scavenge for meat if in the wild, but domestic pigs are usually raised on a grain and vegetable diet—largely because a growing pig can eat double its weight in food each day. That can mean up to nearly 500 pounds of food for some bigger commercial breeds.

Pigs are naturally hierarchical and will fight each other for rank and status. Two pigs of the same sex from the same litter will rarely scuffle as they get older, but introducing a new pig into the mix can create trouble, as I learned from one farmer after I received a carcass that was missing a foot. The farmer told me that the hog had been bitten before getting to the slaughterhouse, and the meat inspector wouldn't let the carcass go without the offending foot being removed. Another farmer regaled me with stories of Hogzilla, an especially large and beastly pig who asserted his dominance over other weaker pigs by bowling them over whenever he was feeling testy. Most pig farmers get to know their animals' unique personalities and behaviors, and provide separate enclosures to manage any problems.

BREEDS

The most common pig is, as noted earlier, the white pig, a cross between the Duroc and Yorkshire breeds that has been bred to eliminate extra fat. If you've seen the film *Babe*, you know what this pig looks like. In the late '70s, when health experts and governments in North America declared that fat in our diet was causing heart disease, pork sales dropped dramatically and pig farmers had to figure out new ways to market their animals. Unfortunately, this led to the fat being bred out of a naturally fatty animal and butchers trimming more fat off carcasses. Luckily, people still lined up for hot dogs and breakfast sausages, so butchers had a home for that fat, but overall it was a disappointing time for pork farmers.

In recent years, chefs have popularized the use of heritage breeds of pigs as food animals. These hogs have had the same bloodline for decades and can normally be traced back to a particular region of the world, where the fat content and genetics adapted to let them thrive in the local climate. Meat from Berkshire and Tamworth pigs in England has received especially high praise from chefs in recent years. The Berkshire breed naturally has a very high intramuscular fat content, resulting in marbling rarely seen in other pork. The Tamworth breed has a long belly that makes excellent cured bacon and has a lower fat content than Berkshires. The wooly Mangalitsa from Hungary is prized for its enormously high fat content and is used primarily for charcuterie, as the fat needs to be cured and/or smoked to be truly appreciated.

Heritage pork is expensive compared with conventional pork, but I would advise everyone to try a heritage pork chop at least once in their life. These hogs truly are the tastiest around, and in my opinion, the flavor difference more than justifies the price.

SHOPPING FOR PORK

Pork is often called "the other white meat" to try to get some of those sweet, sweet chicken sales, I think, but pork meat is only white after it's cooked—and even then, it's really more gray or taupe. Here's what to look for when buying raw pork.

- **Look at the color of the meat.** Fresh pork meat has a rosy appearance, and the fat is snowy white. Avoid grayish meat, which indicates that the pork has been sitting around too long.
- **Look for moisture on the surface of the meat.** No visible moisture on a pork chop or shoulder can mean that it's been in the case too long.
- **If the meat has a bone in it, look at the cut edge.** The bone marrow should be red or pink. A brown bone means the meat might be too old to cook.
- **Ask for fat. Pork that's too lean can be dry once cooked.** Although brining can help add moisture, you really should start with a high-quality, well-marbled cut of pork.
- **Shop at stores that offer different cuts.** A store that offers pork trotters, liver, or bones is probably getting in whole animals, which indicates there are skilled butchers on staff. And skilled butchers tend to have a better eye for fresh meat than grocery clerks do.

Meeting Murray Thunberg

Murray Thunberg was born a farmer, moved to the city as a young man to make his fortune in business, then got tired and decided to be a farmer again. You know how it goes. At first he specialized in heritage eggs from pastured hens. The city went nuts for them. His eggs came in beautiful pastel shades, from baby blue to gold to light green, the flavor was astounding, and the yolks, so orange and rich, were like the ones used to make pasta in Italy. Murray sold his eggs at farmers' markets around town and wanted to supply our shop as well. It wasn't a hard sell. But as it turns out, he had something else he wanted to sell.

"Where do you get your heritage pork from?" he asked one day.

When I told him the name of the farm, he scratched his chin. "Yeah, they're ok . . ." he said. "Do you know if their pigs are registered?"

At that time I had never heard of breed registration. I didn't realize that the pedigree of purebred heritage pigs is as properly documented and registered as that of dogs. Murray explained: "My father was a cattleman. When I was a boy, I rode around in my father's pickup truck as he and I went about our chores. In his glove compartment he kept a book on cattle breeds, with pictures and a ton of info on each one. Leafing through that book got me hooked on breeds, especially making sure the lineage is strong and pure. And to be sure of the lineage, those pigs have to be registered." Registering breeds is an expensive, time-consuming, and just process that Murray firmly believes in. And you can see those beliefs in action at his farm.

When I visited Murray's farm for myself later that day, it didn't take long for me to see the difference. Money was tight when he and his friend Dwayne began raising heritage pigs, and they had built their pig houses with whatever plywood they could find. But those houses were filled with fresh straw, allowing for comfortable farrowing, and the animals had more open space to run, eat, and wallow than most urban condo dwellers.

Murray told me about the different pigs, including lesser-known breeds such as Hereford, Gloucestershire Old Spot, and British Saddleback, all of them properly registered and documented. He's committed to protecting these lines of pigs from disappearing, and this is exactly the type of farming I support. There may be a Murray at the farmers' market near you. Maybe, if you're lucky, he'll have the same sense of humor and honor that Murray Thunberg does.

Pork Cuts

1. Picnic shoulder

2. Butt

3. Shoulder chop

4. Rib chop

5. Rib roast

6. Center-cut chop

7. Boneless loin chop

8. Tenderloin

9. Pork belly

10. Side ribs

11. Back ribs

12. Skirt

13. Sirloin

14. Fresh ham

15. Cutlets

16. Hock

Picnic Shoulder

This lower half of the shoulder is bonier than the butt end (top end) and includes the muscles around the joint between the shoulder blade and the forearm (hock). This cut is typically deboned and used for ground or stew meat or sausages and used whole as a roast for slow-cooking.

Good for: **braising, pressure cooking, roasting, smoking**

Butt

This meatier end of the shoulder is a versatile cut that can be braised, smoked, stewed, or slow roasted. It has a good amount of fat both on the outer portion of the meat and in the interior. This is the most common cut for pulled pork and, at my shop, our preferred meat for kebabs.

Good for: **braising, grilling, pressure cooking, roasting, smoking**

Shoulder Chop

A great bone-in cut from the butt, this chop may be one of my favorite cuts. Also known as a blade steak, it is definitely chewier than a pork rib chop, but the flavor is more pronounced due to the fat and it is definitely juicier, especially when brined or marinated.

Good for: **grilling, pan-frying, smoking, sous vide**

Rib Chop

Just like the rib eyes and prime rib section of beef, this tender cut from the shoulder to the middle of the loin is best suited to roasting, grilling, and pan-frying. These chops typically have less fat on the outside of the meat but have more marbling within.

Good for: **grilling, pan-frying, smoking**

Pork Rib Roast

The rib section of the loin includes up to 13 bones, depending on where the loin was separated from the shoulder. A rib roast is a great easy Sunday supper, and if the whole thing is used, you can loop it into a crown roast as well, which is when you curl the loin and rib bones in a circle to create a crown of meat fit for a king!

Good for: **roasting, smoking**

Center-Cut Chop

This tender chop from the hip to the back of the loin is typically served on the bone. These chops have more fat on the outside of the meat than rib chops but less marbling on the inside. The muscle can be left whole and taken off the bone to make an excellent roast.

Good for: **grilling, pan-frying, smoking**

Boneless Loin Chop

These chops can be cut from any part of the loin, which runs from the shoulder, along the spine, and down to the tailbone. Because they are boneless, these chops are tastiest if cut from the shoulder end, where there is usually more fat. Boneless loin chop is often butterflied, leaving one side attached so it can be opened like a book and stuffed.

Good for: **grilling, pan-frying**

Tenderloin

The leanest cut of pork, the tenderloin is the muscle that runs along the backbone. As its name suggests, it is very tender meat, as it is a "floating" muscle that barely works. And because it is so lean and boneless, the meat can be a little dry if it's overcooked.

Good for: **grilling, pan-frying, poaching, roasting, saautéing**

Pork Belly

One of the fattiest cuts from the pig, the belly meat comes from the underside of the animal. It is most commonly cured, smoked, sliced, and sold as bacon but it's also delicious fresh, either braised or slow-roasted.

Good for: **braising, slow-roasting, smoking**

Side Ribs

Located between the back and spareribs, the side ribs are meaty and can be prepared by smoking, braising, slow-roasting, or poaching. (For more on ribs, see page 100.)

Good for: **braising, grilling, poaching, pressure cooking, slow-roasting, smoking**

Back Ribs

If you remove all of the bones from a pork rib roast, you get the back ribs. They're shorter and leaner than other ribs. (For more on this, see page 100.)

Good for: **braising, grilling, slow-roasting, smoking**

Pork Skirt

This muscle hangs on the inside of the rib cage and is rarely encountered in a grocery store (ask for it where whole pigs are butchered). Keep in mind you only get 2 portions per animal, so don't go asking for enough to feed a party of 10.

Good for: **grilling, pan-frying, sautéing**

Sirloin

The end of the loin between the striploin and the ham (the top of the back leg), this softball-sized muscle can be used for roasts, stir-fry meat, or kebabs. It is usually not very well marbled, so it can be dry.
Good for: **roasting, stir-frying**

Fresh Ham

The upper part of the back leg is often cured and smoked but also makes a great fresh roast. It is leaner than the shoulder, so a little more care may be necessary when preparing it so the meat doesn't dry out.
Good for: **braaising, roasting, pressure cooking, smoking**

Pork Cutlets

Normally cut from a leg muscle like the outside flat, inside round, or eye of round, pork cutlets are thin slices of meat that have been tenderized by pounding them. They are perfect for pork schnitzels.
Good for: **pan-frying, sautéing**

Hock

Pork hock, a.k.a. knuckle, is the bone-in shank muscle from the lower part of either the front or back legs, just above the cartilage-and-bone-filled trotter. It is decent as a raw cut but excellent smoked, as in Choucroute Garnie (page 135) or Cassoulet (page 321).
Good for: **braising, pressure cooking, roasting, smoking, sous vide**

PORK RIBS: ALL YOUR QUESTIONS ANSWERED

As popular as they are, pork ribs can be very confusing to purchase. Here is a little FAQ about ribs and what you should be looking for when you're at the grocery store or butcher shop.

Q. How many bones are in a rack of ribs?

A. A full rack of ribs is usually 12 to 13 bones. There are 15 to 16 rib bones per hog, depending on the breed, and the rib section is separated from the shoulder section between the third and fourth rib, leaving 3 ribs on the shoulder. If your math is as good as mine, that leaves you with 12 or 13 bones on a full rack of ribs.

Q. What's the difference between side ribs and back ribs?

A. The ribs on a pig begin at the spine and curve toward the breast and belly. The first 4 to 4½ inches of ribs starting at the spine are called the *back ribs*—they're closest to the back. These ribs lean up against the loin muscle, which is a fairly tender nonworking muscle, so the meat around the back-rib bones is tender. They are the more expensive cut of the two.

The next 6 inches or so of ribs, from the end of the back ribs toward the breast of the hog, are the *side ribs*, also called *spareribs* in the U.S. The meat around the side rib bones is a little tougher because they're closer to the tough belly muscle. The side ribs are commonly sold in a shape that goes by three names—square cut, center-cut, or St. Louis cut—and means that instead of tapering along the natural line of the rib bones, the butcher has cut them into an even rectangle. This cut has a full rib bone at one end of the rack and only a small bone at the other end, with a higher proportion of meat.

At the end of the side ribs are small bits of cartilage called *feather bones*. These are rarely sold, but a butcher who breaks down whole hogs will have them and sell them for a song. They are bony for sure but have lots of lovely bits of meat in there.

Q. Does it matter which cut I get?

A. Yes. As with any other cut of meat, which ribs to buy depends on how you plan to cook them. The meat on back ribs is leaner and more tender, so they don't have to cook for long. Try back ribs quickly grilled on a barbecue or steamed in a wok like the dishes at a dim sum restaurant. Side ribs need a bit more cooking. Many barbecue restaurants prepare side ribs in a smoker, but they're equally good basted with barbecue sauce and cooked low and slow in a barbecue or oven.

Q. Do I need to remove the membrane from the underside of the ribs?

A. The thin sheet of membrane that covers the bony side of the ribs is called the *peritoneum* and toughens as it cooks. Many people don't like this and choose to remove it. Personally, I don't mind the chewiness too much. The difference is kind of like segmenting an orange. You can go to the trouble of removing all the pith and membrane—or you can just peel and eat it like a normal person. You don't *need* to remove the membrane, but you might *choose* to. Some people say the membrane interferes with the meat absorbing the flavor of rubs and smoke, but I've never found this to be an issue. However, if I were serving ribs to a group of rib-eating purists, I would remove the membrane. It's easier than having to moderate a debate on the subject for the next two hours.

Q. Why don't you sell back ribs that often?

A. Only at butcher shops that break down whole hogs do you hear this question. The answer is simple: We keep our back ribs attached to the loin muscle so we can sell bone-in rib chops, which are the best cut for a grilled pork chop in my opinion. If you want ribs, we offer a lot of side ribs instead. Our customers have gotten used to it, I think.

Q. What are "country ribs"?

A. What Canadians call pork blade or shoulder chops, Americans call country ribs. They're thin steaks cut from the loin end of the blade muscle. While this cut contains no actual rib bones, it can include the cross-cut of the scapula, or paddle bone, in the middle of the cut. These chops are delicious, but I don't think of them as a rib. Because, well, Canada.

Q. Do you have a good rib recipe?

A. Whaddaya know, I have a couple . . . (See pages 129 to 131.)

Ham is a bit of a no-brainer. A good smoked ham is ready for the oven—all you need are some cloves and a roasting pan. The ginger beurre blanc in this recipe is definitely an indulgence, and completely unnecessary, which makes it that much more enjoyable. Serve with Gratin Dauphinois (page 344) and Peas with Pearl Onions, Lettuce, and Mint (page 353).

BAKED HAM WITH GINGER BEURRE BLANC

Preheat the oven to 325°F. Have a roasting pan with an elevated roasting rack ready.

Using a sharp knife, score the skin of the ham, over the curved top side, in a crosshatch pattern at 2-inch intervals. Press a clove into every second X of the crosshatch.

Set the ham on the baking rack and pour 1 can of ginger ale and the water into the roasting pan. Cover the ham with aluminum foil and bake until hot all the way through, about 2 hours. A meat thermometer inserted in the ham should read 150°F.

Remove the foil and bake until the skin is dry and dark golden, about 30 minutes. Remove from the oven and allow to cool on the rack.

While the ham is roasting, make the beurre blanc. Pour the remaining can of ginger ale into a medium saucepan over medium heat. Add the wine, ginger, thyme, bay leaves, salt and pepper, and bring to a simmer. Reduce the liquid to 1 cup, about 5 minutes, then turn down the heat to very low. Gradually add the butter, whisking until the sauce is emulsified. Season to taste with salt and pepper. Strain the beurre blanc through a fine-mesh sieve into a gravy boat.

To serve, slice the ham and arrange it on a platter. Set the beurre blanc alongside.

Serves 10 to 12

1 (about 10 pounds) smoked ham, skin-on and bone-in (ask for shank end)

20 whole cloves

2 (each 12 ounces) cans ginger ale (divided)

1 cup water

1 cup white wine

3 Tbsp chopped fresh ginger

4 thyme sprigs

2 bay leaves (dried is fine)

Salt and pepper

½ cup butter, cold, diced

"Ham" is another word for pork hind leg and it is most commonly smoked. Fresh ham describes a pork leg that hasn't been cured, smoked, or manipulated in any way. Be sure you buy the right cut for this dish!

The lowly fresh pork leg, while one of the most delicious cuts, needs to be loved a bit with a brine to ensure its juiciness after it's been roasted. It's pretty economical, though: you can feed a large crowd for around two dollars a person. Serve this ham with some crusty rolls, mustard, and cheddar cheese for a sandwich buffet.

ROASTED FRESH HAM

Place the salt, sugar, onions, peppercorns, bay leaves, and cloves in a nonreactive stockpot large enough to hold the ham (see note). Bring the brine to a boil over high heat and cook, uncovered, for about 5 minutes. Remove the pot from the heat and allow to cool to room temperature, about 1 hour.

Score the ham over the top curved side in a crosshatch pattern at 1-inch intervals. (If you can, have your butcher do this for you, as they will have sharper knives.) Fully submerge the ham in the brine, cover, and refrigerate for 10 hours. Turn the ham over, cover, and refrigerate for at least another 10 hours.

About 6 hours before you plan to serve the meal, preheat the oven to 300°F. Have a roasting pan with an elevated roasting rack ready.

Remove the ham from the brine, rinse it under cold, running water for about 5 minutes, and then pat it dry with a towel. Place the ham on the roasting rack, scored skin side up, and set the roasting pan on the center rack of the oven. Cook for about 5 hours, or 30 minutes per pound. To test for doneness, insert a meat thermometer in the thickest part of the meat. The temperature should register around 145°F to 150°F. Remove the pork from the oven.

Turn up the oven to 500°F. Once it reaches full temperature, roast the ham until a crackling has developed on the skin, 5 to 10 minutes. Remove from the oven and allow to rest for at least 30 minutes.

To serve, cut the ham into slices and arrange on a platter.

Serves 12 to 16

8 quarts water

2 cups salt

2 cups packed brown sugar

2 onions, quartered

¼ cup black peppercorns

15–20 bay leaves

2 Tbsp whole cloves

1 (10–12 pounds) fresh ham, skin-on and bone-in, shank end preferably

NOTE: Start this roast a full 24 hours before you plan to serve it so the meat has time to soak in the brine.

If you don't have a pot large enough to hold the ham, purchase a brining bag from your local butcher.

Spiessbraten means "spit-roasted" in German. It's a traditional dish made by slowly roasting either pork or beef over a beechwood fire. If you like smoky pork, I urge you to try this delicious dish. Serve with the sweet mustard, dill pickles, and potato salad.

GERMAN SMOKED PORK SHOULDER (SPIESSBRATEN)

Season the pork butt with the garlic and juniper, and salt and pepper. Layer half the onions in the bottom of a nonreactive pan, place the pork on top, and cover with the remaining onions, ensuring the pork is completely covered. Refrigerate for 24 hours.

To make the sweet mustard, mix together the mustard, honey, molasses, and caraway seeds in a small bowl until well combined, then cover and refrigerate until needed.

Fill your hot smoker with the wood chips. Traditionally, this recipe is made with dried beechwood, but I've never seen it in North America. Applewood is one of my go-tos. Preheat the smoker to 250°F. If you don't have a smoker, you can use a charcoal barbecue for this dish. Arrange the charcoal on one side of the grill and preheat the barbecue to 250°F. Soak 3 cups of wood chips in cold water for 30 minutes, then scatter them on the hot coals to create the smoke. Close the lid of the barbecue and adjust the air vents so the temperature inside remains around 250°F. Smoke for 5 to 6 hours, adding more wood chips every couple of hours and checking the temperature and the smoke periodically. (The pork will become too dark and bitter if the heat is too high.) Make sure you have enough charcoal to get you through the 6 hours. To do this, heat up more charcoal in your starter chimney before adding it to the kettle, or use a propane grill and a smokebox instead. Heat one side of the grill to 250°F and place the smokebox full of wood chips beneath it. Place the pork on the cooler side of the grill, with a drip pan underneath to catch any fat.

Transfer the pork from the pan to a cutting board, leaving the top layer of onions on the meat. Roll up the shoulder like a pinwheel, enclosing the onions within the meat, then tie up the roast (page 27).

Hot-smoke the pork until a thermometer inserted in the thickest part of the meat reads 165°F, 4 to 5 hours.

Serves 8 to 10

SMOKED PORK

8 pounds boneless pork butt, butterflied open

6 garlic cloves, minced

2 Tbsp ground juniper berries

Salt and pepper

3 Spanish onions, thinly sliced (divided)

3 cups wood chips

SWEET MUSTARD

1 cup Dijon mustard

½ cup honey

½ cup fancy molasses

2 Tbsp caraway seeds, toasted and ground

NOTE: You'll need a smoker or charcoal barbecue for this recipe, and leave yourself enough time to start a full 29 hours before you plan to eat.

Remove the rolls from the smoker and wrap them first in aluminum foil and then in a towel so they retain their moisture as they cool.

Once the rolls reach room temperature, unwrap them and slice them thinly. Arrange slices on individual plates. Place the bowl of sweet mustard where everyone can help themselves.

I've cooked many foods on my charcoal barbecue, but one of my favorite ways to do so is hot-smoking pork butt using plenty of wood chips to impart a strong smoky flavor. Don't worry if you smell a bit like a campfire after making this: a quick T-shirt change and a hair wash will easily solve that problem. And the shoulder itself is so glorious—sweet, caramel-hued, and so, so succulent—that any inconveniences are quickly forgotten. Pork butt comes from the shoulder of the pig and runs from the top of the pork rack to the base of the head. A lot of people, myself included, love eating the meat around the bone because it tends to be a little fattier and juicier than the rest of the muscle, but whether you make this recipe with bone-in or boneless pork butt isn't going to make a huge difference to the overall flavor.

SIMPLE HOT-SMOKED PORK BUTT

Rub the meat all over with the sugar and salt. Place the pork in a bowl or casserole and refrigerate, uncovered, overnight.

In the morning, soak the wood chips in water for 30 minutes. About 6 hours before you plan to eat, preheat your charcoal barbecue to 300°F. Once the coals are piping hot, arrange them on one side of your barbecue.

Remove the pork from the fridge and drain off any liquid, then place the pork on the cooler side of the barbecue, away from the fire. Throw a handful of the soaked wood chips directly on the hot charcoal, then close the lid of the barbecue and adjust the air vents so the temperature inside remains around 300°F. Smoke for 5 to 6 hours, adding more wood chips every couple of hours and checking the temperature and the smoke periodically. (The pork will become too dark and bitter if the heat is too high.) Make sure you have enough charcoal to get you through the 6 hours. To do this, you can heat up more charcoal in your starter chimney before adding it to the kettle. Or use a propane grill and a smokebox instead. Heat one side of the grill to 300°F and place the smokebox full of wood chips beneath it. Place the pork on the cooler side of the grill, with a drip pan underneath to catch any fat.

Once the meat is fork-tender, transfer the pork to a cutting board, cover it loosely with aluminum foil, and allow to rest for about 20 minutes.

To serve, cut into slices and arrange on a serving platter.

Serves 8 to 10

1 (8–10 pounds) whole boneless
   pork butt
½ cup brown sugar
½ cup salt
3 cups wood chips

NOTE: Begin this dish a day ahead so the meat has time to take on the flavor of the rub.

A whole picnic shoulder weighs between 9 and 11 pounds and can feed at least eight people—or four with generous leftovers—which makes it a simple and inexpensive way to treat a lot of people. The prune sauce in this recipe works really well with the pork and makes an interesting change from the classic applesauce. Serve with Creamy Mashed Potatoes (page 342).

OVEN-ROASTED PORK PICNIC SHOULDER WITH PRUNES

For the roast, mix the salt, pepper, cinnamon, allspice, and cloves in a small bowl. Using a sharp knife, or a box-cutter, score the skin of the pork in a crosshatch pattern at 1-inch intervals. Using your hands, rub the mixture all over the roast, pressing the seasoning into the scored skin and all the crevices. Set the roast on a plate and refrigerate, uncovered, for 8 to 12 hours.

About 7 hours before serving time, remove the roast from the fridge and allow it to come to room temperature for 1 hour.

Preheat the oven to 275°F. Have a roasting pan with an elevated roasting rack ready.

Place the roast on the roasting rack and set the roasting pan in the oven. Roast the pork, basting it with the drippings every 30 minutes or so, until a fork inserted in the meatiest part of the shoulder sees the meat yield easily, about 5 hours. Remove the pork from the oven and transfer it to a baking tray. Reserve the roasting pan to make the sauce.

Turn up the oven to 450°F. Once the oven reaches temperature, return the roast to the oven and cook until the skin has crackled up, 15 to 20 minutes. Remove from the oven, tent with aluminum foil, and set aside to rest.

To make the sauce, drain all but 2 Tbsp of the fat from the reserved roasting pan. Place the pan over medium heat and add the shallots. Using a wooden spoon, scrape all the delicious drippings from the bottom of the pan. Once the shallots start to brown, add the garlic and continue stirring.

recipe continues

Serves 8 to 10

DRY-RUBBED PORK

3 Tbsp salt

2 Tbsp pepper

1 tsp ground cinnamon

1 tsp ground allspice

½ tsp ground cloves

1 (9–11 pounds) whole pork picnic shoulder, skin-on and bone-in

PRUNE SAUCE

½ cup chopped shallots

2 garlic cloves, minced

2 cups pitted prunes

1½ cups prune juice

1½ cups red wine

2 cups Beef Stock (page 361)

4 thyme sprigs

3 bay leaves

2 Tbsp unsalted butter, cold, cubed

Salt and pepper

Lemon juice

NOTE: Start this dish the day before you plan to serve it so the meat has time to absorb the flavor of the dry rub.

Place the prunes in a medium saucepan with the prune juice and simmer over medium heat until the juice has reduced by half, about 5 minutes.

Once the garlic has caramelized in the roasting pan, pour off the excess fat. To do this, turn off the heat, tilt the pan, and let the bottom edge rest on the lip of a frying pan. Move the solids to the top of the roasting pan, then use a tablespoon to scoop out and discard the fat.

Return the roasting pan to medium heat and deglaze with the wine, scraping up all the remaining bits of caramelized meat juice. When the wine has reduced by half, about 4 minutes, add the stock, thyme, and bay leaves. Simmer for about 5 minutes, or until the sauce just coats the back of a spoon.

Strain the sauce into the saucepan with the prunes and prune juice. Bring this mixture to a simmer, then gradually add the butter, stirring constantly, until the sauce is completely emulsified. Season with salt, pepper, and lemon juice. Remove the saucepan from the heat.

To serve, remove the aluminum foil from the roast, carve the meat into slices around the joint, and arrange them on a platter. The skin should easily come off in pieces. I like to break up this crackling and serve it alongside the pork. Pour the prune sauce into a gravy boat and set it alongside the pork.

Opening a new store is both exhilarating and exhausting. Between sorting out the contractors, the artists (yes, artists are involved), the bankers, and the staff, I barely have time to remember how to put my pants on. However, no matter what kind of day I'm having, I make a point of sitting down to dinner with my family every night. There's only one problem with this plan: our son needs to eat at 6:00 p.m. Not only have I had to reset my body clock—my wife, Alia, and I never ate before 8:00 p.m. before our son Des came along—but I've had to rethink my menus to make them fast and easy to prepare. Luckily, I have just the thing in the shop: smoked pork chops. Also known as Kassler chops, they're cut from the loin, seasoned, and smoked in the same way bacon is (but they are much leaner), and they're great in any season. All you really have to do is fry them for about 4 minutes per side over medium heat and they can be served with anything. Try them with this quick mustard sauce that kids, both young and old, will definitely love and a cabbage slaw, potato salad, or really any kind of nice warm vegetable. Enjoy!

SMOKED PORK CHOPS WITH MUSTARD SAUCE

In a large frying pan over medium heat, heat the oil. Add the chops and fry until golden brown on each side and hot all the way through, 4 to 5 minutes per side.

While the chops are cooking, make the sauce. In a small saucepan, simmer the onions and vinegar over medium heat for about 2 minutes, or enough just to soften the onions. Add the mustard, sugar, and apple juice, bring to a simmer, and whisk until the sugar is melted. Pour into a gravy boat.

To serve, place a chop on each plate and serve the sauce alongside.

Serves 4

2 Tbsp vegetable oil

4 smoked pork chops

1 Tbsp finely diced red onions

1 Tbsp red wine vinegar

2 Tbsp Dijon mustard

1 Tbsp packed brown sugar

2 Tbsp apple juice

This simple and delicious dinner for a warm summer night is perfect when the cherries are ripe and the rosé is flowing. Serve with boiled green beans tossed in a little salted butter, lemon, chives, and toasted almonds.

GRILLED PORK CHOPS WITH A CHERRY SALSA

In a large bowl, toss the chops with the garlic, thyme, and oil. Liberally season with salt and pepper, mix again, and refrigerate, uncovered, for 1 hour.

Preheat your barbecue to high on one side and low on the other.

While the grill is heating, make your salsa. In a large bowl, toss the cherries, onions, celery, basil, chives, and pepper with the vinegar and oil. Mix well, season to taste, and allow to sit at room temperature until your pork chops are cooked. Or make the salsa ahead of time, cover, and refrigerate for up to 4 days.

When the barbecue is hot, place the chops on the hot side of the grill and sear both sides to a golden brown, then move them to the cooler side to finish the cooking. To test for doneness, insert a meat thermometer near (but not touching) the bone. When the temperature reads 145°F, remove the chops from the grill and allow them to rest for 10 minutes.

To serve, arrange the chops on a platter. Spoon the salsa into a serving bowl and drizzle it over the chops.

Serves 4

GRILLED PORK CHOPS

4 pork rib chops

4 garlic cloves, minced

4 thyme sprigs

2 Tbsp olive oil

Salt and pepper

SALSA

1 cup sweet black cherries, pitted and chopped

¼ red onion, minced

½ celery stalk, finely diced

2 Tbsp finely chopped basil

1 Tbsp finely chopped chives

1 Tbsp pepper

¼ cup balsamic vinegar

2 Tbsp olive oil

Salt

A full rack of pork has 13 rib bones; each bone represents a portion (ok, a hefty portion, but still . . .). Before you begin, count the number of people you're having over and figure out how much of the rack you'll need.

MAPLE SMOKE-ROASTED PORK RACK

In a nonreactive pot large enough to hold the pork rack, combine the salt, sage, rosemary, and cloves with the syrup and water. Bring to a boil over medium heat and then immediately remove from the heat and allow to cool completely. Add the pork rack, cover, and refrigerate overnight.

Soak the wood chips in a bowl of water for 30 minutes. Place the soaked chips in a smokebox or enclose them in an aluminum packet. Preheat one side of your barbecue to high. Leave the other side off. Set the smokebox (or aluminum packet) on the hot side of the grill and wait until it starts smoking. A charcoal grill would work beautifully for this recipe. If you do use one, keep the temperature consistently low and smolder the wood chips directly on the coals.

Set your pork rack directly on the cooler side of the barbecue. Close the lid, *leaving it open a small crack*. (I prop a pair of metal tongs between the barbecue and the lid.) Smoke for 30 minutes.

While the pork rack is smoking, preheat the oven to 350°F.

Open the lid of the barbecue completely after 30 minutes. Plenty of smoke should erupt. The pork should be starting to brown on the outside and feel a little firm. Transfer the pork to a roasting pan.

Place the pan in the oven and roast until a thermometer inserted in the thickest part of the pork reads 150°F, 30 to 45 minutes. Remove the pork from the oven and allow to rest for 10 minutes.

To serve, slice the pork rack into individual chops and arrange on individual plates.

Serves 8

½ cup salt

1 bunch sage

1 bunch rosemary

1 Tbsp whole cloves

½ cup maple syrup

1 quart water

8-bone pork rack, chine bone removed

2 cups wood chips

NOTE: Begin this recipe the day before you plan to serve it so the pork has time to infuse overnight.

A bone-in pork rib roast (or "rack," as I like to call it) is a wonderful Sunday roast. The loin is a very tender cut, and roasting it on the bone provides plenty of opportunity to eat the most delicious bits of meat around each rib. This recipe calls for a delicious walnut crust, which gives this dish a very cool-weather feel. Perfect for an autumn harvest meal.

WALNUT-CRUSTED PORK RACK WITH SAGE PAN SAUCE AND APPLE CHUTNEY

Serves 4

4-bone skinless pork rib roast, chine bone removed

Salt and pepper

WALNUT CRUST

1 cup walnuts, shelled

½ cup bread crumbs

Salt and pepper

2 Tbsp honey

2 Tbsp Dijon mustard

CHUTNEY

½ cup apple cider vinegar

½ cup packed brown sugar

4 tart apples, peeled and cut in small dice

2 Tbsp water

1 Tbsp lemon juice

1 Tbsp minced ginger

1 Tbsp minced garlic

1 tsp whole mustard seeds

1 tsp salt

½ tsp ground cinnamon

PAN SAUCE

1 small onion, diced

2 garlic cloves, minced

6 sage sprigs

1 cup apple cider or apple juice

1 cup Chicken Stock (page 360)

2 Tbsp butter, cold, diced

Preheat the oven to 350°F. Have a roasting pan with an elevated roasting rack ready.

Season the meat liberally with salt and pepper. Place the roast on the roasting rack, skin side up, and place the pan in the oven. Roast your pork until a thermometer inserted into the thickest part of the meat reads 145°F, about 1¾ hours.

recipe continues

While the roast is cooking, make the walnut crust. Spread the walnuts in a single layer on a baking tray and roast in the oven alongside the pork until golden brown. This only takes a few minutes, so keep a close eye on them in case they burn. Let the nuts cool slightly, then place them in a food processor, add the bread crumbs and salt and pepper to taste, and pulse until finely chopped. Set aside. In a small bowl, mix together the honey and mustard until well combined.

To make the chutney, place the vinegar and sugar in a medium nonreactive saucepan, bring to a simmer over medium heat, and cook, stirring occasionally, for about 10 minutes. Remove from the heat. Place the apples in a bowl, add the water and lemon juice, and coat the apples well to prevent discoloration. Add the apples, ginger, garlic, mustard seeds, salt, and cinnamon to the sweetened vinegar and bring to a simmer over medium heat. Cook until the apples are tender and the mixture has thickened, 8 to 10 minutes. Remove from the heat, pour into a small bowl, and set aside to cool.

To apply the walnut crust, remove the roast from the oven after 1¾ hours. Brush the meat with the honey-mustard mixture, then sprinkle the walnut mixture all over the roast, patting it down into the honey-mustard. Return the roast to the oven for another 15 minutes. The roast is ready when a thermometer inserted into the thickest part of the meat reads 145°F.

Transfer the roast to a cutting board, cover with aluminum foil, and allow to rest for 20 minutes while you make the pan sauce.

To make the pan sauce, spoon off most of the fat from the roasting pan, leaving about 2 Tbsp, and place the pan over medium heat. Add the onions, garlic, and sage, stirring every few minutes until they are translucent and scraping up the roasted bits from the bottom of the pan. When the onions are slightly caramelized, deglaze with the cider (or apple juice) and reduce by half, about 5 minutes. Add the stock and bring it to a simmer. Season to taste, then turn off the heat and gradually add the butter, whisking until the sauce is emulsified. Strain the sauce through a fine-mesh sieve into a gravy boat.

To carve the roast, use a slicing knife to remove the loin from the rib bones, then cut the pork loin into slices and arrange them on a serving platter. Cut between each rib bone to separate them. Arrange the ribs alongside the sliced loin. Serve with the chutney and sauce on the side.

Soft and sweet Gorgonzola paired with bitter and charred grilled radicchio is fantastic—especially if used to stuff pork tenderloin. This tender cut is always a hit at my table, but tenderloin often needs help to step up its flavor, usually with a marinade or a sauce. Here I've done both of those things *and* stuffed it. Because why wouldn't you?

PORK TENDERLOIN STUFFED WITH RADICCHIO AND GORGONZOLA CHEESE

Using a thin boning knife, create a hole down the center of each pork tenderloin, about a ½-inch wide, being careful not to cut through either side of the meat. Think of it like you're cutting a hollow tube down the center of the tenderloin, like the air channel in a drinking straw. In a bowl large enough to hold the tenderloins, stir together ¼ cup of the oil, the soy sauce, and vinegar. Add the tenderloins, toss well, and cover with plastic wrap. Refrigerate for 3 to 4 hours.

When you're almost ready to eat, toss the radicchio with the sugar in a separate bowl. Add just enough cold water to cover the radicchio and set aside for 30 minutes. Drain and pat dry with paper towel.

Preheat the oven to 450°F. Line a baking tray with parchment paper.

Toss the radicchio with the remaining ¼ cup of oil and the onions. Season with salt and pepper. Arrange the radicchio mixture in a single layer on the baking tray and roast until slightly golden, about 30 minutes. Remove from the oven and allow to cool completely on the tray. Turn down the oven to 400°F.

Place the radicchio mixture in a bowl and add the Gorgonzola and vinegar. Season with salt and pepper, toss gently, and set aside.

Drain the marinade from the pork and pat the meat dry. Using a tablespoon, scoop radicchio stuffing into the center of the meat, generously filling each tenderloin. Drizzle along the outside of the tenderloin with oil.

Place a large ovenproof frying pan over medium heat. Once it's hot, add the tenderloins and brown on all sides. Transfer the pan to the oven, roast for 15 minutes, then remove from the oven and allow to rest for another 10 minutes. Slice the tenderloin into rounds and serve.

Serves 4

2 pork tenderloins (each about 12 ounces), cleaned of silverskin and excess fat

½ cup olive oil (divided) + more for drizzling

¼ cup soy sauce

¼ cup sherry vinegar

1 head radicchio, cut in 8 wedges

2 Tbsp sugar

½ red onion, cut in 4 wedges

Salt and pepper

½ cup Gorgonzola cheese

2 Tbsp balsamic vinegar

NOTE: Start marinating the pork 4½ to 5 hours before you plan to serve it.

Breaded Cutlets

Breading and frying meat is the cornerstone of comfort food—and it's so easy that everyone should know the few easy steps it requires. There are exceptions to these steps—for example, not all meats are pounded first—but overall, I guarantee great results if you follow them.

CHOOSE THE RIGHT CUT. Most butchers will use leg cuts, such as the inside round, outside flat, or sirloin tips, of pork and veal for cutlets because they are inexpensive and easily tenderized. While these cuts make perfectly good—sometimes great—fried cutlets, my favorite cut is a boneless loin because it is more tender and generally has more marbling and more flavor.

POUND YOUR MEAT. If you're pan-frying a breaded cutlet, the meat needs to be evenly thin. The thinner the better, because a thick cut of meat won't be properly cooked by the time the bread crust is golden. A good friend of mine who lived in Munich tells me the butchers there pound the meat until it's almost translucent. To do the job properly, you need a good mallet, but a small heavy pot will do. To pound the meat into a flat a cutlet:

1. Place your cutting board on a solid part of your work surface.
2. Unroll two large sheets of plastic wrap—one to cover the cutting board and a second to place on top of the cutlet. These will keep your mallet clean while you're pounding the meat.
3. Flatten the cutlet by pounding the meat away from you with the flat side of a mallet. By tapping lightly and evenly, you can easily see which areas need more flattening. When you're done, set the cutlet on a clean tray. Repeat with the remaining cutlets.

CREATE A DREDGING STATION. To bread meat properly, you need to coat it with flour, dip it in egg, and coat it with bread crumbs. To keep your kitchen clean, set up a dredging station before you begin to cook:

1. Fill a large flat container like a plate or a baking pan with at least 2 cups of flour (all-purpose is best). Season the flour with salt and pepper (take this into account when you season the meat).
2. Beat the eggs well in a large, shallow bowl. This is your egg wash.
3. Fill a roasting pan with fine bread crumbs. Use the freshest bread crumbs you can find, and if they seem chunky, sift them through a medium-mesh sieve to get rid of the larger bits.
4. Arrange the bowls of flour, eggs, and bread crumbs in a row, then add a final baking tray or plate large enough to hold the finished cutlets. Have parchment paper or aluminum foil on hand to prevent the breaded cutlets from sticking together as you layer them.

BREAD YOUR MEAT EFFICIENTLY. To keep your hands as clean as possible, use one hand to pick up the raw meat and place it in the flour. We'll call this your "wet" hand because it touched wet meat. Use your other hand, your "dry" hand, to scoop flour over the cutlet, flip it around, and ensure it is thoroughly coated (see image 1). Then, use your dry hand to drop the cutlet into the egg wash (see image 2).

Use your wet hand to completely cover the flour-dusted cutlet with egg, lift the meat and let the excess egg drip off, then set it into the bread crumbs. Using your dry hand, scoop some bread crumbs over the cutlet, coating evenly (see image 3). Set the cutlet on your baking tray. Repeat with the remaining cutlets.

FRY YOUR CUTLET. Choose a large frying pan deep enough to hold at least 1 inch of oil. Heat the oil over medium-high heat until it looks slightly shimmery, about 1 minute. Toss a pinch of bread crumbs into the oil. If they sizzle and pan-fry right away, the oil is ready. Immediately, using a pair of tongs, place a cutlet in the oil, setting down the edge closest to you first. Pan-fry for a couple of minutes, then peek at the underside. Once it's golden, turn the cutlet over to brown the other side. Transfer the cutlet to a clean baking tray to keep warm while you fry the remaining cutlets.

CLEAN YOUR FRYING PAN REGULARLY. After every two batches, pour off the leftover hot fat into a dry metal bowl. Use a dry paper towel to wipe out the pan before returning it to the stovetop, refilling it with oil, and frying more cutlets. DO NOT USE WATER TO CLEAN THE HOT PAN as it can warp the pan and cool it down.

Once you get the hang of these steps, you can add grated Parmigiano-Reggiano cheese or hot sauce to the egg wash. Or put garlic powder in the flour or dried oregano in the bread crumbs. Or try breading underripe tomatoes, shrimp, or mozzarella sticks. Now you know the basics, go forth and fry!

Pay attention to the details in this recipe. The baking soda, the vinegar, and the evenly trimmed belly will all add up to the perfect final dish: rich and delicious meat with a super-puffy crackling. You'll need six bamboo skewers.

Be sure to start this dish 2 days before you plan to eat it so the meat has time to absorb the flavors of the rub and the marinade.

CRISPY ROASTED PORK BELLY

Ask your butcher to trim the pork belly so it will lie very flat on an even surface. This ensures all the skin will get puffy and crackle at the same time when it is cooked. Tightly tape together six bamboo skewers so the pointed ends are aligned. Use the skewers to prick the skin, just getting through the tough collagen but not penetrating all the way into the meat. Make as many holes as possible (up to 1,000!) so the rub can get into the skin and draw out the moisture, which will help in the crackling process.

In a small bowl, mix together the baking soda and salt until well combined. Sprinkle the mixture evenly over the skin, using a pastry brush or a spoon to lightly spread it and coat the belly. Place the meat in a nonreactive casserole dish, cover, and refrigerate overnight.

The following day, thoroughly rinse the pork belly under cold, running water to remove as much of the rub as possible. Pat it dry and sprinkle a little cider vinegar over the skin. The vinegar will react with any remaining baking soda and cause it to foam. Run the belly under running water again, and repeat until it does not foam when sprinkled with vinegar.

To make the marinade, place the cider or juice, soy sauce, vinegar, and maple syrup in a large bowl. Add the garlic, shallots, ginger, star anise, bay leaves, thyme, sage, peppercorns, and salt and pepepr to taste, stir well, and bring to a simmer over medium heat. Remove the pot from the heat and cool. Pour the marinade into a nonreactive casserole dish large enough to hold the meat, then add the belly, skin side up. Keep the skin out of the marinade and as dry as possible. Refrigerate for another 24 hours.

About 2½ hours before serving, remove the belly from the marinade, reserving the marinade. Preheat the oven to 325°F. Using a box cutter or very sharp knife, score the skin of the belly in a crosshatch pattern, at 1-inch intervals. The belly will be easier to portion once it's roasted this way. Season the belly liberally all over with salt and pepper.

Serves 8 to 10

1 (5 pounds) pork belly, 12 inches square, skin-on

3 Tbsp baking soda

3 Tbsp salt

Pepper

Cider vinegar

MARINADE

2 cups apple cider or apple juice

½ cup light Japanese soy sauce (shoyu)

¼ cup cider vinegar

¼ cup maple syrup

4 garlic cloves, sliced

4 shallots, sliced

2 Tbsp sliced fresh ginger

6 whole star anise

6 bay leaves

6–8 thyme sprigs

6–8 sage sprigs

2 Tbsp black peppercorns

Salt and pepper

Place the belly on a wire rack set over a baking tray. Make sure it is very flat and even. Roast until fork-tender, about 1½ to 2 hours. Make a glaze while the belly is cooking.

Pour the reserved marinade into a saucepan. Bring to a simmer over medium heat and reduce until it coats the back of a spoon, about 10 minutes. Strain the glaze through a fine-mesh sieve into a side dish.

Remove the belly from the oven and allow it to rest while you turn up the oven to 550°F or as high as it will go. Once the oven has reached temperature, return the belly to the oven and roast until the skin gets crispy, about 10 minutes. Remove from the oven and allow to cool slightly on the rack.

Slice the belly into individual portions and arrange on a platter. Serve with the glaze on the side.

The idea for this recipe was born when I visited the tremendous outdoor market in Lyon, France. Next to the stalls filled with fruits, charcuterie, and spices was a man tending a rotisserie. As the chickens cooked, their juices dripped down onto slabs of pork belly with the bone still attached. This was a revelation to me because, as a chef, I was used to cooking pork belly with no bone as bacon or as slow-roasted pork belly. When I got home, I tinkered with the idea of the bone-in belly and came up with this delicious, hearty recipe, which is perfect for a summer evening meal under the stars.

GRILLED BONE-IN PORK BELLY

Score the skin of the pork belly in a straight line at ½-inch intervals, running in the same direction as the rib bones. (It will help when portioning the belly later and allow the marinade to penetrate the meat.) Season the belly liberally with salt and pepper—a large piece of belly needs a good amount of salt to flavor it well.

Place the garlic, lemon zest and juice, parsley, fennel seeds, rosemary, chili flakes, and oil in a food processor. Pulse until the mixture becomes a purée. Using your hands, rub this marinade all over the pork belly, massaging it well into the meat. Place the belly in a nonreactive bowl, wrap tightly with plastic wrap, and refrigerate for 3 days.

The day before you plan to serve the belly, preheat the oven to 350°F.

Place the belly in a roasting pan and add hot water until it reaches halfway up the belly. Cover the pan and roast for about 3 hours, or until the meat yields easily when a knife is inserted in the center of the roast. Take the belly out of the oven, then turn up the oven to 475°F.

Return the roast to the oven, uncovered, and cook until the skin puffs up and crackles, about 15 minutes. Remove the belly from the oven and allow it to rest for 1 hour, then wrap it tightly in plastic wrap and refrigerate overnight.

About 30 minutes before you plan to serve the belly, preheat your barbecue to medium-high. Unwrap the belly and discard the plastic. Using a sharp knife, cut between the rib bones. You should have 8 evenly sized belly chops.

Serves 8

1 pork belly from the shoulder end, 8 side rib bones left attached

Salt and pepper

16 garlic cloves, chopped

4 lemons, zest and juice + 2 lemons, cut in wedges, for garnish

1 cup chopped Italian parsley

¼ cup fennel seeds, toasted until fragrant and golden

¼ cup chopped rosemary

2 Tbsp chili flakes

½ cup olive oil

½ cup red pepper jelly

NOTE: Start marinating the pork belly 4 days before you plan to eat it.

recipe continues

Melt the red pepper jelly in a small saucepan over low heat.

Place the belly chops on the barbecue and brush them with the melted jelly. Grill, turning every few minutes, and basting with the jelly until they're nicely charred on the outside and a thermometer inserted into the center of one reads 160°F, 15 to 20 minutes total.

To serve, arrange the chops on a platter and serve immediately with lemon wedges on the side.

Ribs are a bit of a thing here in North America. Every summer, another RibFest seems to pop up in a new town, bringing smoker trailers, food trucks, rib stands, and dive-bar blues bands to a park where the masses line up to stuff their faces with deliciously slow-roasted pork, sucked off the bone. But you don't have to line up in the blazing heat to enjoy delicious pork ribs: they are easy enough to make at home, and there you can play whatever music you want while those babies slow-cook! Memphis-style ribs are simply dry-rubbed and basted with a juice-vinegar mixture while they roast slowly over wood smoke. I like to use a charcoal grill to cook the ribs, but a regular barbecue works just fine too.

MEMPHIS-STYLE BARBECUED SIDE RIBS

To remove the membrane from the underside of the ribs, slide a paring knife under the membrane at the cut edge of one of the middle bones. Lift up a few inches of the membrane, then grasp it with a paper towel and pull the rest of the membrane away from the bones. Discard the membrane.

Mix the spice rub with the sugar. Place the ribs in a large nonreactive pan and cover them all over with the rub, using your hands to massage it right into the meat. Cover and refrigerate overnight.

Preheat the barbecue to 250°F. If you are using a charcoal grill, soak 1 cup of wood chips in water for 30 minutes while the barbecue is preheating. When the grill is hot, toss half of the wood chips on the coals. (Add the other half partway through the cooking time.) If using a propane grill, preheat to 250°F and smolder the soaked wood chips in a smoker box.

Place the ribs on the grill, cover, and cook for 3 to 4 hours, or until the meat is pulling away from the rib bones. Stir the juice and vinegar together and baste the ribs every 15 minutes or so.

To serve, cut the ribs between each bone, arrange on a platter, and serve immediately.

Serves 2 to 3

1 rack of side ribs
1 cup BBQ Dry Rub (page 376)
¼ cup packed brown sugar
1 cup wood chips
1 cup apple juice
3 Tbsp apple cider vinegar

NOTE: Begin this dish the day before you plan to serve the ribs so they have time to absorb the flavor of the rub.

While this recipe won't be winning any traditional rib contests (it's not barbecue), it will win the hearts of your friends, family, and anyone else who loves a messy, lip-smacking, tender rib. I like to use back ribs here, as I find they are a bit more tender and work well with the braising technique. Serve with Sweet and Sour Baked Beans (page 355).

BAKED SAUCY RIBS

To remove the membrane from the underside of the ribs, slide a paring knife under the membrane at the cut edge of one of the middle bones. Lift up a few inches of the membrane, then grasp it with a paper towel and pull the rest of the membrane away from the bones. Discard the membrane.

Place the ribs in a large nonreactive pan and, cover them with the dry rub, using your hands to massage it right into the meat. Cover and refrigerate overnight.

Preheat the oven to 300°F.

In a large frying pan over medium-high heat, heat the oil. Sear the ribs, one bit at a time, until browned all over. You will need to maneuver the ribs around the pan a few times, but it's not as difficult as it might sound.

Place the ribs in a roasting pan and pour in 2 cups of boiling water. Cover the pan tightly with aluminum foil and bake until the meat yields easily when pierced with a knife, about 2 hours. Remove the pan from the oven and turn up the temperature to 400°F.

Line a baking tray with parchment paper. Place the ribs on the baking tray, baste well with ¾ cup of the sauce, and roast for 10 minutes. Baste the ribs with the remaining sauce and roast until caramelized, about 5 minutes. Remove from the oven and allow to cool slightly.

To serve, cut between each rib and arrange on individual plates. Serve immediately.

Serves 2 to 3

1 rack of back ribs
1 cup BBQ Dry Rub (page 376)
1 Tbsp vegetable oil
1 cup Dad's BBQ Sauce (page 369) or your favorite barbecue sauce (divided)

NOTE: Begin this dish the day before you plan to serve the ribs so they have time to absorb the flavor of the rub.

I came up with this recipe on a cool fall night when Des was around nine months old. He was just starting to eat whatever we ate and he loved soft stewed meat. Serve this with crusty country bread.

PORK AND WALNUT STEW

Preheat the oven to 350°F and line a baking tray with aluminum foil or parchment paper.

Heat the oil in a large ovenproof pot over medium heat. Place the pork in a large bowl and season liberally with salt and pepper, tossing it well. Working in batches, add the pork to the hot oil, stirring often to brown the meat all over. Using a slotted spoon, return the meat to the bowl.

Add the onions, carrots, celery, and garlic to the pot and season with salt and pepper. Turn the heat down to medium-low, stir the vegetables, and cover the pot. Sweat the vegetables, stirring them every few minutes, until soft and slightly caramelized, about 10 minutes.

While the vegetables are cooking, arrange the walnuts in a single layer on the baking tray. Roast in the oven until golden, about 15 minutes, then remove from the oven and allow to cool on the pan. Leave the oven on.

When the vegetables are cooked, remove the lid and add the pork. Turn the heat back up to medium. Add the wine and simmer until it is reduced by half. Add the stock and herb bundle, bring to a simmer, and cover. Place the pot in the oven and braise for 1 hour. Add the squash, stirring gently, cover again, and return the stew to the oven until the meat is soft, 30 minutes. Remove from the oven and discard the herb bundle.

Set a large fine-mesh sieve over a clean pot. Strain the stew through the sieve to collect the braising liquid. Place the sieve full of pork and vegetables over a bowl and set aside.

Place the pot of braising liquid over low heat and add three-quarters of the roasted walnuts. Using an immersion blender, purée the walnuts in the pot. (Or purée them with the braising liquid in batches in a blender. You want a smooth, emulsified sauce.)

Add the pork, vegetables, and the remaining walnuts to the puréed walnuts in the pot. Bring to a gentle simmer and season to taste. To serve, ladle the pork stew into individual bowls.

Serves 8

2 Tbsp olive or vegetable oil

3½ pounds pork shoulder, cut in 1½-inch cubes

Salt and pepper

¾ cup medium-diced onions

¾ cup medium-diced carrots

½ cup medium-diced celery

6 garlic cloves, chopped

2 cups walnuts, shelled

2 cups white wine

2 cups Chicken Stock (page 360)

1 herb bundle (8 thyme sprigs, 4 parsley sprigs, 3 bay leaves) (page 36)

1 cup diced butternut squash

NOTE: For best results, make sure the vegetables are diced the same size—a bit smaller than the meat cubes.

This simple Alsatian dish takes some time to make but it is rustic comfort food at its best and should be an essential part of your repertoire. On the next cold night, invite some friends over and throw this popular French bistro dish in the middle of the table with a baguette, some good mustard, a jar of gherkins, and plenty of Riesling. You'll be a star.

CHOUCROUTE GARNIE

In a heavy-bottomed pot over medium heat, melt 1 Tbsp of the butter with the bacon. Add the onions and garlic and sweat until translucent.

Add the ham hock, turn down the heat to medium-low, and cover the pot. Sweat for 15 minutes, then add the cabbage and herb bundle. Stirring frequently, cook for 30 minutes, or until the cabbage is translucent. Add the sauerkraut and wine, cover, and simmer for 1½ hours.

Turn the heat off the cabbage and keep warm. Using a pair of tongs, remove the ham hock and cool slightly. When cool to the touch, discard the skin and the bone, and shred the meat. Add the shredded hock meat back to the pot with the smoked pork chops, smoked sausages, weisswurst, and wieners. Cover and steam for 12 to 15 minutes.

While the meats are steaming, bring a medium pot of salted water to a boil over high heat. Add the mini potatoes and boil until fork-tender, 12 to 15 minutes. Drain the potatoes, return them to the pot, and toss with the remaining 1 Tbsp of butter and the chives. Season with salt and pepper.

Using a slotted spoon or tongs, transfer the chops, smoked sausages, weisswurst, and weiners to a cutting board. Slice them into attractive, bite-sized pieces. Taste the cabbage, and season with salt and pepper, if needed.

To serve, pile the cooked cabbage stew onto a large platter and arrange the smoked meats on top. Serve with the mini potatoes.

NOTE: This dish is traditionally made only with sauerkraut (*choucroute* is the French word for "sauerkraut"), but I prefer to add fresh cabbage to lighten the flavor of the dish. If you prefer to go classic, omit the fresh cabbage and double the amount of sauerkraut.

Serves 8 to 10

2 Tbsp butter (divided)

½ pound sliced bacon, cut in medium dice

3 large onions, thinly sliced

4 garlic cloves, minced

1 large smoked ham hock, 1¼ pounds, cut in quarters (ask your butcher to cut it on the band saw)

1 small head Savoy cabbage, shredded

1 herb sachet (1 Tbsp juniper berries, 10 thyme sprigs, 6 bay leaves) (page 36)

2 cups sauerkraut, drained

2 cups dry white wine (Riesling, Gewürztraminer, and Pinot Gris are all good choices)

4 smoked pork chops (Kassler chops)

4 large good-quality smoked pork sausages

4 weisswurst (found at German/ Eastern European delis)

4 pork wieners (hot dog–style)

1 pound mini potatoes, washed

1 Tbsp sliced chives

Salt and pepper

Over the years I have seen many different recipes for porchetta (pronounced "por-ketta"). It can be made with a whole pig, a loin, or, in this case, a shoulder wrapped in a belly. I prefer using the shoulder, as it is more succulent, but use a boneless pork loin if you like a leaner porchetta. You'll need to use the belly either way. Ask your butcher to cut the belly to the same length as the shoulder so it covers the entire shoulder. I also like to butterfly the shoulder and belly meats, as I get more of the delicious seasoning throughout this way. Serve porchetta as is with a side of roasted potatoes or pile some slices on good-quality ciabatta or brioche rolls.

PORCHETTA

Preheat the oven to 350°F. Have ready a roll of kitchen twine.

Arrange the fennel seeds on a baking tray and toast until slightly golden. Cool slightly, then crush the seeds lightly in a mortar and pestle or on a cutting board, using a clean, heavy pot.

Place the crushed seeds in a bowl, add the lemon zest, garlic, parsley, rosemary, chili flakes, salt, pepper, and oil, and mix thoroughly until well combined. Set aside.

Using a box cutter or very sharp knife, score the pork belly skin in a crosshatch pattern at 1-inch intervals. Then butterfly the belly, as if you're opening a book (see images 1 and 2 on the following page). Do the same with the pork butt, but make two cuts, opening the shoulder like a brochure (you want three flaps, see images 3 and 4).

Place the open pork butt on your work surface in front of you and slather the open side of the meat with half of the marinade.

Open the belly so the skin is facing down and to the left (like the front cover of the book, when open). Place the belly, meat side down, on top of the marinated shoulder. The skin side of the belly will be resting on your work surface, to the left of the shoulder. Rub the top side of the belly with the remaining marinade. You should have one long rectangle of meat, all with marinade on top (see image 5).

recipe continues

Serves 8 to 10

MARINADE

1 cup fennel seeds

5 lemons, zest only

12 garlic cloves, minced

½ cup finely chopped Italian parsley

¼ cup finely chopped rosemary

¼ cup dried chili flakes

¼ cup salt

2 Tbsp pepper

6 Tbsp olive oil

PORK ROAST

1 (3½ pounds) boneless pork belly, skin-on, cut in a square with the nipple end removed

1 (6 pounds) skinless, boneless pork shoulder, butt end (also called the capicollo)

2 Tbsp olive oil

Salt and pepper

NOTE: Be sure to start this recipe 1½ days before you plan to serve it so the pork has time to take on the flavor of the marinade.

Starting from the right side of the shoulder, fold the shoulder meat on top of the belly meat and roll it toward the left (see images 6 and 7). You should have a roll of roast with the dry skin exposed. Use the kitchen twine to tie the roast well (see images 8 and 9), then place it in a nonreactive container, cover, and refrigerate for 24 hours.

When you're ready to cook, preheat the oven to 450°F. Have a roasting pan with a V-shaped roasting rack ready.

Place the roast, skin side up, on the V-rack and rub the oil all over the meat. Season the skin with salt and pepper. Place the roasting pan in the oven and roast until the skin is crispy and dark golden brown, about 30 minutes. Turn down the oven to 275°F and continue cooking until a thermometer inserted in the thickest part of the meat reads 160°F, about 3 hours. Remove the porchetta from the oven, tent it with aluminum foil, and allow it to rest for 45 minutes.

To serve, slice the porchetta thickly. (Note that because of the butterflying technique, the roast will fall apart and your slices will not be perfect. That's part of the charm of this dish for me.) Arrange the porchetta slices on a serving platter or load them onto fresh buns.

LAMB

Lamb

I DIDN'T GROW UP EATING MUCH LAMB; in fact, I think I was 17 years old before I ate it for the first time. My mother had roasted a lamb for Easter supper, and I realized that night that I needed to eat more lamb. The leg meat was delicious—tender and mild, with a hint of the grassy gaminess lamb is known for, and it was served with mint jelly. I was hooked. Then, when I started cooking in restaurants, I realized there's some kind of unwritten rule that says there should be one lamb dish on the menu. I quickly got the hang of cooking each restaurant's lamb dish—tasty cuts such as rack of lamb, lamb T-bone, lamb sirloin, and braised lamb shank. Since opening the butcher shop, where I only bring in whole lambs to butcher, I've had to get familiar with cooking all the different cuts so I can discuss them with my customers. Which, to be honest, is a great problem to have. My entire family loves the flavor of lamb, and feeding them has opened up a whole new world of dishes and cooking techniques for me.

RAISING SHEEP

Lamb has a unique fresh, grassy, earthy, herbaceous flavor that's due to a fatty acid that only sheep contain. The flavor of the lamb depends hugely on its diet. In New Zealand, sheep get a steady—actually, pretty much exclusive—diet of grass, and they're prized for their mild grassy flavor. Lamb from the U.S. and Canada can have less of that flavor, as grain finishing is prevalent here in North America. The distinctive taste of lamb can evoke strong reactions, both positive and negative. I find that when it's prepared well, with appropriate side dishes and sauces, lamb can win over almost all naysayers. That said, the flavor becomes more robust as the animal ages. My customers seem to prefer the taste of younger, milder-tasting lambs; the lambs I bring in to the shop are usually between 5 and 10 months old, and the finished carcass is about 50 pounds.

Mutton refers to meat from a sheep that is over a year old. I've had mutton from animals that are up to two, even three years old, and it was delicious. Yet finding someone who raises sheep for mutton is a very difficult task because the sheep take longer to raise, they require more food and care than younger lambs, and the market for mutton is small. It's true that the older the animal, the tougher the meat; however, mutton makes a perfect stewing or braising meat. Its flavor is like lamb with all of the "lambiness" accentuated, and it pairs well with similarly strong flavors like dark beer or curry. One of my favorite cooking methods is to slowly stew the meat with red wine and orange zest until it falls apart and then use it as a meat pie filling.

SHOPPING FOR LAMB

Lamb meat should be rosy pink, and its fat white. Lamb that has been sitting around too long is tacky to the touch; old lamb has a tremendously sour smell that you will recognize if you come across it. I prefer to buy fresh lamb, but frozen is fine as long as it is thawed slowly in the fridge. Don't run frozen lamb (or any meat, for that matter) under water to thaw it, as that could ruin the integrity of the product.

When you're shopping for fresh lamb, your shop should be able to tell you where the lamb came from. If it's Canadian or American, the flavor profile will be mild and sweet; if it's Australian or New Zealand, it will be grassier and more gamey flavored. Try both to decide which you like best.

CLASSIC FLAVOR PAIRINGS FOR LAMB

This list is not exhaustive, but playing around with any of these flavors should yield good results.

- **Anchovy**: Particularly good in marinades, the fish flavor mellows as the lamb cooks.
- **Curry spices**: Strong spices like coriander, cumin, and fenugreek pair very well with lamb, especially when they are toasted first and then ground.
- **Dates**: The sweetness of dried fruit pairs very well with the herbaceous lamb.
- **Fresh lemon**: Acid from a squeeze of lemon juice at the end of cooking really cuts through the fat in lamb and lends a fresh aroma to it.
- **Garlic**: Good garlic is essential in any lamb dish.
- **Mint**: The classic go-to for a jelly or sauce.
- **Olives**: Salty olives are a common ingredient in Mediterranean and Middle Eastern lamb dishes.
- **Preserved lemon**: A great companion to lamb. Use only the peel.
- **Rosemary**: Another classic herb pairing, especially when mixed with garlic and lemon.

Meeting the Forsyths

It's a cool and wet late summer's day, and I'm visiting the Forsyths at their farm on a patch of bedrock in Grey County, near Georgian Bay. The soil's not great for growing many crops outside of the barley and peas they use as feed during the harsh Ontario winters, but when Shane moved here in 1980 with a flock of thirty sheep it was what he could afford. Brenda joined him a year later, and thus began their family business.

"You better hold on tight!" he says as he slams his foot on the gas of the off-road four-wheeler we're using to herd a flock of sheep that has escaped the pasture where they were *supposed* to be. I grasp the crossbar in front of me and my bones rattle as the wheels dip in and out of seemingly every rut and crevice. "To herd them, you have to go back and forth along their flank," he explains, "just close enough to get them moving." They are moving as one, jumping and running across the field, through a thicket of trees, and down a lane to their original pasture. Just as they are about to reach it, something spooks the leader and they all run off down the lane in the opposite direction. "Oh," says Shane, "it's going to be one of those days."

The Forsyths have about 400 ewes, and each one gives birth about three times every two years. Unlike many other animals, sheep are not raised exclusively for meat. There are breeds that have better coats for wool, like the Delaine Merinos, and then there are breeds such as East Friesians that produce an abundant supply of milk. For Shane and Brenda, it's all about the breed that produces the best meat, and for them it's the Dorset Horn. Brenda explains: "We try to choose our breeding stock based on meat qualities. We tend to stay away from animals raised for the showring, as those don't necessarily reflect a good carcass."

One of the reasons I've been working with the Forsyths for over a decade is because their lamb is consistently flavorful, with a lean finish and firm muscle. When I ask how they maintain this consistency, Shane tells me it's probably because they prefer to raise their lambs in a more traditional way. He explains: "In modern lambing, lambs are weaned from their mothers at around 6 weeks, then fed a soy-based formula that quickens their development. I prefer to keep them with their mothers for at least 3 months. Then I'll wean them off, having them eat as much grass as possible. When they get up to eighty pounds, we'll finish them with lot of hay, and some dried peas, barley, and oats. This will get their weight up to about 110 pounds or so; that's when they're ready for market. Sometimes they'll hit that weight at 5 months, sometimes at 10 months; it all depends on the animal."

Sheep farming is hard work; the animals never take vacation and their needs are relentless, and the hours are very long. The life of a farmer is a bit like driving a four-wheeler hastily through a pasture. If you're going to survive like Shane and Brenda, you better hold on tight.

Lamb Cuts

1. Neck

2. Foreshank

3. Shoulder/shoulder chops

4. Rack/rib chops

5. Short loin/saddle/T-bone chops

6. Sirloin

7. Bone-in leg roast

8. Leg steak

9. Boneless leg roast

10. Belly

Neck

The neck can be a very flavorful and economical cut, prepared either on the bone or boneless as a small roast (for two people). As the meat is very tough, it requires a long cooking time to make it tender.

***Good for:* braising, pressure cooking**

Foreshank

A lamb has four shank muscles in total, but the best cut is from the front of the animal. The foreshank is meatier with a smaller bone, and one shank easily serves one person. This is another tough but flavorful cut that requires a long cooking time to make it tender.

***Good for:* braising, pressure cooking**

Shoulder/Shoulder Chops

The shoulder can be prepared boneless or bone-in, ground or whole, or even cut into chops. It is a working muscle, but because lambs are younger, you can get some tender chops from the shoulder.

***Good for:* braising, grilling, pressure cooking**

Rack/Rib Chops

The rack refers to the entire line of ribs that run along the back and sides of the animal. It is the most tender cut of lamb and can either be served whole or cut into chops.

***Good for:* grilling, pan-frying, roasting**

Short Loin/Saddle/T-Bone Chops

The short loin comprises the striploin and tenderloin because the tenderloin is really too small to be sold on its own. These cuts are typically left on the bone and cut across to create lamb chops. Alternatively, both muscles can be taken off the bone but kept whole and tied together to create a delicious roast.

***Good for:* grilling, pan-frying, roasting**

Sirloin

The sirloin muscle along the back is either left attached to the leg or, more often, separated from it. The sirloin is tender and may be dry-roasted, or even diced and used on a skewer.

Good for: **roasting, grilling, sautéing**

Bone-In Leg Roast

The whole leg includes the sirloin muscle and aitchbone; ask your butcher to remove the aitchbone to make carving easier. The quintessential springtime Sunday roast.

Good for: **grilling, roasting**

Leg Steak

The cross cut of the thigh, the leg steak (a.k.a. chop) is an excellent economical choice for pan-frying, grilling, or broiling.

Good for: **grilling, pan-frying**

Boneless Leg Roast

Boneless leg is sold either butterflied or tunnel-boned (the bones are removed, leaving the meat intact). A tunnel-boned leg is great if you want to stuff the leg before roasting, as it provides a natural pocket. A butterflied leg is a perfect barbecue roast, charred and slowly cooked.

Good for: **grilling, roasting**

Belly

Lamb belly is the meat from the flank and can be quite fatty, but it's a solid cut if you take the time to stuff it, roll it, and braise it. It is also commonly used to make spiedino, an Italian skewered meat for the barbecue. I've had lamb bacon made successfully from belly as well.

Good for: **braising, grilling**

Slowly cooked in liquid so it is super succulent and tender, this lamb roast—from the shoulder rather than the more traditional leg—can blow your expectations out of the water. I like to pair this dish with a Simple Herbed Risotto (page 349) and some Carrots in Vinaigrette (page 354).

SLOW-COOKED LAMB SHOULDER

NOTE: Begin marinating the meat the day before you plan to serve this roast.

To prepare the roast, have ready a few feet of kitchen twine. Place the meat on your work surface in front of you. It should look rectangular except for a flap where the neck was. Cut off that flap and place it on top of the butterflied meat.

In a bowl, mix the parsley, chives, lemon zest, thyme, rosemary, and anchovy paste with the 3 Tbsp of minced garlic, the capers, oil, mustard, and vinegar to make a marinade. Season the lamb shoulder with salt and pepper, then use a spoon or a pastry brush to spread half the marinade all over the inside of the lamb. Starting at one edge, tightly roll up the meat and tie it with the twine.

Spread the remaining marinade over the outside of the roast, place it in a casserole dish just large enough to hold it snugly, cover, and refrigerate overnight.

About 4 hours before you plan to serve the roast, preheat the oven to 325°F.

Heat a little oil in a heavy-bottomed, ovenproof pot on medium heat. Add the roast and sear all over until well browned. Remove from the pot and set aside.

To the same pot, add the chopped garlic, the onions, carrots, turnips, parsnips, and celery, and sauté until caramelized. Season with salt and pepper, stir in the tomato paste, and cook for about 5 minutes, just to let the flavors meld.

recipe continues

Serves 6 to 8

1 boneless lamb shoulder, butterflied (about 5 pounds)

1 cup chopped Italian parsley leaves

½ cup minced chives

3 Tbsp lemon zest

1 Tbsp chopped thyme

1 Tbsp chopped rosemary

1 tsp anchovy paste

4 garlic cloves, chopped + 3 Tbsp minced garlic

3 Tbsp chopped capers

3 Tbsp olive oil + more for searing

2 Tbsp Dijon mustard

1 Tbsp red wine vinegar

Salt and freshly cracked black pepper

1 onion, cut in medium dice

1 carrot, cut in medium dice

1 turnip, cut in medium dice

1 parsnip, cut in medium dice

1 celery stalk, diced

2 Tbsp tomato paste

2 cups red wine

2 cups Chicken Stock (page 360)

1 herb bundle (4 rosemary sprigs, 4 thyme sprigs, 2 parsley sprigs, 2 bay leaves) (page 36)

2 Tbsp butter, cold, cubed

Deglaze the pot with the wine, return the lamb to the pot, and add enough stock to completely cover it (you might need more or less than 2 cups). Add the herb bundle. Bring the liquid to a simmer, cover with a lid, and roast in the oven until the meat is fork-tender, about 3 hours.

Remove the roast from the oven and allow it to cool in its cooking liquid for about ½ hour. Transfer the meat to a cutting board and discard the herb bundle.

In a blender, purée the braising liquid and the vegetables. Strain this liquid through a fine-mesh sieve into a clean pot and cook over medium heat until it coats the back of a spoon, about 10 minutes. Remove from the heat and gradually add the butter, whisking until the sauce is emulsified.

To serve, carve the roast into slices and arrange on a serving platter. Spoon some of the sauce on top and serve the rest in a gravy boat alongside.

A tagine is a cone-shaped cooking vessel traditionally used in Moroccan cooking. Meat (commonly lamb, chicken, and beef), vegetables, and liquid are placed in the shallow base, the lid is set on top, and as the food cooks, the steam inside the tagine falls back into the ingredients, creating a delicious combination of flavors. You don't need a tagine to make this dish—a Dutch oven will do the trick—but the flavor of the broth will be more intense if you do. Tagines are traditionally made from ceramic or unglazed clay and placed directly over a fire, so if you're using one, cook directly over a gas flame or on a charcoal grill. (The tagine could crack if placed on a heated electric or ceramic-topped element, but to prevent this you can use a heat diffuser, which are widely available to purchase online.) Feel free to double this recipe if your tagine is large enough. Serve with steamed couscous and plenty of flatbread to mop up the delicious juices at the bottom of the pot.

LAMB SHANK TAGINE

Serves 2

1½ tsp harissa paste (see note)

1 Tbsp olive oil

3 tsp salt (divided)

2 lamb shanks (each about 12 ounces)

1½ tsp pepper

½ tsp ground cumin

½ tsp ground coriander

¼ tsp ground ginger

¼ tsp ground cinnamon

½ tsp smoked or regular paprika

2 shallots, sliced into ¼-inch-thick rings

3 garlic cloves, chopped

1 small carrot, quartered lengthwise, and cut in 2-inch lengths

1 medium potato, peeled and cut in ½-inch wedges

1 celery stalk, cut in 2-inch lengths

¼ bulb fennel, cut in ½-inch wedges

10 black olives, pitted or whole

6 dried apricots

1 preserved lemon, peel only (see note)

3 bay leaves (dried are fine)

2½–3 cups Chicken Stock (divided, page 360)

In a medium bowl, mix together the harissa, oil, and 1½ tsp of the salt to form a paste. Using your hands, rub the paste all over the shanks, cover, and refrigerate for 6 hours.

If you don't have a gas stove, preheat the oven to 350°F. In a small bowl, mix together the remaining 1½ tsp salt, the pepper, cumin, coriander, ginger, cinnamon, and paprika.

recipe continues

Line the base of your tagine or Dutch oven with the shallots. Sprinkle the garlic over the top, and then place the lamb shanks on top of the shallots, crossing one on top of the other. Sprinkle half of the spice mix over the meat and shallots.

Arrange the vegetables over the lamb in a pyramid. Sprinkle the vegetables with the rest of the spice mix.

Scatter the olives, apricots, preserved lemon skin, and bay leaves around the vegetables. Pour 2½ cups of the stock into the base of the tagine or Dutch oven (don't pour it over the vegetables and meat).

To cook on a gas stovetop, cover the tagine (or Dutch oven) and place over very low heat. Bring the liquid to a simmer and cook for 2 hours. (If you're using the oven, cover the Dutch oven with a tight-fitting lid, bring to a simmer over medium heat, then transfer to the oven until the meat is tender, about 2 hours.) After 2 hours, check the tagine. If the liquid has reduced to a sauce consistency, add another ½ cup of stock and cook until the meat pulls away from the bone, about 1 hour.

Remove the tagine from the heat and allow to cool for 20 minutes. Bring the dish to the table and remove the lid in front of your guests for a "wow" effect.

NOTE: Harissa is a spice paste typical of North African cookery that generally includes a mix of roasted chili peppers and fennel. It can be found in most large grocery stores or online. If you can't find it, substitute 2½ Tbsp chili powder, 1 Tbsp ground fennel, 1 tsp garlic powder, and 1 tsp ground cumin mixed with 1½ tsp olive oil.

Preserved lemons are sold in jars in large grocery stores or online. I like to cut the lemon in quarters and then cut out and discard the flesh, which can be very bitter, saving the peel for use in the recipe. If you can't find preserved lemon, use the zest of a fresh lemon instead, peeled into strips.

Start this dish the morning of the day you plan to serve it so the meat has time to marinate.

I was raised Catholic. I was baptized and confirmed, and I went to confession a whole lot. I sang in the choir, was an altar boy for a couple of years, and went to Catholic school too. Yet I never understood why at Easter, we showed our respect and gratitude by eating a ton of chocolate eggs and cooking lamb. (Actually, in my family we never had lamb—we had ham. But Ham of God just doesn't sound right.) Ritual played a huge role in my life at that time. As an adult, I realize that religious rituals tied to feasting are a rare occasion for many a family to sit down and break bread together. So feasting with family is my religion now. The kitchen is my sacristy, our chairs are pews, the dinner table my altar. We eat beef roasts at Christmas. We eat pancakes on Shrove Tuesday. We eat lamb—like this roasted leg with tzatziki—at Easter. And we give thanks to the farmers, the grocers, and the cooks. Pair this with spring vegetables like asparagus, wild leeks, and peas.

ROASTED LEG OF LAMB WITH TZATZIKI

Rub the lamb leg all over with the marinade, wrap it in plastic, and refrigerate for at least 24 hours. If you have the time, 48 hours is preferable.

Preheat the oven to 300°F. Better yet, preheat a charcoal grill, adjusting the airflow to achieve 300°F. (I prefer to roast a leg of lamb on my charcoal grill. The flavor of the smoke that licks the meat on the grill just isn't replicated in the oven.) Have a roasting pan with an elevated roasting rack ready.

Place the marinated lamb leg on the roasting rack and place the roasting pan in the center of the oven. If you're using a charcoal grill, place the lamb slightly beside the charcoal, to avoid flare-ups. Roast until a thermometer inserted into the thickest part of the meat reads 135°F (for medium), about 2½ hours.

While the lamb is roasting, make the tzatziki. Place the grated cucumber in a serving bowl, salt it lightly, and allow to sit at room temperature for 1 hour. Drain any liquid from the bowl and, using your hands, squeeze the excess water from the cucumber. Add the yogurt, and then the mint, garlic, and lemon juice to the bowl, stir well, season with salt and pepper, and allow to sit at room temperature for another hour.

Transfer the lamb to a cutting board, tent it with aluminum foil, and allow to rest for at least 30 minutes. To serve, slice the lamb and arrange on a serving platter with the tzatziki on the side.

Serves 8 to 10

1 (6–7 pounds) bone-in lamb leg, aitchbone removed

1 cup Middle Eastern Marinade (page 374)

TZATZIKI
½ English cucumber, grated

Salt and pepper

2 cups thick Greek-style yogurt

3 Tbsp chopped mint leaves

½ tsp minced garlic

1 Tbsp lemon juice

NOTE: Start marinating the lamb at least a day before cooking it.

This recipe is based on a couple of French country recipes I've played with over the years. You start it right after breakfast, it cooks slowly while you go about with your day, and you finish it when your guests show up. Easy-peasy, really. I call this a roast, but it's really more of a braise—a long, slow cook with moisture. It also seems like a lot of garlic, but it sweetens as it cooks and produces an excellent sauce.

SEVEN-HOUR ROASTED LEG OF LAMB WITH LOTS OF GARLIC

Preheat the oven to 500°F. Have a roasting pan with an elevated roasting rack ready.

Season the lamb with salt and pepper and rub in the 2 Tbsp of oil. Place the lamb on the roasting rack and set the roasting pan in the oven. Roast until golden, about 20 minutes. Remove the lamb from the oven, and turn down the oven temperature to 250°F.

In an ovenproof casserole dish just large enough to fit the leg of lamb, heat the remaining 1 cup of oil over medium heat. Add the garlic and rosemary and fry until the garlic starts to release its aroma. Place the browned lamb leg on top of the garlic, then add the stock over and around the lamb. Bring to a simmer, cover with a lid, and place in the oven. Roast for 7 hours, or until fork-tender.

Remove the casserole dish from the oven and carefully transfer the lamb to a serving platter (it will want to fall off the bone) and cover with aluminum foil while you make the sauce.

Using a ladle, skim off and discard as much fat as possible from the top of the roasting juices (without removing the brown juice). Discard the rosemary stems (the leaves will still be in the pot—that's ok).

Place the casserole over medium heat and bring to a simmer. Add the lemon juice and salt and pepper to taste. Strain the roasting juices through a fine-mesh sieve into a clean pot, using the back of the ladle to push the cooked garlic through, puréeing it as you do so. Scrape the underside of the strainer, ensuring all the good bits of garlic get into the sauce. Discard the solids from the strainer. Bring the sauce to a simmer over medium heat, season to taste, and pour into a gravy boat.

To serve, remove the foil from the lamb and set the garlic sauce alongside. Pull chunks of the lamb away from the bone and serve.

Serves 8 to 10

1 (6–7 pounds) bone-in leg of lamb, aitchbone removed

Salt and pepper

1 cup + 2 Tbsp olive oil (divided)

4 bulbs garlic, split into whole, peeled cloves (30–40 cloves)

6 rosemary sprigs

2 cups Beef Stock (page 361)

2 Tbsp lemon juice

Rack of lamb is a special cut, usually reserved for dinner parties with friends you want to impress. The rack is basically the prime rib of the lamb world (so good we used it for the cover of this book!): it has very tender meat and a lovely bit of fat and is an all-around excellent cut. It can be cut into individual chops and grilled, or roasted whole, as in this recipe.

BALSAMIC-GLAZED RACK OF LAMB WITH PISTACHIO MINT PESTO

In a small bowl, mix together the vinegar and molasses, then season with salt and pepper. Brush the marinade all over the lamb and place it in a large bowl with the garlic and rosemary. Cover and refrigerate for 6 hours.

Preheat the oven to 350°F. Line two baking trays with parchment paper. Have ready two sheets of aluminum foil.

Pour 1 Tbsp of the oil into a large frying pan set over high heat. Remove 1 rack of lamb from the marinade and place it in the pan, fat side down. Sear for 4 minutes, or until golden brown on one side. Turn it over, sear the other side, and transfer to a baking tray. Wipe the frying pan clean, add another 1 Tbsp of oil, and repeat with the second rack of lamb.

Fold a sheet of aluminum foil around the rib bones on each rack to prevent them from scorching while they cook. Place the lamb, bone side down, on the baking trays.

Using a slotted spoon, remove the rosemary and garlic from the marinade and chop them finely. (You'll have to pick the rosemary leaves off the stems first.) Return them to the marinade, stir well, then spoon the mixture over the lamb loin. Roast the lamb until a thermometer inserted into the thickest part of the loin reads 135°F, about 20 minutes. Remove from the oven and allow to rest for 10 minutes.

To make the pesto, place the remaining 2 Tbsp oil, the anchovies, pistachios, mint, parsley, and lemon zest in a blender. Purée until smooth, adding more oil, 1 tsp at a time, if needed. Season with salt and pepper and spoon into a small serving bowl.

To serve, discard the foil from the lamb. Cut between the bones and arrange the lamb chops on a serving platter. Serve the pesto alongside.

Serves 4

2 Tbsp balsamic vinegar

2 Tbsp fancy molasses

Salt and pepper

2 (each 1½–2 pounds) racks of lamb, bones frenched (ask your butcher to do this)

4 garlic cloves, crushed with the side of a knife

4 rosemary sprigs

4 Tbsp olive oil (divided)

2 small anchovies

½ cup shelled pistachios, toasted

3 Tbsp chopped mint leaves

2 Tbsp chopped Italian parsley leaves

1 tsp minced lemon zest

NOTE: The flavor and texture of the lamb don't need any help from a marinade, but I like how the balsamic vinegar and molasses complement the rack. You can skip the marinade and just season the meat with salt and pepper if you prefer.

If you plan to use the marinade, start half a day ahead; if not, this is a very quick recipe.

I first started making this dish at Mistura, where we stuffed the lamb with foie gras and truffles. Nowadays, at the shop, we make this version with dried cranberries, Parmigiano-Reggiano cheese, and red wine around holiday time, as it looks spectacular and feels quite decadent. We call this a "royale" due to its luxurious nature, and I'm sure your guests will feel like royalty when digging in. This recipe is perfect for a dinner party because you can prep everything hours in advance, then throw the chops in the oven 30 minutes before serving. Serve with Rosti (page 345).

LAMB CHOP "ROYALE"

Place the lamb chops on a cutting board and cut out the smaller rib bones so it looks like each chop has only one bone. Arrange the chops on their side, with the "eye" facing up. Use a meat mallet to flatten each lamb to half of its original thickness. Season each chop with salt and pepper.

Place a large frying pan over high heat and add the oil. When it's hot, sear the lamb chops on both sides, just enough to give them a golden-brown crust, about 3 minutes per side. The lamb should still be blue-rare. (If your pan is large enough to hold all the lamb chops with at least 1 inch between them, sear them all at once. If not, sear them in batches.) Transfer the chops to a baking tray to cool.

Place the cranberries and wine in a small saucepan over medium-high heat and bring to a simmer. Cook until the wine is reduced by half, then remove the pot from the heat and allow to cool. Strain out the cranberries, reserving the wine. Set aside.

In a small frying pan over medium heat, melt the 1 Tbsp of butter. Add the shallots, garlic, and carrots and sweat until translucent. Add the thyme and chives, and season with salt and pepper. Remove from the heat and set aside to cool. Once cool, fold in the cranberries, bread crumbs, and cheese. Set aside.

To prepare the cabbage, fill a large bowl with ice water. Bring a large pot of water to a boil over high heat and season it with a generous pinch of salt. Have ready some paper towels or a towel.

Serves 4

1 rack of lamb, bones frenched (about 1½ pounds, ask your butcher to do this), cut in 4 even "double" chops (each chop should have two rib bones)

Salt and pepper

2 Tbsp olive oil

½ cup dried cranberries

½ cup red wine

1 Tbsp + ¼ cup butter, cold, cubed (divided)

2 shallots, minced

2 garlic cloves, minced

1 small carrot, finely diced

1 Tbsp finely chopped thyme

1 Tbsp finely chopped chives

2 Tbsp bread crumbs, preferably panko

2 Tbsp finely grated Parmigiano-Reggiano cheese

4 large Savoy cabbage leaves (+ 3 or 4 extra for "just in case")

4 caul fat sheets, about 8 inches square (see note)

½ cup Beef Stock (page 361)

1 thyme sprig

recipe continues

Place a cabbage leaf on your cutting board. Using a paring knife, cut a triangular wedge from the core of the leaf. You should end up with something resembling a leafy Pac-Man. Repeat with the remaining cabbage leaves. When the water is at a rolling boil, blanch the cabbage leaves until translucent, about 1 minute. Using a slotted spoon, gently transfer the leaves to the ice water bath, doing your best to keep them intact. (If your leaves fall apart, try again with the "just in case" leaves.) Once the leaves are cold, drain them well and dry on the towel.

Preheat the oven to 400°F. Line a baking tray with parchment paper.

To assemble a royale, place a seared lamb chop on your cutting board. Add a heaping Tbsp of the cooked cranberry stuffing on top of the chop, centered on the loin meat. Place a cooked cabbage leaf on top of the stuffing, with the "V" of the leaf surrounding the lamb rib bone. Wrap the cabbage leaf around the entire chop and set aside on a plate. Repeat with the remaining stuffing, cabbage leaves, and chops.

Wipe down your cutting board and arrange a sheet of caul fat on top. Place the lamb chop, stuffing side down, on top. Tightly wrap the chop with the fat, nesting any excess fat on the underside (the non-stuffing side) of the wrapped chop, and place, stuffing side up, on the baking tray. Repeat with the remaining chops and then roast the royales until the fat is golden and a thermometer inserted into the loin meat reads 135°F, 25 to 30 minutes. Remove from the oven and allow to rest for 10 minutes.

To make the sauce, pour the reserved red wine into a small saucepan. Add the stock and thyme and bring to a simmer over medium heat. Reduce the sauce by a quarter, then remove from the heat. Gradually add the ¼ cup butter, whisking until the sauce is emulsified. Discard the thyme, then season with salt and pepper.

To serve, place the royales on individual plates. Pour the sauce into a gravy boat and serve alongside.

NOTE: Caul fat is a thin lacy membrane of fat that surrounds the internal organs of pigs, cows, and sheep. It is flavorless and odorless, and when it's laid out it looks like delicate webbing. Caul fat is not sold in individual sheets; instead, you'll buy a 1- or 2-pound ball from a butcher. Each ball will most likely contain a few sheets of membrane wrapped up around each other and frozen. Thaw the ball slightly, then unwrap it to get a few sheets to use in this recipe. Pack the rest of the ball into a resealable plastic bag and freeze for another time.

Lamb T-bone chops, also known as lamb loin chops, are delicious little chops cut from the saddle, or shortloin, of the lamb. There are two muscles at play here: the striploin and the tenderloin. Both are very tender and very tasty. You can broil or pan-fry lamb chops, but I really like them charred on a charcoal grill, though propane or gas will do nicely as well.

LAMB T-BONE CHOPS WITH ROASTED ONIONS

In a large casserole dish, mix the garlic and chopped parsley with ¼ cup of the oil until well combined. Add the chops, toss well, and season with salt and pepper. Cover, refrigerate, and allow to marinate for 4 hours.

Preheat the oven to 450°F. Line a baking tray with parchment paper.

In a bowl, mix the onions with the remaining ¼ cup of oil, sugar, paprika, and salt to taste, until well coated. Arrange the onions on the baking tray, cut side down, and roast in the oven until caramelized and cooked through, about 30 minutes. Remove from the oven and allow to cool. Preheat the grill to high.

When the onions are cool enough to handle, peel and discard the skins. Cut each half onion into thick wedges and place them in a bowl. Add the green onions, whole parsley leaves, and vinegar, and toss well. Arrange the mixture on a serving platter.

Grill the chops, turning often, until lightly charred on the outside. To test for doneness, use a thermometer inserted in the thickest part of the meat near the bone. When it reads 145°F, the chops are cooked (they will be medium near the bone and medium-well done closer to the edge). Remove from the grill and allow to rest for 10 minutes.

To serve, place the chops on the bed of the roasted onions. Serve immediately.

Serves 4

6 garlic cloves, minced

2 Tbsp chopped Italian parsley leaves

½ cup olive oil (divided)

12 (each about 1 inch thick) lamb T-bone chops

Salt and pepper

2 pounds red onions, unpeeled and cut in half from north to south

1 Tbsp sugar

1 tsp smoked (not spicy) paprika

3 Tbsp sliced green onions

3 Tbsp whole Italian parsley leaves

1 Tbsp red wine vinegar

NOTE: Allow 4 hours for the chops to marinate before you cook them.

Reverse-searing involves cooking a piece of meat at a very low temperature for a long time to achieve the desired internal temperature before searing it over high heat to get a crispy crust. This technique works well for large cuts of steak, like thick striploins, rib eyes, and porterhouse, where the meat will slowly get to the right color and temperature without being under- or overcooked. I like to reverse-sear lamb sirloin—a great family cut that averages 1 to 1½ pounds—because the long, slow roast with dry heat tenderizes the muscle, leaving it slightly pink without drying it out. This technique also works well for a whole butterflied leg of lamb. Serve with Grilled Asparagus with Mediterranean Flavors (page 352).

REVERSE-SEARED LAMB SIRLOIN

In a casserole dish large enough to hold the lamb, mix together the rosemary, parsley, garlic, lemon zest and juice, oil, and salt and pepper to taste. Add the lamb, spoon the marinade over the meat until it's well coated, cover, and refrigerate for at least 12 hours.

Preheat the oven to 200°F. Have a roasting pan with an elevated roasting rack ready.

Place the lamb on the roasting rack, place the pan in the oven, and roast for 2½ hours. To test for doneness, insert a thermometer in the thickest part of the meat. (I like medium-well done, so I would take it out when the thermometer reads 145°F.)

Heat a large frying pan over high heat. Sear the lamb on each side until golden and slightly charred, about 4 minutes per side. Remove from the pan and allow to rest for 5 minutes.

To serve, cut the lamb into slices and arrange them on a serving platter.

Serves 3 to 4

2 Tbsp chopped rosemary

2 Tbsp chopped Italian parsley

1 Tbsp minced garlic

1 Tbsp grated lemon zest

1 Tbsp lemon juice

1 Tbsp olive oil

Salt and pepper

1 (1½–2 pounds) lamb sirloin roast

NOTE: Allow the lamb to marinate for a day before you cook it.

BEEF

Beef

WHEN I WAS A YOUNG COOK learning the ropes in kitchens, the grill cooks were the ones we all looked up to. They're the ones entrusted with making sure everyone's proteins are cooked properly, every single time. Most often working alone, the grill cook quickly seasons, flips, adds to, and removes a lot of different cuts from the grill or pan for up to 4 hours nonstop. And beef is always the most stressful protein to cook. Blue, rare, mid-rare, medium, mid-well, well done. First, you must know all of these colors by touch—no instant-read thermometers allowed. Second, you must be able to tell the difference in colors for different cuts of meat. A medium tenderloin feels different from a medium striploin, for example. Third, you have to time the meat so it rests for the perfect amount of time before being plated. And you are responsible for correctly seasoning each cut, controlling the heat source, and often slicing the meat for plating. In other words, it helps to have a cool head on your shoulders when cooking beef—whether it's beef roast or steak for a celebratory meal or ground beef for a quick Tuesday night dinner. Beef's versatility is its true strength, and my wish is that you understand, ask for, and use different cuts. There is a delicious world beyond striploin steaks, tenderloin steaks, stewing beef, and ground beef.

RAISING BEEF (AND VEAL)

To talk intelligently about beef, you need to know the difference between cows, heifers, steers, and bulls.

- **Cows:** Females that have had at least one calf and are raised for dairy production, or cow-calf operations that produce meat calves.
- **Heifers:** Unbred females that will not be mothers and are raised for meat production.
- **Steers:** Castrated males that are raised for meat.
- **Bulls:** Bred to sire and are generally the kings of a beef farm.

What's the Deal with Veal?

Veal is the retail term for bull—read male—calves, usually about 5 to 7 months old, or when the calf is heavy enough to "go to market." When a cow gives birth, the dairy farmer will generally check the sex, and a female will be kept and raised as another producer of udderly delicious milk (c'mon, that joke is amazing), whereas a male will be shipped off to another farm about a week after his birth to be raised with other little dudes.

Some veal calves are raised in outdoor hutches, which look like big, white, plastic doghouses. I'm not convinced the calves love this arrangement, since they're chained to their hutches. Other calves are raised in indoor stalls, which provide more protection during crappy winter weather. And still other calves are raised in indoor pens—sometimes crowded, sometimes not. Although farmers check up on the calves regularly, sometimes shit goes down. I'm not a fan of any of these conventional methods of raising veal.

Whenever possible, I try to get veal from organic dairy farmers who raise Holsteins for their milk. These farmers keep the bull calves with their mother from the time they are born until they are ready for market (a delightful euphemism for the less palatable "for slaughter"). The animals I buy have been fed by their moms until they were slowly weaned with some molasses-covered grain and then left to eat grass with everybody else. Once the calves reach market weight, the farmers call me and let me know they're ready to go.

Veal raised in this way doesn't come into the market very frequently, and after the last veal I bought was passed over for beef steaks, chicken breasts, and leg of lamb—I almost decided not to carry it anymore. But then I remembered a pastured veal sirloin steak I cooked for Alia and me, simply grilled with some sautéed mushrooms. The veal's tender meat, with a bit of chew and slightly herbaceous, sweet taste, made for a special meal. If you've never tried pastured veal, I highly recommend it.

You'll find two types of veal at the retail level: white and red. White veal is from a calf that has only eaten a skim milk solution loaded with vitamins and nutrients, which ensures a creamy colored meat and extremely mild, almost neutral flavor. White veal chops are very popular in posh restaurants. Red veal is from a calf that gets a skim milk solution and then has corn and grains gradually introduced to its diet, which results in a meat with more robust, stronger flavor than white veal.

Let's Be Clear about Steer

Male calves raised beyond their veal years become beef steers. Steers and heifers are raised primarily in open fields, eating grasses and pasture during the warmer months and hay and silage (fermented grass) in the colder months. The animals reach market weight between 18 months and 2 years. Many beef cattle get a ratio of grain and corn throughout the winter to keep their weight up, and regardless of season, many steers and heifers are fed a good amount of grain in the last three months of their lives, give or take, to fatten them up and promote intramuscular marbling. Cattle that are "corn-fed," "grain-fed," or "corn-finished" are typically fed corn, soy, and other high-starch, high-carbohydrate foods to increase their size at a much quicker rate and get them deliciously fat. Grain-fed beef fat is sweet and velvety, and the number-one choice in North America. Common breeds raised for beef are Angus, Hereford, and Limousin, or a genetic combination of the three. Increasingly popular is meat from cattle that are "100% grass-fed," which means they have been on a diet of grass, hay, and silage their whole lives.

BREEDS

There are many different breeds of cattle and they each have their own unique characteristics. In my travels, I have found that each country has different preferences when it comes to the beef they raise. France, for example, loves the lean, long muscles of a Charolais, whereas Japan prizes its ultra-marbled Wagyu. Here are some of the more popular meat breeds and what they bring to the table.

Angus
The most common breed raised in North America, Angus beef is prized for its large muscle content, consistently high marbling, and ability to thrive in difficult environments like Canadian winters.

Charolais
The most common French breed, Charolais is well muscled but, in my experience, quite lean. It's great cross-bred with a smaller Angus, for example, to increase its muscle size while retaining the classic Angus marbling.

Chianina
One of the oldest domesticated breeds of cattle in the world, the Italian Chianina is known for its huge frame. It is a very tall and heavy animal that produces a high yield of quality meat, used in the classic *bistecca alla fiorentina*. It thrives in hot, sunny climates, is a great forager, and is fairly uncommon in North America.

Hereford
One of the most common breeds originating from England is the Hereford. Its tawny-brown coat and white face are a common sight on country roads in Canada,

the U.S., or pretty much any country in the world. It is often cross-bred as it contributes hardiness to the genetic line.

Limousin

Many of the farmers I work with raise Limousin cattle, a breed originally from France that has a very high muscle content and large loins. For consumers, this means big rib eyes and striploins that are great for sharing! The Limousin is often cross-bred for its hybrid vigor, which means it improves the yield of other breeds.

Wagyu

The word Wagyu actually refers to four breeds, all originally from Japan, with the Japanese Black being the most common of the four. The animals are bred and fed to produce muscle with an extremely high intramuscular fat content. In fact, the loins in the highest grades of Wagyu beef will have more visible white fat than red meat. Traditionally, Wagyu beef is sliced very thinly and seared on a hot stone or frying pan, just to warm the meat through and melt the fat. In North America we like our beef steaks cut thickly, which doesn't work with Wagyu beef. The fat doesn't render properly and the steak isn't pleasant to eat, which isn't what you want after you've shelled out $200. My friend Chef Danny McCallum of Jacob's Steakhouse in Toronto has figured out the best of both worlds: he cuts a small cube of Wagyu beef, sears it on all sides over an intensely high heat, and then slices it thinly before serving. The result is beef that has steakhouse-char on the outside but is meltingly delicious on the inside.

SHOPPING FOR BEEF

Beef has a longer shelf life than any other protein, and it is sometimes purposely left to dry out in a fridge for a few weeks, so color is not always a good gauge of quality. A dry-aged steak that is black and leathery on the outside can open to a beautiful rosy bloom of steak inside.

When a steer is slaughtered, the carcass is usually hung for around 7 days to allow the beef to relax after it's gone through rigor mortis. Then the carcass is broken down into quarters. The front quarter includes the rib section and the shoulder, and the hind quarter includes the short loin and the hip. The quarters are further broken down into primal cuts, large cuts like the loin, the blade, and the rounds; it's then further processed into sub-primals like steaks and roasts, which are then packaged in vacuum bags and shipped to the grocery store or butcher shop.

Beef can age in the vacuum bags—this is called *wet-aging*—during which time the naturally occurring enzymes in the meat break down the muscle tissue, yielding a more tender beef. It can also age in the air. The bright red color of beef is due to myoglobin, a purplish-red iron-containing protein in the muscle of the beef. When a steak is cut from the whole muscle and exposed to oxygen, the surface of the steak becomes a bright, somewhat cherry-red oxymyoglobin (are you following, kids?). In most supermarkets, steaks are placed on trays and wrapped in a special plastic that allows in just enough oxygen to keep them looking cherry red for few days. At my butcher shops, our steaks are kept exposed to the air all the time in the butcher case, so they turn a deeper, darker purple color after a day or so. Those steaks are in the metamyoglobin stage and will still be excellent to eat for a few days. The darker, drier steaks can be mistaken for being not good and fresh, but I assure you they are delicious. In fact, I have quite a few customers who want the oldest, blackest steak I can give them. And believe me, they know what they're talking about.

Dry-aging beef means allowing the meat to slowly mature and tenderize in a chilled open-air environment. Butchers will normally reserve the loin or rib section of a steer and hang it in the cooler for longer than the standard 7-day period. This aging process allows the enzymes to tenderize the muscle fibers, but the beef also actually loses moisture, creating a finer grain of beef that is tighter and more pleasant to chew. Aging also changes the flavor: beef adopts an umami-rich blue-cheese flavor and a warm, nutty, popcorn-like savoriness as it ages. We find that aging the beef in a well-ventilated, humidity-controlled cooler set to between 35°F and 37°F for 35 days produces optimal tenderness and flavor. It takes a while to get the conditions right, but when you do, dry-aged beef is a culinary wonder. It's not easy to replicate the conditions to dry-age beef at home, however, so buy it from a butcher or ask your grocery store to carry it.

It will be hard to tell just by looking at steaks if they're dry-aged or not, so be sure to ask. Non-dry-aged beef can sweat out excess moisture—water weight—after it's been cut. It's the reason the pads that line Styrofoam meat trays were created and it's not a sign of poor quality. Too much liquid, though, is a sign the beef may have been previously frozen—a reputable grocery store will be transparent and label these products—although that's not necessarily an issue for braising cuts like beef cheek or oxtail.

Shopping for ground beef can be tricky, as you can't see what the beef looks like until you get it home and open it up. Ground beef can oxidize rather quickly, and it can look gray or brown in the middle of a package. This is not a problem unless it has an off-smell. Bad beef smells sour, and it isn't a smell you can ignore. Discard that beef right away and call the store you bought it from to get your money back.

Beef should be slightly tacky to the touch, and the grains of meat should feel strong. If you get beef that has no body—we call it "floppy" because it has poor muscle-fiber quality and little to no intramuscular fat—use it only for grinding.

Meet the Sculthorpes

James Sculthorpe and his brother Ian have been running their beef business for about as long as I've owned my butcher shop. They're young farmers whose passion for grass-fed beef is contagious. Ian got his first steer when he was 12 years old and hasn't looked back. He has studied how cattle are raised in Argentina and New Zealand, two of the world's top producers of 100% grass-fed beef, and brought this knowledge to the family farm, which occupies 50 acres of land lush with grass and clover near Lake Ontario. These animals eat well.

Raising cattle exclusively on grass can take 6 to 12 months longer than fattening animals on grain, but it promotes the slow growth of muscles and produces beef that is naturally higher in omega-3 fatty acids (the good ones), contains a beneficial fatty acid called conjugated linoleic acid (CLA), and is much lower in monounsaturated fat. What does that mean for you? Think leaner beef with greater health benefits, in particular cardiovascular health, and an overall mild herbaceous flavor due to the animal's diet. I also find that the fat from grass-fed beef lacks the greasy mouthfeel that grain-fed beef can sometimes have.

James left a career in finance to focus on building this business, and he and I have had many discussions about the future of grass-fed beef. It costs more to raise these cattle, both because they require more time to reach market weight and because they need more land to forage for grass. Ten years ago there was little demand for this meat, but some of our customers now request it regularly. To be truly sustainable, however, farmers raising grass-fed cattle need to work with restaurant owners to grow the market; for example, one large restaurant committed to offering 100% grass-fed beef burgers can help farmers raise and process more animals. This is how the industry will grow.

Some consumers believe that because the meat from grass-fed cattle is leaner and lacks the intense marbling of grain-fed meat, it could be dry or tough. This is not at all true. James and Ian have even brought in a few Devon bulls from New Zealand in an effort to combat this misconception. This breed's genetic makeup allows for decent marbling for grass-fed beef, especially when crossed with the Angus breed, and the result has been consistently improved marbling in this beef year after year. On one of my visits to their farm the Sculthorpes surprised me. "See that bull over there?" James asked, pointing at a rather large, ahem, well-testicled beast, "That's one of the Devon bulls. We call him Peter, Duke of Kensington." Well, I was certainly chuffed. I can finally show my Alia what kind of bull I'm responsible for!

Beef Cuts
STEAKS

1. Rib eye

2. Bone-in rib steak/cowboy steak/
côtes de boeuf

3. Minute steak

4. Striploin

5. Tenderloin

6. T-bone and porterhouse

7. Top sirloin

8. Coulotte/picanha

9. Flank steak

10. Bavette steak

11. Skirt steak

12. Petite tender

13. Flat iron/paleron/blade steak

14. Chuck tail flap

15. Denver steak

16. Hanger

STEAKS

Rib Eye

The rib eye comes from the boneless rib section between the shoulder blade and the striploin. It is very tender and tends to have a greater interior fat content than the other loin steaks. The rib eye from closest to the shoulder end will have a larger portion of the spinalis dorsi muscle. The spinalis dorsi has a bit more chew than the loin, but the juiciness and flavor are well worth it.

Good for: **grilling, pan-frying, sous vide**

Bone-In Rib Steak/Cowboy Steak/Côtes de Boeuf

All these different names describe the steaks that are cut from between each rib bone when these bones are left surrounding the rib muscle. Each steak is normally 1 to 2 inches thick, depending on the size of the loin, and can weigh up to 2 pounds. The rib bone is either cut short or cleaned of excess meat and fat or "frenched" and left long for an impressive presentation.

Good for: **grilling, pan-frying, sous vide**

Minute Steak

A minute steak is a quick-frying or grilling steak cut from the hip muscles such as outside flat or inside round. Since these steaks are cut from hardworking muscles and are naturally quite tough, they are sliced very thinly and sometimes tenderized with a mallet or perforator machine to improve the eating experience.

Good for: **grilling, pan-frying**

Striploin

The striploin, sometimes referred to as a New York cut or sirloin, is the part of the loin that moves from the rib eye toward the hip. This premium steak is similar to a rib eye in terms of tenderness, and when well marbled can be as juicy and satisfying. The striploin has less interior fat than the rib eye, but more exterior fat (i.e., fat cap), a little of which should be left on the steak to savor once cooked.

Good for: **grilling, pan-frying, sous vide**

Tenderloin

The tenderloin is a nonworking muscle that hangs inside the carcass, just on the other side of the spine from the striploin, and increases in size as you move toward the rear of the animal. It is the leanest and most tender cut of beef available. It is most typically prepared as a steak, grilled or pan-fried over high heat and sometimes finished in the oven. It can also be served raw as beef carpaccio or steak tartare.

Good for: **grilling, pan-frying, poaching, sous vide**

T-Bone and Porterhouse

The T-bone is a cross-cut of the long loin section, with the striploin on one side and the tenderloin on the other. It is often quite large and can be a good steak for two people to share. Porterhouse are the last two to three T-bone steaks closest to the rear of the animal and are typically cut 2 inches thick. A porterhouse will include a full piece of the tenderloin.

Good for: **grilling, pan-frying**

Top Sirloin

A large muscle from the very back of the loin section, this cut is very versatile and can be made into roasts and steaks. It is fairly tender and very lean. It can be a less expensive substitute for tenderloin, especially in a raw preparation like tartare.

Good for: **grilling, pan-frying, sous vide**

Coulotte/Picanha

Also known as the picanha or top sirloin cap, the coulotte is a triangular muscle that sits on top of the top sirloin. It can be sold whole as a large tender grilling roast or cut into portions as steaks, often with the fat cap left on. It is an excellent and economical large-format steak to cook for six or more people.

Good for: **grilling, pan-frying, roasting, sous vide**

Flank Steak

One of three belly steaks from cattle, the flank is quite lean and has medium tenderness. It is often marinated, as the long grain absorbs a lot of flavor. It is most often grilled or pan-fried but can also be used as a quick braising steak. After cooking it should be sliced thinly and across the grain.

Good for: **braising, grilling, pan-frying, sous vide**

Bavette

Also known as flap meat, the bavette also comes from the belly area. It has more fat, especially intramuscular, than flank steak, but overall is leaner than the skirt. *Bavette* means "bib" in English and describes the shape of the muscle, which can vary in thickness but is consistently packed with flavor. Like the flank, it should be sliced thinly across the grain after cooking.

Good for: **braising, grilling, pan-frying, sous vide**

Skirt Steak

The third of the belly steaks, the skirt steak has the most fat of the three and is also the most tender. Since it is such a thin steak, it is best cooked quickly over very high heat. Skirt is often marinated before cooking and is used in a lot of Latin dishes. There is both an "inside" skirt and an "outside" skirt on a carcass: they can be used interchangeably, but the outside is slightly thicker than the inside.

Good for: **grilling, pan-frying**

Petite Tender

This interior muscle on the blade (upper part of the shoulder) takes a fair amount of skill to cut, which is one reason it's not as readily available as other cuts. Because it comes from the shoulder, the petite tender is a bit chewy but very flavorful. It is shaped like a pork tenderloin and takes well to quick cooking using dry methods such as grilling and pan-frying.

Good for: **grilling, pan-frying**

Flat Iron/Paleron/Blade Steak

The flat iron comes from the shoulder, where it is protected on two sides by bone. It is actually two muscles bisected by a thick layer of connective tissue. To cut a flat iron, the butcher has to remove the inedible connective tissue and fabricate two long, thin, tender muscles. It's considered the second-most tender cut of steak (after tenderloin). When cross-cut, this steak is commonly known as a blade steak or paleron.

Good for: **braising, grilling, pan-frying**

Chuck Tail Flap

This muscle sits in the shoulder between the chuck short ribs and the blade eye. It is a continuation of the short rib muscle and can be used in similar recipes or as a thin grilling steak. Its intense intramuscular marbling makes it extra juicy.

Good for: **braising, grilling, pan-frying**

Denver Steak

Cut from the boneless blade, which is butterflied open, the Denver steak is extracted from the center where the muscle grains are quite tight and the meat slightly more tender than the rest of the blade. Due to the small number of steaks it produces and amount of labor involved, this cut isn't as popular as others, but it is a very tasty option if you come across it.

Good for: **grilling, pan-frying**

Hanger

The hanger, also known as back steak or onglet, quite literally hangs off the interior of the carcass. Classified as an offal (page 261), the hanger is rich in iron and has a deep flavor. The muscle fibers are looser than those of other steaks, and the whole muscle needs to be cleaned well of any silverskin or connective tissue before cooking.

Good for: **grilling, pan-frying**

STEAK: ALL YOUR QUESTIONS ANSWERED

In the land of a butcher's display cooler are many delights. There are hills of oxtails and valleys of bacon. There are the plains of lamb, which aren't very plain at all. There are the towers of pork chops, sometimes piled to such a precarious height that I wonder when they'll topple onto the pork roasts. Across from the tower of pork, over the plains of lamb, are the fields of beef steaks. Muscled and fatty, the steaks are kings of the land. They are the cuts shoppers drool over most. In North America, steaks are considered the best thing you can serve when the boss comes over. (By the way, I'm still waiting for an invite from any of my staff . . .) Many butcher shops carry over 12 types of steak, so it can be daunting to choose one. Don't be afraid to ask your butcher about different cuts and how best to prepare them. Or listen in on this typical conversation:

Q. Can I get a steak?

A. Yes. Yes, you can.

Q. What kind of steaks do you have there?

A. We carry quite a few cuts. Almost always we have rib eyes, striploins, tenderloins, top sirloins, and bone-in rib steak. We also have a dry-aged beef program, where we age beef for a minimum of 35 days—we use the beef rib section for that. We also have a special few not-so-popular-but-super-tasty cuts we always want people to try, such as flank, bavette, hanger, skirt, petite tender, eye of round, and flat iron. Does that help?

Q. I want something super tender. What should I get?

A. Tenderloin or flat iron. Tenderloin is also sometimes called the filet mignon. It is by far the most tender steak you can get. The flat iron is a cut from the shoulder that comes a close second to tenderloin's tenderness. It is super fashionable on restaurant menus due to its relatively low price, great flavor, and said tenderness. Highly recommended.

Q. What if I like my steaks to have a bit of fat?

A. Take anything from the rib section. This includes rib eye, cowboy steak, côtes de boeuf, and bone-in rib steak. These are all steaks taken from the rib muscle of the steer. It is hands down the most luscious and fatty steak you can get. Not to mention delicious.

Q. How do I cook the steak?

A. Turn to page 210. Basically, the only way you can screw up is if it's burnt shoe-leather. Otherwise, even a well-done steak can be enjoyable.

Q. What should I eat it with?

A. A big red wine. A friend or lover. And a smile. As humans, we are privileged to be able to experience such enjoyment, so savor it.

Beef Cuts
ROASTS

1. Prime rib

2. Top sirloin

3. Eye of round

4. Outside flat

5. Inside round

6. Sirloin tip

7. Boneless blade

8. Shoulder clod/cross rib

OTHER CUTS

1. Chuck short ribs (English, flanken, Miami-style)

2. Back ribs

3. Brisket

4. Shank

5. Cheek

6. Oxtail

7. Tongue

8. Heart

ROASTS

Prime Rib

This cut is the same muscle as the rib eye, which is to say it comes from the rib section between the shoulder blade and the striploin, but it's cut with the bone in. It is also very tender and has great interior fat content—the quintessential roast beef.

Good for: **roasting, smoking**

Top Sirloin

When the top sirloin is cleaned properly and the connective tissues have been removed, it makes a delightful small roast, between 2 and 3 pounds, perfect for a smaller group. At my shop, we like to tie some of the fat cap on the top to give it a bit of extra moisture while cooking.

Good for: **roasting**

Eye of Round

The lean eye of round comes from the leg and is a little tougher than any of the belly steaks, the flat iron, or the top sirloin steaks. As a steak, it can be marinated and cooked quickly over high heat or it can be cooked as a dry roast and sliced very thinly before serving.

Good for: **braising, grilling, roasting**

Outside Flat

This leg cut is most often used as a less expensive dry roast or a thin steak suitable for quick frying. It is tougher than the eye of round but similar in terms of fat content. When cleaned properly, thinly sliced, and served with a rich gravy it is actually quite a pleasant, affordable roast.

Good for: **grilling, pan-frying, roasting**

Inside Round

Another leg cut that is much larger than the outside flat but can be treated in much the same way.

Good for: **braising, grilling, pan-frying, roasting**

Sirloin Tip

This very lean muscle sits at the top of the hip. It is great as either a thinly sliced cutlet, a dry roast, or a pot roast.

Good for: **braising, grilling, pan-frying, roasting**

Boneless Blade

Also referred to as chuck or blade eye, this shoulder muscle is most commonly used for pot roasts and stewing beef. Large pockets of fat between the blade muscles must be removed before serving.

Good for: **braising, pressure cooking, stewing**

Shoulder Clod (Cross Rib)

The shoulder clod, also known as the cross rib, is a roast cut from the shoulder, closer to the rib section. It is commonly sold boneless, but sometimes has the rib bones attached. It is a very hardworking muscle and makes for an excellent and succulent pot roast.

Good for: **braising, pressure cooking, roasting, stewing**

OTHER CUTS

Chuck Short Ribs

The first four ribs from the loin can be cut several different ways. Cut across the bone they are flanken cut. Cut with the bone they are English cut. Both flanken and English cuts are thick and need to be braised. When cut thinly across the bone they are suitable for grilling and known as Korean-cut ribs or Miami-style ribs.

Good for: **braising, grilling, pressure cooking, smoking**

Back Ribs

The plate of ribs left over after the rib bones have been removed from the rib eye, the beef back ribs are a great-value barbecue cut. They aren't as meaty as chuck short ribs, but the meat is very tender and therefore doesn't need to be cooked for an extended period.

Good for: **braising, grilling, pressure cooking, smoking**

Tri Tip (*not shown*)

The tri tip is a triangular muscle found on the bottom sirloin of the animal. It is meaty and lean, and while slightly less tender than the top sirloin, it is traditionally prepared in the same way. It is commonly roasted whole and sliced thinly against the grain.

Good for: **braising, grilling, pressure cooking, roasting, smoking**

Brisket

Brisket is another slow-cooking cut. The brisket can be divided between the flat (or single), which typically has more fat on the surface of the meat, and the point (or double), which has less surface fat but more interior fat. The fattier pieces are typically better for drier cooking methods (like smoking), to help keep the meat moist.

Good for: **braising, pressure cooking, smoking**

Shank

Essentially the shin of the animal, this very tough cut requires long cooking times and benefits from added moisture to prevent it from drying out.

Good for: **braising, pressure cooking**

Cheek

Beef cheeks are lean, tough muscles that are excellent in dishes where the meat is shredded, such as chilies, tacos, and ragùs.

Good for: **braising, pressure cooking**

Ground Beef (*not shown*)

Ground beef can be made from a single part of the animal or from a selection of cuts. We use boneless blade meat for ground beef at the shop, but bits of sirloin, rib eye, and hip cut trim find their way as well. Grocery stores typically sell three versions: extra lean, lean, and regular. Lean is a good all-purpose ground beef. Regular is too fatty for anything other than burgers.

Good for: **grilling, pan-frying**

Oxtail

The tail of the steer is a very flavorful cut when braised for a long time. It has a ton of lip-smacking collagen, and the marrow from the tail bones is especially tasty. Usually cut between the joints in medallions, oxtail can also be chopped up on the band saw in 2-inch cubes for a stew or curry.

Good for: **braising, pressure cooking**

Tongue

Beef tongue, while officially an organ meat, is actually a very tough muscle that becomes very tender after hours of gentle simmering. It is fantastic pickled or corned, and it makes a great sandwich meat.

Good for: **braising, poaching, pressure cooking**

Heart

Another muscle that gets lumped in as an organ, the heart is a lean and very tender muscle that benefits from quick cooking. It needs to be carefully cleaned of the veins and connective tissue to be enjoyed properly.

Good for: **grilling, pan-frying, smoking**

Sometimes, in the dead of winter, nothing warms your bones like a slow-cooked piece of beef. A pot roast is a braise, and it works well with any tough cut of beef. I like to serve this dish with plain buttered noodles.

SIMPLE POT ROAST

Preheat the oven to 450°F. Have a roasting pan with an elevated roasting rack ready.

Season the beef liberally with salt and pepper, then rub it with the oil. Place the beef on the roasting rack and roast until golden brown all over, about 30 minutes. Leave the oven switched on.

While the beef is browning, place the bacon and onions in a large ovenproof pot over medium heat, stir well, cover the pot, and let cook for 5 minutes. Add the garlic, carrots, celery, and rutabaga, stir, and cover again, sweating all of the vegetables until fragrant and softened, about 10 minutes. Add the tomato paste and stir well, then deglaze the pot with the wine.

Add the herb bundle to the pot, and season the contents of the pot with salt and pepper. Add the browned beef and turn down the oven to 300°F.

Add the stock to the pot and bring it to a simmer over medium heat, ladling off and discarding any scum as it rises to the surface. Once it's simmering, cover the pot and place in the oven for 1 hour.

Lift the lid, turn the beef over, and return to the oven until fork-tender, about 1½ hours. Carefully transfer the meat to a cutting board and tent it loosely with aluminum foil to keep it warm. Discard the herb bundle.

Strain the braising liquid through a fine-mesh sieve and discard the solids. Place the liquid in a small saucepan and bring to a simmer over medium heat. Taste and season with more salt and pepper, if needed.

In a small bowl, whisk together the cornstarch and cold water. Slowly pour the cornstarch slurry into the braising liquid, whisking to incorporate, and simmer until thickened. If the sauce seems too thin, make a little more slurry and add it in the same way.

Serves 6 to 8

1 (4 pounds) blade roast, trimmed of silverskin and excess fat, tied (page 27)

Salt and pepper

2 Tbsp vegetable oil

4 slices bacon, cut in medium dice

1 large onion, chopped

4 garlic cloves, chopped

2 medium carrots, chopped

2 celery stalks, chopped

1 cup chopped rutabaga,

1 Tbsp tomato paste

1 cup red wine

1 herb bundle (4 rosemary sprigs, 4 thyme sprigs, 3 bay leaves) (page 36)

3 cups Beef (or Chicken) Stock (page 361)

2 Tbsp cornstarch

2 Tbsp cold water

NOTE: You could use any tough working muscle, such as eye of round, in this recipe. I like to use the blade because it has a good fat-to-meat ratio. A leaner cut like eye of round can come out dry and stringy; a fattier cut like blade has more flavor.

To serve, slice the beef and arrange it on a serving platter. Drizzle with some of the sauce and pour the rest into a gravy boat to serve alongside.

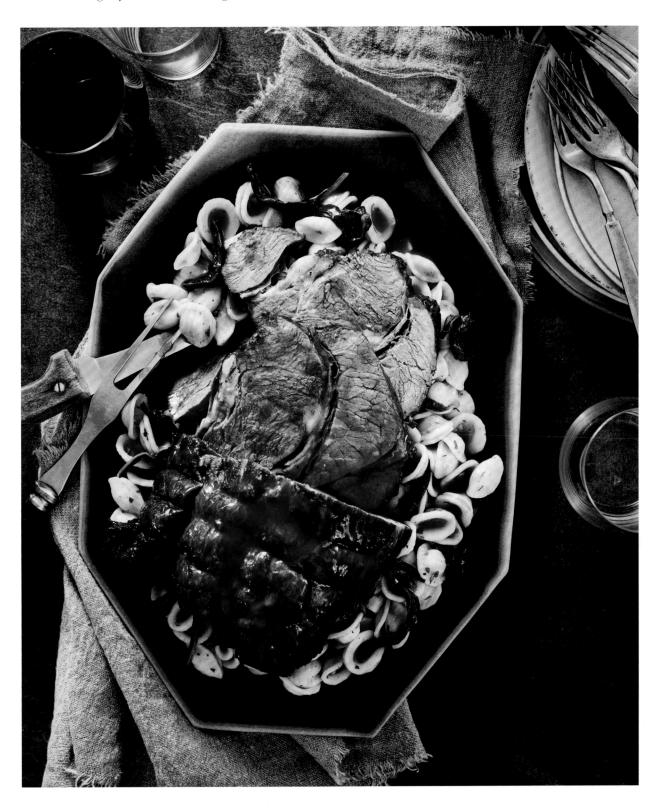

Paleron, more commonly known as a top blade steak, is a classic example of a cut that has lots of flavor but is tricky to work with. It's a cross cut of the top blade (a.k.a. flat iron) muscle that isn't cleaned of the nerve or silverskin before portioning, which basically means that you have two super-tender muscles surrounded and bisected by inedible gristle. A paleron is not the best grilling steak; the best way to cook this steak is to let it swim in red wine, beef stock, and aromatics in an ovenproof pan for a couple of hours. Slow-cooking the meat this way will break down the nerve and silverskin and allow them to soften, therefore rendering the whole cut edible—and delicious. Serve with Roasted Cauliflower and Cheddar Risotto (page 350).

PALERON STEAK IN RED WINE

Preheat the oven to 300°F. Place the flour in a small shallow bowl. Pat the steaks dry with a paper towel and season liberally with salt and pepper.

In an ovenproof pan large enough to fit all of the steaks without crowding, melt 2 Tbsp of the butter over medium-high heat. Dredge each side of the steaks in flour, shaking off any excess, and place them in the pan. Cook on both sides until golden brown, about 3 minutes per side. Transfer the steaks to a cutting board and allow them to rest.

Turn down the heat to medium-low, return the pan to the heat, and add 1 Tbsp of the butter. Add the onions and garlic and sweat until translucent, about 10 minutes. Season with salt and pepper, and then add the herb bundle, shiitake mushrooms (if using), and wine. Simmer to reduce the wine by a quarter.

Add the stock, bring back to a simmer, and then add the steaks, making sure they are completely submerged. If not, add more stock. Cover with a lid and braise in the oven until a steak knife can easily pierce the nerve in the middle of the steak, about 2½ hours.

At the 2-hour point, melt the remaining 1 Tbsp of butter in a clean frying pan over medium-low heat. Add the bacon (if using) and the pearl onions and sweat until the onions are slightly golden, about 5 minutes. Season with salt and pepper. Add the carrots and cook for another 5 to 10 minutes, or until all the vegetables are quite golden. Stir in the mushrooms and cook until they release their liquid and shrink a little. Season the vegetables to taste and keep warm.

Serves 4

½ cup all-purpose flour (for dredging)

4 (each about 9 ounces) paleron (top blade) steaks

Salt and pepper

4 Tbsp butter (divided)

1 cup minced onion

4 garlic cloves, minced

1 herb bundle (6 sprigs each of thyme, parsley, and rosemary; 2 bay leaves) (page 36)

8 dried shiitake mushrooms (optional)

2 cups full-bodied red wine

2 cups Beef Stock (page 361)

1 cup finely diced bacon (optional)

1 cup pearl onions

2 carrots, cut in small dice

2 cups button (or your favorite) mushrooms, quartered

2 Tbsp chopped chives

When the steaks are cooked, transfer them to a plate, cover, and keep warm. Discard the herb bundle and shiitake mushrooms (if using).

Place the pan with the braising liquid over medium heat, bring to a simmer, and reduce until it coats the back of a spoon, about 8 minutes. Add the carrots, button mushrooms, pearl onions, and chives, and toss gently to combine. To serve, arrange the steaks on a serving platter and pour the sauce over top.

I came up with this recipe when I was hosting an Oscars party a few years back. It turned out so well that I now use it for any get-together when tasty meat snacks fit the bill. These little bad boys taste like a savory candy bar, but in a good way.

SHORT RIB CANDY

Preheat the oven to 325°F.

Season the ribs with salt and pepper. Place the oil in a heavy-bottomed ovenproof pot set over medium-high heat. When the oil is hot, add the beef and brown it on all sides. Transfer to a plate and set aside.

Turn down the heat to medium-low, place the onions, garlic, and ginger in the pot, and sweat them, stirring every couple of minutes, until the onions are soft and caramelized, about 10 minutes. Add the carrots, celery, star anise, and ssamjang (or Sriracha), and cook for another 10 minutes.

Deglaze the pot with 2 cups of the root beer and the stock and bring to a simmer. Return the beef to the pot, making sure the meat is completely submerged. If not, add the remaining 1 cup of root beer. Cover with a lid and braise in the oven until the bones easily slip out of the ribs, 2½ to 3 hours.

Transfer the meat to a clean pot, then strain the braising liquid through a fine-mesh sieve over the ribs. Allow to cool to room temperature, cover, and refrigerate overnight.

The next day, use a spoon to skim off and discard the solidified fat from the top of the braising liquid. Place the pot over medium-low heat to warm the meat in the sauce a little, remove the ribs from the braising liquid, and set aside.

Turn up the heat to medium-high and reduce the braising liquid until the sauce coats the back of a spoon, about 12 minutes.

While the glaze is reducing, pop the bones out of the ribs and discard. Place the meat on a cutting board and cut it into bite-sized pieces. Add to the pot with the glaze and stir until the meat pieces are all shiny.

Serves 4 to 6

4 beef short ribs, flanken cut, 1½ inches thick

Salt and pepper

2 Tbsp olive oil

1 onion, sliced

2 garlic cloves, sliced

2 Tbsp sliced ginger

1 carrot, chopped

1 celery stalk, chopped

6 star anise pods

2 Tbsp ssamjang (Korean spicy bean paste) or Sriracha

2–3 cups root beer (divided)

2 cups Chicken Stock (page 360)

1 cup salted peanuts, roasted

3 Tbsp sliced green onions

NOTE: Start this recipe a day ahead of time, then dig in: your party is going to be a smashing success!

Place the roasted peanuts in a food processor and pulse them until they're chunky. Add the green onions and salt, to taste, and pulse just until the mixture looks like very coarse bread crumbs. Transfer this mixture to a bowl.

Using a knife and a fork, and working in batches, dip the sticky, warm meat pieces in the peanuts and roll them around until well coated. Arrange the meat bites on a clean plate and serve immediately.

This stew originates from Belgium and uses delicious rich Belgian ale rather than the more usual red wine. The unique combination of sweet brown sugar, sour cider vinegar, and caramelized onions gives this stew a richness you and your family will go bananas for. Serve this dish with some crusty bread, buttered egg noodles, or french fries.

CARBONNADE FLAMANDE (FLEMISH BEEF AND BEER STEW)

Place ½ cup of the flour in a small, shallow bowl.

Place a large, heavy-bottomed ovenproof pot over medium heat. Add 2 Tbsp of the oil and 2 Tbsp of the butter. Place half the beef in the bowl of flour, toss well, and season liberally with salt and pepper. Shake off any excess flour and add the beef to the pot. Brown the beef, stirring frequently until dark golden all over, about 8 minutes. Transfer to a plate and set aside. Repeat with the remaining beef, flour, oil, and butter. Transfer to the plate and set aside.

Turn down the heat to medium-low and add the bacon. Allow the bacon to render its fat, about 5 minutes, then add the onions and garlic. Add a healthy pinch of salt and pepper, stir well, and cover the pot. Slowly caramelize the onions, stirring with a wooden spoon every 10 minutes or so and scraping up the browned bits of beef and bacon from the bottom of the pot, for between 45 minutes and 1 hour. When the onions are golden and have released all their liquid, turn up the heat to medium-high.

Preheat the oven to 325°F. Return the beef to the pot and add the herb bundle. Deglaze the pot with the beer, and then add the sugar and vinegar. Bring the liquid to a simmer and reduce by one-quarter, 5 to 8 minutes, then add the stock. Bring back to a simmer, cover, and braise in the oven until the beef is tender, about 1½ hours. Discard the herb bundle.

To serve, spoon the stew into a casserole dish and serve hot.

Serves 4 to 6

1 cup all-purpose flour (divided)

4 Tbsp vegetable oil (divided)

4 Tbsp butter (divided)

2 pounds beef blade, cut in 1½–2-inch cubes

Salt and pepper

6 slices bacon, cut in medium dice

2 large Spanish onions, thinly sliced lengthwise

4 garlic cloves, minced

1 herb bundle (4 thyme sprigs, 2 parsley sprigs, and 2 bay leaves) (page 36)

2 cups Belgian-style dark beer

1 Tbsp packed brown sugar

2 Tbsp apple cider vinegar

1 cup Beef Stock (page 361)

NOTE: If you make this stew the day before you want to eat it, the flavors will develop overnight, making for an even better-tasting stew.

There used to be a small Mexican restaurant around the corner from my house. One of my favorite taco fillings on their taco platter was *suadero,* which is beef that tastes like it's been cooked slowly in its own fat, like a leg of duck confit. I researched the cut used, but my studies showed it's a long, thin cut of muscle that rests between the flank and the outside of the carcass—basically something we just don't harvest here in Canada. So I experimented with my favorite stewing cut—blade—et voilà! The taqueria may be long gone, but I can still enjoy this tasty filling whenever I want. I make my tacos with two tortillas per serving (as it makes the taco stronger) and classic toppings, but feel free to use a single tortilla and go nuts with salsas, hot sauces, guacamole, cheese—whatever your family enjoys!

TACOS DE SUADERO

Preheat the oven to 325°F.

In a large ovenproof pot over medium heat, melt the fat. Add the diced onions, sauté until translucent, and then stir in the cumin and allspice, followed by the beef. Season with salt and pepper and cook, stirring well, to brown the beef all over, about 10 minutes.

When the beef is brown, add the water and bring to a simmer. Give the meat a good stir, cover with a tight-fitting lid, and braise in the oven for 3 hours, stirring every 30 minutes or so. The beef is done when the meat falls apart when you stir it.

While the beef is braising, mix the sliced red onions with the lime juice and a pinch of salt in a small bowl. Set it aside to allow the onions to lightly pickle.

When the meat is cooked, place the pot on the stovetop over medium heat. Remove the lid and allow the meat to simmer, stirring constantly, for 10 to 15 minutes. The water will evaporate, leaving the beef simmering in its own fat. Allow the beef to caramelize lightly on the bottom of the pot, scraping it up with a wooden spoon until the contents of the entire pot are golden brown. Remove from the heat and strain the beef through a fine-mesh sieve to remove the excess fat. (Refrigerate this fat and use it in place of butter or olive oil to cook potatoes or other vegetables.)

To serve, arrange the tortillas on a serving platter and scoop the beef into a large serving bowl. Place the pickled red onions, cilantro, and lime wedges in separate bowls and invite everyone to assemble their own tacos.

Serves 6 to 8

6 Tbsp rendered beef fat (or vegetable shortening)

½ cup small-diced onion

¼ tsp ground cumin

¼ tsp allspice

2½ pounds beef stew, preferably cut from the blade

Salt and pepper

2 cups water

½ cup thinly sliced red onion

2 Tbsp lime juice

12–24 corn tortillas

½ bunch cilantro, washed and picked of large stems

1 lime, cut in wedges

NOTE: I usually make this in a pressure cooker rather than the oven. If you use a pressure cooker, reduce the water to 1 cup, set the pressure cooker to high, and cook the beef for 60 minutes.

Bread sauce is a wonderful sauce traditionally made by rehydrating stale bread and seasoning it with warm spices. It is usually served in Britain alongside roasted game birds, and I first came across it while working for Chef Jason Bangerter at Auberge du Pommier. He had worked in England for a while and brought the idea back to serve with a roasted squab. Later, at Mistura, I collaborated with Massimo Capra to create an Italian spin on bread sauce that worked really well with beefy flat iron steak. Paired with some pan-roasted cippolini onions and sautéed greens, this is a simple yet elegant main course.

FLAT IRON STEAK WITH BREAD SAUCE AND ROASTED CIPPOLINI

Preheat the oven to 375°F. Have a sheet of aluminum foil and a baking tray ready.

Place the garlic cloves on the foil, drizzle with 2 Tbsp of the oil, and fold the foil into a pouch to completely encase the garlic. Set the pouch on the baking tray and bake until the garlic is golden brown, about 30 minutes. Remove from the oven and set aside.

Pour the milk into a small saucepan and add 4 of the thyme sprigs, 2 of the bay leaves, the cloves, peppercorns, and nutmeg. Set the saucepan over medium heat, bring to a simmer, and cook for 5 minutes. Remove from the heat and allow the spices to infuse for 10 minutes. Strain the milk through a fine-mesh sieve into a clean, medium-size saucepan and discard the solids from the sieve.

Add the roasted garlic to the milk and use an immersion blender to purée the mixture until smooth. (Or use a countertop blender and pour the mixture into a small clean saucepan.) Set aside.

Cut the bread into quarters, place them in a food processor, and pulse to create fresh bread crumbs.

Return the milk mixture to low heat and whisk in the bread crumbs to thicken the sauce. It should be thick enough to coat the back of a spoon. Season with salt, then strain the sauce through a fine-mesh sieve again. Keep warm until ready to serve.

Serves 4

8 garlic cloves, peeled

4 Tbsp olive oil (divided)

1 cup milk

8 thyme sprigs (divided)

3 bay leaves (dried will do, divided)

2 whole cloves

1 tsp whole black peppercorns

½ tsp freshly grated nutmeg

10 slices white sandwich bread, crusts removed

Salt and pepper

3 Tbsp butter (divided)

8 cippolini onions or pearl onions

1 cup Chicken Stock (page 360)

4 (each about 8 ounces) flat iron steaks

1 bunch Swiss chard, washed and chopped

recipe continues

Place a large frying pan over medium heat and add 2 Tbsp of the butter. When it's melted, add the cippolini onions (or pearl onions). Season with salt and pepper and cook until caramelized, about 4 minutes per side. Add the stock and the remaining 4 thyme sprigs and 1 bay leaf, and turn down the heat to a simmer. Cover the pan and simmer until the cippolini are fully cooked, about 10 minutes Set aside and keep warm.

Set a large, heavy-bottomed frying pan over high heat. Season the steaks liberally with salt and pepper, then rub them with the remaining 2 Tbsp of oil.

When the pans are scorching hot, cook two steaks at a time for about 4 minutes per side, until golden brown. Remove from the pan and allow to rest for 5 minutes before slicing.

In a large frying pan over medium heat, add the remaining 1 Tbsp butter and sauté the Swiss chard. Season with salt and pepper and set aside.

To plate the steaks, spoon 3 Tbsp of the bread sauce into the center of each plate. Pat dry the cooked Swiss chard on some paper towel and arrange in the center of the bread sauce. Slice the flat iron steak against the grain and arrange the slices attractively in a tower on top of the chard. Arrange the cippolini onions (or pearl onions) and 2 Tbsp of their cooking sauce around the steak and serve.

Internationally, a London broil is a cut of steak, traditionally flank, that has been marinated overnight, broiled in the oven under high heat, rested, and sliced across the grain. Somewhere along the line, however, butchers in Toronto and the surrounding area stuffed a whole flank steak with seasoned ground meat and sold it as a roast. This is the London broil I grew up with, so this is the version I'm showing you how to make. The pickle gravy is my addition, and it brings this closer to a traditional German *rouladen*.

LONDON BROIL WITH PICKLE GRAVY

Preheat the oven to 425°F. Have some kitchen twine and a roasting pan with an elevated roasting rack ready.

Using a sharp knife, butterfly the flank steak along the long side, being careful not to cut through the steak. You should be able to open the flank like a book. Set aside.

Melt the butter in a large frying pan over medium heat. Add the onions and garlic and sweat until the onions are just browning. Add the mushrooms and thyme, and cook, stirring frequently, until the moisture from the mushrooms evaporates. Season with salt and pepper, deglaze the pan with the brandy, and remove from the heat.

Place the ground beef in a large bowl. Add the mushroom mixture, parsley, and Worcestershire sauce, and mix everything thoroughly. Season with salt and pepper. Check the seasoning by taking a small bit of the filling and microwaving or pan-frying it until cooked through.

Lay the flank open on your work surface with the middle of the "book" parallel to the edge of your work surface in front of you. Spread the mustard all over the meat, making sure the surface is completely covered. Spoon the ground beef mixture into a tube shape along the first third of the flank, parallel to your work surface. Fold the bottom edge of the flank over the filling and roll it up like a cigar. Using good strong kitchen twine, tie the tube of flank at 1-inch intervals. Rub in the oil and season with salt and pepper.

Serves 6

LONDON BROIL

1 (about 2 pounds) whole flank, trimmed of silverskin

1 Tbsp butter

1 cup finely chopped onion

2 garlic cloves, finely chopped

3 cups chopped cremini or white mushrooms

1 Tbsp chopped thyme leaves

Salt and pepper

2 Tbsp brandy

1½ pounds ground beef

2 Tbsp chopped Italian parsley

1 tsp Worcestershire sauce

3 tsp English mustard

2 Tbsp vegetable oil

PICKLE GRAVY

2 Tbsp butter

2 Tbsp minced shallots

1½ Tbsp all-purpose flour

3 Tbsp red wine

3 Tbsp pickle juice

2 cups Beef Stock (page 361)

1 large pickle, finely diced

recipe continues

Put the roast on the rack and set the roasting pan in the oven, then roast, turning once, until a thermometer inserted directly into the center of the roast reads 150°F, about 20 minutes. Transfer the roast to a plate, cover with aluminum foil, and allow to rest for about 15 minutes.

While the roast is resting, make the gravy. Place the roasting pan over medium heat and melt the butter. Add the shallots and sweat until translucent, 5 to 8 minutes. Stir in the flour, creating a roux, and cook for 2 minutes. Deglaze with the wine and pickle juice, then add the stock, bring to a simmer, and reduce by one-quarter.

Strain the gravy through a fine-mesh sieve into a saucepan, bring back to a simmer, and stir in the diced pickles to warm them through. Remove from the heat and pour into a gravy boat. To serve, thinly slice the meat and arrange on a serving platter. Serve with the pickle gravy alongside.

Very slowly cooking a steak at low temperature until it reaches the desired internal temperature and then searing it quickly over high heat to get a crust is known as reverse-searing, and it takes a lot of the guesswork out of cooking a steak perfectly. In this recipe, I use the sirloin cap—the triangular muscle that sits on the top sirloin—called a *coulotte* in France and a *picanha* steak in Brazil. Whatever you call it, this cut has a natural fat cap, which I leave on while cooking so the rendered fat bastes the steak. If you prefer, you can remove the fat or ask your butcher to do it for you. See image on page 213.

REVERSE-SEARED SIRLOIN CAP STEAK WITH CHIMICHURRI SAUCE

NOTE: Start this at least 12 hours before you plan to eat.

Serves 4

Place the garlic, thyme, vinegar, oil, and a pinch of salt in a small bowl and mix together.

Using the point of a sharp knife, score the fat side of the sirloin cap in a crosshatch pattern. Place the steak in a baking dish, and season both sides liberally with salt and pepper. Rub the marinade all over the steak, and refrigerate, uncovered and fat cap facing up, for at least 8 hours.

An hour and a half before you want to eat, preheat the oven to 275°F. Take the steak out of the fridge and bring to room temperature. Place the steak in the oven and cook until an internal thermometer inserted into the middle of the steak reads the desired temperature (page 41). Take the steak out of the oven and set aside.

Place a large, heavy-bottomed frying pan over high heat. Discard the garlic and thyme, and then sear the sirloin cap, fat side down, in the hot pan. Turn the steak over when golden, and sear the other side. The whole process should take about 1 minute per side. Remove from the pan and set on a cutting board to rest for 5 minutes.

To make the chimichurri sauce, place the cilantro in a blender and purée with the sugar, oil, lime juice, and vinegar. Pour the mixture into a serving bowl and stir in the red onion, garlic, and lime zest. Season with salt and pepper.

To serve, slice the steak against the grain and arrange on a serving platter with the chimichurri alongside.

STEAK

3 garlic cloves, sliced in half

6 thyme sprigs, cut in half

3 Tbsp red wine vinegar

3 Tbsp olive oil

Salt and pepper

1 sirloin cap, 2–2½ pounds, fat cap left on, silverskin removed

CHIMICHURRI SAUCE

2 cups cilantro, leaves picked and washed

1 tsp granulated sugar

3 Tbsp olive oil

2 Tbsp lime juice

1 Tbsp red wine vinegar

½ red onion, finely diced

2 garlic cloves, minced

1 tsp grated lime zest

Salt and pepper

How to Cook a Steak

I get asked this question often, and for good reason. Steak is considered by many people to be the epitome of a luxury meal in North America. It's what many people want to cook when they're having friends over, or order when they're going out for a celebratory meal. It can also make a delicious and simple weeknight meal. There are many different cuts of steak, some tougher than others, some fattier than others. Here's a breakdown of cooking tips to make sure you get the best out of your cut of choice.

Tender	Lean	Luxurious (anniversary steak meal)	Foodie (on the look-out for undiscovered steaks)	Bistro (when steak frites is on the menu)	Weeknight (steak because it's a Tuesday!)
Tenderloin	Tenderloin	Dry-aged cuts	Hanger	Hanger	Top sirloin
Striploin	Flank	Rib eye	Chuck flap	Bavette	Coulotte
Rib eye	Petite tender	Côtes de boeuf/cowboy	Denver steak	Flat iron	Skirt
Top sirloin	Minute steak	Porterhouse		Top sirloin	Minute steak
Flat iron		Striploin		Paleron	

CHOOSE YOUR STEAK. There are no hard and fast rules about which type of steak you should cook for dinner. It all depends on what you feel like eating! The chart above shows each cut of steak's common characteristics.

CHOOSE YOUR COOKING METHOD. The three most common methods people use to cook steaks at home are pan-frying, grilling, and broiling. Pan-frying is better for medium-sized (1-inch) steaks with a flat surface area (for browning), grilling works great for thicker (1- to 2-inch) steaks that may need a bit more time to cook, and broiling is perfect for thinner (less than 1 inch) steaks that can cook very quickly. If you don't have a barbecue, you can cook any steak in a pan.

PAN-FRYING

Great pan-frying cuts: top sirloin, flank, flat-iron, tenderloin, petite tender, minute steak, bavette, hanger, Denver steak, paleron, coulotte/picanha

- Heat a heavy-bottomed frying pan over a high heat. I prefer flat-bottomed cast iron pans because they retain the heat excellently and you can get a great caramelization on the surface of the steak. A grill pan (to make the marks) works well too, although I prefer an over-all golden crust on my pan-fried steaks.
- Season the steak generously with salt and pepper, then rub with vegetable or olive oil.
- Sear the steak in the hot pan until all sides are golden brown. The timing depends on the size and thickness of the steak, but as a rule of thumb, searing the steak for a

minimum of 3 minutes per side will achieve the desired golden brown-ness.

- With a flat-bottomed pan, you can flip as many times as you think necessary, but aim for one flip during the cooking time. For thinner (less than 1 inch) steaks that means 2 minutes per side, and for thicker (2-inch) steaks that means 4 minutes per side. You'll find the timing gets easier with practice.

- After the steaks are golden brown, turn the heat down to medium, add 2 Tbsp of butter to the pan with 2 sprigs of thyme, and finish cooking until the desired internal temperature has been reached (see page 41).

- For thick steaks (1 inch or thicker), rest the meat for a minimum of 8 minutes before serving. For thinner steaks (less than 1 inch), rest for 2 minutes before serving.

GRILLING

Great grilling cuts: Rib eye, striploin, cotes de boeuf/cowboy steak, T-bone/porterhouse, flank, skirt, bavette, chuck flap, Denver steak, coulotte/picanha

- If you're using propane/gas, heat half of your grill to high, and the other half to medium heat. If you're using charcoal, arrange the hot coals on only one side of the grill.

- Season the steak generously with salt and pepper, then rub it with vegetable or olive oil.

- Sear the steak on the hot side of the grill, and flip it until it's golden brown on both sides. The timing depends on the size and thickness of the steak, but as a rule of thumb, searing the steak for a minimum of 3 minutes per side will achieve the desired golden-brown crust. Be aware of how fatty your steak is, as melting marbling can cause flareups if you're not paying attention.

- Some cooks like cross-hatch grill marks on a steak. To do this, just turn the steak 90 degrees after about 1½ minutes during the searing phase. Aim (with practice) for one flip during the cooking time. For thinner (less than 1 inch) steaks that means 2 minutes per side, and for thicker (2-inch) steaks that means 4 minutes per side. You'll find the timing gets easier with practice.

- Move the steak to the cooler side of the grill and finish cooking until the desired internal temperature has been reached (see page 41).

- For thick steaks (1 inch or thicker), rest the meat for a minimum of 8 minutes before serving. For thinner steaks (less than 1 inch), rest for 2 minutes before serving.

BROIL

Great broiling cuts: top sirloin, tenderloin, skirt, coulotte, chuck flap, Denver

- Preheat the broiler to high heat. If cooking thick steaks (1 inch or thicker), place the oven rack on the second-highest position in the oven. If cooking thinner steaks (less than 1 inch), place it on the highest position.

- Season the steak with salt and pepper, then rub with vegetable or olive oil.

- Place the steak on a heavy-bottomed tray. (Ovens sometimes come with these; otherwise use a shallow ovenproof frying pan that will fit inside the oven with the door closed. A baking tray *can* work, but it might buckle due to the high temperature.)

- Place the tray under the broiler and cook until golden brown, about 2 minutes, flip the steak, and repeat with the other side.

- Continue flipping to finish cooking until the desired internal temperature has been reached (see page 41). If the steak is thin (less than 1 inch), a single flip should be sufficient, but if it is thick (1 inch or thicker), it may take two or three flips to evenly cook the meat.
- For thick steaks (1 inch or thicker), rest the meat for a minimum of 8 minutes before serving. For thinner steaks (less than 1 inch), rest for 2 minutes before serving.

KNOW WHEN THE STEAK IS DONE. This is possibly the most difficult technique to master. The only way to get comfortable with internal temperatures is by practicing cooking steaks. There are two methods—one slightly more accurate than the other—you can use to get started. But remember, if you're eating good meat—that is, cattle raised with care and fed properly to maintain growth and fat content—your steak will be good no matter what. Trust me, I've had better well-done steaks from good farms than perfectly cooked medium-rare steaks from a factory farm.

- **The Finger Test:** Simply touch your thumb to your pinky finger on one hand. Using your the index finger of your other hand, touch the meaty part of your thumb, near the base. That's what a well-done steak feels like. Now touch your thumb with your ring finger: that's medium. Touch your thumb with your middle finger: that's medium-rare. Finally, touch your thumb to your index finger: that's blue rare. I recommend trying this technique close to when you think the steaks are finished cooking. It's common to see grill cooks in restaurants constantly touching the steaks, using their intuition and experience to judge when to take the steak off the grill.

- **Internal Thermometer:** This method is more exact, but it also depends on the quality of the thermometer and the thickness of the steak. For example, it's great on a big côte de boeuf, but pretty useless with a skirt steak. The thicker the steak, the more accurately the internal temperature can be read. If the steak is thin, heat will travel through the muscle fibers more quickly, distorting the true internal temperature of the meat. Additionally, you'll want to take a steak off the heat when it is 5 or 10 degrees cooler than the target temperature, as it will continue cooking for a bit as it rests.

Rare	115°F to 120°F
Medium-rare	120°F to 125°F
Medium	130°F to 135°F
Medium-well	145°F to 150°F
Well-done	160°F

LET IT REST. Resting a steak before serving it is always a good plan, as it allows the juices to settle back into the muscle fiber and prevents the juice from flowing away once the steak is cut. You'll always have some juice come out of a steak, but resting minimizes it.

SLICE THE STEAK. If I'm having company over for steak, I tend to choose a larger steak like a striploin or rib eye, and slice it before serving. This encourages people to eat what they want, instead of expecting them to finish a 14-ounce steak on their own. However, if the steak weighs less than 6 ounces, I'll almost always serve it on its own and let my guest slice it. It's all about reading the room and serving accordingly.

*Reverse-Seared Sirloin Cap Steak
with Chimichurri Sauce (page 209)*

Stuffing a steak isn't something I normally do, but it really works here. The briny flavor of the main ingredients is a nice contrast to the beefy flank. Make sure you cook it and cut into it in front of people—it's a guaranteed showstopper. Serve with Orzo Salad with Peas, Chili, Mint, and Feta (page 351).

FLANK STEAK STUFFED WITH FETA, SUNDRIED TOMATOES, AND OLIVES

Cut the flank into 6 thin, evenly sized steaks. To do this, place the steak on a work surface with the long side parallel to you. Cut the flank in half through the muscle grains. Then, cut each half into thirds, along the muscle grain.

Cut a pocket into each flank steak. To do this, use a thin boning knife. Holding the knife parallel to your work surface and starting at the thickest end of the steak, plunge the knife blade into the meat, being careful not to cut all the way through. Wiggle the knife a little to create a pocket. Think of the steak like a pillowcase—you're creating the opening in which to put the pillow. In this case, the pillow (stuffing) is delicious. Once you have cut the pocket in each steak, remove the knife, set the meat on a plate, and refrigerate, uncovered, while you make the stuffing.

To make the stuffing, heat the oil in a pan over medium heat. Add the onions and garlic and sweat until slightly caramelized. Add the olives and sun-dried tomatoes and cook until fragrant, about 2 minutes. Stir in the bread crumbs, parsley, and green onions and cook, stirring frequently, until the bread crumbs are slightly toasted. Remove from the heat and stir in the feta cheese. Mix thoroughly to combine and set aside to cool.

Arrange the steaks on a cutting board. Using a tablespoon, stuff the olive mixture into the pocket of each steak. Seal the end of each steak with a couple of toothpicks. Rub each steak with some oil and season with salt and pepper. Cover and refrigerate for at least 4 hours, and as long as overnight.

To cook the flank, you can either grill or pan-fry it. Either preheat your barbecue to hot on one side and warm on the other or preheat the oven to 400°F.

recipe continues

Serves 6

1 (about 2½ pounds) whole flank steak, trimmed of any silverskin

2 Tbsp olive oil + more for rubbing the steaks

1 cup minced onion

4 garlic cloves, minced

1 cup green olives, pitted and chopped

1 cup sun-dried tomatoes in oil, drained and chopped

1 cup bread crumbs

½ cup chopped Italian parsley

½ cup thinly sliced green onions

1 cup crumbled feta cheese

Salt and pepper

NOTE: Start this at least 4½ hours before dinner so it has time to marinate (from the inside out!).

To grill the steaks, place them on the hot side of the barbecue and sear, until golden on both sides, about 5 minutes per side. Transfer the steaks to the warm side of the grill. The steaks are done when a thermometer inserted into the thickest part of the meat registers 140°F. To pan-fry the steaks, heat two ovenproof frying pans over medium-high heat. When hot, add the steaks and brown on one side. Turn the steaks over and place the pans in the oven until the steaks are cooked, about 5 minutes. Remove the steaks from the heat, discard the toothpicks, and allow to rest for 5 minutes.

To serve, slice the steaks into ½-inch rounds, and serve either on a platter or on individual plates.

Stuffed cabbage has gone out of style in recent years, unfortunately, though a few old-school Eastern European joints in Toronto still make cabbage rolls. If you don't have access to those restaurants or to a grandmother who still makes cabbage rolls, you are missing out! I heartily recommend this recipe when you're having a group of friends or family over, or any time you need to feed a group without breaking the bank. Serve these with a loaf of crusty bread.

CABBAGE ROLLS

Fill a large pot with water, season the water with plenty of salt, so it is just shy of tasting like seawater, and set over high heat to come to a boil. Fill a large bowl with ice water.

Using a paring knife, pull the individual cabbage leaves away from the whole head, trying to keep them intact. You only need 8 evenly sized leaves, but a few extra never hurt anyone. Using tongs, drop the leaves in the boiling water and blanch until soft, 3 to 5 minutes, then transfer them to the ice water to stop the cooking.

Melt 1 Tbsp of the butter in a saucepan over medium heat. Add the onions and garlic and sweat until translucent. Stir in the carrots, thyme, and allspice, and cook until the carrots have released their moisture and are starting to caramelize. Season with salt and pepper, then remove the pan from the heat.

In a large bowl, combine the ground beef and pork with the rice. Add the onion and carrot mixture and stir well. Season to taste, and test the filling by either frying up a small piece or microwaving it for a few seconds. Using a spoon, divide the filling into 8 portions and roll each one into a ball with your hands.

Drain the cabbage leaves and pat dry with paper towel. Using a paring knife, cut out the core in a triangular wedge and discard it. Place a cabbage leaf on a work surface and set a ball of filling on top. Fold the sides of the cabbage leaf over the stuffing and then, starting at the bottom edge, roll the leaf up. Place the roll seam side down on a plate and set aside. Repeat with the remaining cabbage leaves and filling.

Serves 8

1 whole cabbage (preferably Savoy, as its loose leaves separate easily)

3 Tbsp butter (divided)

1 medium onion, finely diced

4 garlic cloves, minced

2 carrots, grated

1 Tbsp chopped thyme

1 tsp allspice

Salt and pepper

1 pound ground beef

1 pound ground pork

2 cups basmati or long-grain cooked rice, at room temperature

3 cups Basic Tomato Sauce (page 367)

1 cup Chicken Stock (page 360)

1 Tbsp paprika

recipe continues

If I have time, I like to refrigerate the rolls so they hold their shape while cooking. To do this, place a small sheet of plastic wrap on your work surface, set a cabbage roll on top, and wrap it tightly, twisting the ends of the plastic wrap so the roll holds its shape. Repeat with the remaining rolls. Refrigerate for 1 hour.

Preheat the oven to 350°F. Have ready some plastic wrap, a roll of aluminum foil, and a casserole dish large enough to hold all the rolls in a single layer.

Place the tomato sauce, stock, and then the paprika in a medium saucepan over medium-high heat. Once hot, ladle half of this mixture into the casserole dish. Unwrap the cabbage rolls, discarding the plastic wrap, and carefully arrange them on top of the tomato sauce mixture. Pour the rest of the sauce over the rolls, and then dot the rolls with the remaining 2 Tbsp of butter. Cover the casserole with plastic wrap, then with aluminum foil and bake in the oven for 45 minutes.

Remove the foil and plastic wrap and bake until a thermometer inserted in the center of the middle-most roll reads 150°F, about 20 minutes.

To serve, carefully transfer the rolls to a serving platter and enjoy hot.

When I left high school, I went straight to work in restaurants. Unlike my siblings who left home to study at university, I was surrounded by good food and never went hungry. Then, as now, many students moved away from home barely knowing how to heat a can of soup, let alone eat well on a budget. This recipe is for them and other cash-strapped reluctant cooks.

HOMEMADE HAMBURGER HELPER

Fill a large pot with water, add the 1 Tbsp of salt, and bring to a boil over high heat.

While the water is coming to a boil, set your biggest frying pan over medium heat and add the oil. When it's hot, add the 1 tsp of salt, the onions, and pepper. Turn down the heat to low, cover the pan, and allow the onions to cook, stirring every minute or so, for 5 minutes. Stir in the garlic, cover, and cook for 5 more minutes.

Add the beef, then turn up the heat to medium. Using a spoon, mash the beef so it browns all over. Stir in the paprika and cook, uncovered, for 8 minutes or until the beef is no longer red.

When the water comes to a boil, add the pasta, stir, and cook according to the directions on the package until al dente. Drain and set aside.

Stir the chopped tomatoes and tomato paste into the beef mixture and allow to cook for 10 minutes.

Stir the sour cream into the beef mixture and turn down the heat to low. Stir until the beef is well coated and saucy, then add the drained pasta and cheese, stirring well to allow the cheese to melt into the sauce.

To serve, scoop the hamburger helper into a large serving bowl and sprinkle with chopped green onions. Ta-dah!

Serves 6

1 Tbsp + 1 tsp salt (divided)

1 Tbsp olive oil or vegetable oil

1 medium onion, cut in medium dice

½ tsp pepper

2 garlic cloves, finely diced

1 pound ground beef

1 Tbsp paprika

1 pound pasta of your choice (small noodles work best)

1 (10 ounces) can chopped tomatoes (do not drain the juices)

2 Tbsp tomato paste

3 Tbsp sour cream

1 cup grated cheddar cheese

½ bunch green onion, chopped

How to Make a Great Hamburger

A great hamburger patty starts with the right ingredients. The keys to a juicy, well-seasoned burger are the fat content and the salt.

USE FATTY, FLAVORFUL MEAT.

The best burgers come from meat with at least 20%–25% fat content. You can get that from chuck or brisket, or from short ribs if you're feeling decadent. Some customers ask for rib eye or striploin to be ground into burger, but I much prefer chuck because it's reasonably priced and it's from a hardworking muscle (it holds up the neck), so it naturally has more flavor and fat throughout. Remember, burgers are "everyman" food; this isn't the time to get hung up on heart health or fancy cuts of meat.

OPT FOR DRY-AGED BEEF.

If you live near a good butcher who dry-ages beef ribs for fancy steaks and such, you might want to ask for their trim. They'll charge you a bit more for it, but using up to 50% dry-aged beef trim creates a burger with a really special flavor. This option is a total nonessential but now that you can buy dry-aged beef in big grocery stores, it might be a bit more available.

CHOOSE A COARSE GRIND.

Many butcher shops, mine included, double-grind their beef because a finer grind breaks apart really well in sauces and meatloaf, creates a cool "wave" pattern that looks great in the display case, and better breaks up the bits of fat that some customers find off-putting. For burgers, you want to see clear bits of meat and fat in your grind because they provide good texture—think of it as "steak burger": meat you can chew on a bit instead of inhaling like the slips of meat you get from fast-food joints.

REMEMBER THE SALT.

Use a good amount of salt to draw out that beef flavor. We use 13 grams of salt to every kilogram of beef (metric measurements are more accurate for seasonings than imperial ones and help us make a consistent product). That's 1.3%, which sounds like a lot but is really worth it.

AND THE BLACK PEPPER.

Very few spices go with beef as well as black pepper does. We find 6 grams of pepper for every kilogram of meat to be a good balance.

BONUS: GRIND YOUR SEASONINGS INTO THE MEAT.

There is much debate about how to season a burger. While many of my respected colleagues advise seasoning the outside of the burger right before it hits the heat (like you would a steak), I like to mix the flavor into the meat—and the most consistent way to do this is when the meat is being ground. If you have a grinder, ask your butcher for the whole pieces of beef and grind them yourself at home. Season the meat with your salt and pepper *before* you put it through the grinder so the seasoning gets incorporated throughout the burger without your having to mix the meat that much. If you don't have a grinder, loosely toss the ground meat with the seasoning before forming a patty. Overmixing causes the fat to be emulsified into the meat, which can lead to a greasy mouthfeel. Skip this step if you don't have a grinder—it's not really going to make a huge difference.

There's a saying that goes something like: "There's no such thing as bad sex or bad hamburgers, there are only variations of good." Or maybe it's pizza instead of hamburgers, I'm not sure. What I do know is that even shitty dime-store frozen patties do the trick if you're camping, you're half in the bag, and you can't see anything other than the campfire. But when you're after a damn good burger, this is it. Serve these on good-quality brioche buns, dressed (or undressed) as you like.

SANAGAN'S MEAT LOCKER'S DRY-AGED BEEF HAMBURGERS

Place both sets of beef in a bowl, add the salt and pepper, and mix to combine (do not overmix). Grind once through the regular-sized plate, then, using your hands, form the mix into 6 balls. Flatten the balls into ¾-inch-thick patties.

Heat a cast-iron frying pan over medium heat. When hot, set the patties in the pan to allow the fat to render and lubricate the pan. Using a spatula, press down lightly on the patties to flatten them and then allow to cook for 5 minutes.

Turn the patties over, press down lightly with the spatula again, and cook until caramelized brown and crunchy on both sides, about 5 minutes in total. At this point the burgers will be medium-well, which is perfect for most people. If you like your burger less cooked, be sure to use freshly ground meat and cook it until an internal thermometer shows 135°F (medium-rare) or 145°F (medium).

Serves 6

1 pound whole boneless blade, cut in grindable chunks

1 pound dry-aged beef trim, cleaned and cut in grindable chunks

1 scant Tbsp salt

1 tsp pepper

Chili is one of those dishes that people can be passionate about; I have a friend who swears that making it with ground beef is a sin, and that it should be made with stewing blade meat, stewed with spices for hours. I don't disagree, but I just think this dish doesn't need to be argued over—especially when this recipe, created by one of my cooks, Matt Crossley, is obviously the best. Serve with steamed rice, as my mother did with her chili when I was growing up, or on toasted white bread, as I did when I was a teenaged stoner.

CHILI CON CARNE

In a large pot over medium heat, brown the beef in 2 Tbsp of the oil. Once brown, drain off the excess oil, transfer the beef to a plate, and set aside.

Return the pot to the heat and add the remaining 1 Tbsp oil. When the oil is hot, add the onions and sweat until translucent, about 5 minutes. Add the garlic and sweat until fragrant, about 2 minutes. Add the celery and bell peppers and continue cooking and stirring for another few minutes.

Turn down the heat to low, stir in the chili powder, paprika, coriander, and cumin, and cook for 5 minutes, or until fragrant. Finally, add the tomato paste and water, stir well to create a loose paste, and simmer, uncovered, for 10 minutes. Season with salt and pepper.

Pass the tomatoes and chipotle peppers through a food mill or food ricer. (If you don't have one, use a food processor—but the seeds may add a bitter taste to your chili.) Add this puréed tomato mixture, the cooked beef, kidney beans, and stock to the pot and stir well to combine. Bring the chili to a simmer over low heat, cover, and simmer for 1¾ hours. Stir every once in a while to prevent the meat from sticking to the bottom.

Add the black beans and cilantro, then stir in the sugar and lime juice. Season to taste: the chili should be tangy and spicy with a hint of sweetness. Cook until the beef is tender, about 15 minutes.

To serve, pour the chili into a large serving bowl and pass the bowls.

NOTE: Chili, like people, improves with age. Make this recipe a day or two before serving and refrigerate to allow the flavor to develop.

Serves 6 to 8

2 pounds ground beef, preferably from the blade

3 Tbsp vegetable oil (divided)

1 medium onion, finely diced

2 Tbsp minced garlic

1 celery stalk, finely diced

½ red bell pepper, seeded and finely diced

2 Tbsp chili powder

1 Tbsp Spanish paprika

2 tsp ground coriander

2 tsp ground cumin

1 tsp dried oregano

⅓ cup tomato paste

⅓ cup water

Salt and pepper

1 (16 ounces) can plum tomatoes (do not drain juices)

1 Tbsp chipotle in adobo sauce

1 heaping cup canned red kidney beans, rinsed and drained

1 cup Beef Stock (page 361)

1 heaping cup canned black beans, rinsed and drained

3 Tbsp chopped cilantro

1 tsp brown sugar

1 Tbsp lime juice

A Bolognese sauce doesn't actually use a lot of beef. In fact, there's more veal and pork than beef in it, but I include it here because most people think of it as a beefy sauce. That's probably because this ragù has so much flavor. It's great tossed with a bit of pappardelle pasta, or better yet, layered with béchamel sauce in a classic Northern Italian lasagne. Keep in mind that if you do make a lasagne, you won't be doing anything else that day; it takes time to prepare from scratch, and after eating some, you won't want to move for a while.

BOLOGNESE SAUCE

Preheat the oven to 325°F.

Melt 1 Tbsp of butter in a large pot over medium heat, add the onions and pancetta, and sweat until fragrant and translucent.

Strain the porcini mushrooms through a fine-mesh sieve, reserving the liquid in a bowl. Chop the mushrooms and add them to the pot along with the garlic, carrots, celery, and bay leaves. Cook until soft, about 5 minutes, then add all three ground meats, the salt, and pepper. Using a potato masher, mash the meat in the pot, separating the grains. Allow the meat to brown slightly.

Add the cheese rind and milk to the pot and bring to a simmer. Simmer until the milk has evaporated, about 10 minutes, and then stir in the reserved porcini water, the tomatoes, wine, stock, and finally the nutmeg. Bring to a simmer, cover, and braise in the oven until the meat is very tender, about 4 hours.

When the meat is cooked, make the flavored butter. In a small saucepan over medium-high heat, melt the 1 cup of butter with the thyme, rosemary, and sage. Continue cooking the butter until it turns slightly brown and becomes very nutty and fragrant (but keep a close eye, as it can turn from brown to black very quickly). Strain the butter through a fine-mesh sieve directly into the sauce, stirring well to incorporate. Now it's ready for you to toss with pasta or use to make lasagne!

NOTE: This sauce will keep in your fridge for up to 5 days and the flavor continues to deepen over that time. It also freezes very well for up to 3 months. This recipe makes a large batch, so you'll be in the sauce for weeks!

Makes enough sauce for one large lasagne or for 12+ over pasta

1 cup + 1 Tbsp butter (divided)

1 large onion, finely diced

¼ pound pancetta, skin removed and cut in small dice

2 Tbsp dried porcini mushrooms soaked in 1 cup of water

4 garlic cloves, minced

3 carrots, finely diced

1 celery stalk, finely diced

4 bay leaves

2 pounds ground pork

2 pounds ground veal

1½ pounds ground beef

2 Tbsp salt

1 Tbsp pepper

¼ pound Parmigiano-Reggiano cheese rinds/chunk

3 cups milk

3 (each 14 ounces) cans of plum tomatoes, chopped

1 cup white wine

1 cup Beef Stock (page 361)

½ tsp grated nutmeg

½ bunch thyme

½ bunch rosemary

½ bunch sage

At the start of every winter, a little ditty plays in my head: "I really can't sauté, (Baby, it's cold outside), I've got to go braise, (Baby, it's cold outside)." Then I think to myself that I should really spend some time fleshing out these lyrics, make a music video to put up on YouTube, and use it to get more customers to the shop in harsh weather conditions. Because that's how social media works, right? And when I picture people braving the wind and the blowing snow and the icy driving conditions, I think to myself that I just want to curl up on my couch and eat meatballs. So yeah, that idea wins every time. These meatballs take a couple of hours to make, but once they're done, they're great to have on hand in your fridge or freezer. I stuff them inside crusty bread, pile them on a mountain of spaghetti, or simply eat them on their own without the sauce.

MEATBALLS

Preheat the oven to 450°F. Line a baking tray with parchment paper.

In a large bowl, mix together the beef, pork, prosciutto, onions, garlic, cheese, parsley, salt, pepper, and oregano until well combined. Pinch off bits of the meat mixture and roll them into balls about 1 to 1½ inches in diameter. Place the meatballs on the baking tray, set it in the oven, and bake until golden brown, about 30 minutes, turning once as they cook.

Heat the sauce in a large pot over medium-low heat until it is simmering. Add the baked meatballs, cover, and simmer for 1½ hours.

To serve, remove from the heat and enjoy. On your couch.

NOTE: When making the meatballs, don't overwork the mix as it can result in a "springy" texture to the balls. After combining the meat with the seasonings, you only need to roll them between your palms for a few seconds to shape the ball.

Makes 15 to 20 meatballs

1 pound ground beef

1 pound ground pork

1 ounce prosciutto, finely diced

¼ cup finely chopped onions

2 Tbsp chopped garlic

2 Tbsp grated Parmigiano-Reggiano or Grana Padano cheese

2 Tbsp chopped Italian parsley

1 Tbsp salt

1 tsp pepper

1 tsp dried oregano

1 batch Basic Tomato Sauce (page 367)

This recipe calls for careful reading, so make sure you follow all the steps. First, brine the beef overnight to season the meat throughout. Second, keep the oven at 500°F for 15 minutes before you cook the roast to ensure the oven retains its heat during the cooking time. And third, slice the cooked roast very thinly to give the illusion of tenderness.

BEEF EYE OF ROUND ROAST WITH MUSTARD SAUCE

Place the salt, sugar, garlic, peppercorns, bay leaves, and water in a medium saucepan and set over high heat until the sugar and salt dissolve. Remove from the heat, add the ice, and refrigerate, uncovered, until completely cool.

Using a sharp boning knife, clean the silverskin from the eye of round but leave the fat cap on. Using a sharp paring knife, poke holes in the ends of the roast, in the direction of the grains of meat. Make about 10 holes in each end. Place the beef in a large pot, cover the roast with the brine, and refrigerate, uncovered, for 12 hours.

The following day, remove the roast from the container and discard the brine. Rinse the meat under cold, running water, set it on a plate, and allow to come to room temperature.

Three hours before you plan to serve the roast, preheat the oven to 500°F. Have a roasting pan with an elevated roasting rack ready. Once the oven reaches temperature, wait for 15 minutes. You want the oven to be super hot and retain its heat as the beef cooks.

To make the seasoning, mix together the garlic salt, pepper, paprika, and oil until well combined. Using your hands, rub this seasoning all over the beef. Place the roast, fat side up, on the rack, set the roasting pan in the oven, and turn down the heat down to 475°F. Cook for 7 minutes per pound. Turn off the oven but *do not open the door for 2 hours.*

Remove the roast from the oven, cover with aluminum foil, and allow to rest for 20 minutes more.

To make the mustard sauce, place the mustard, capers, onions, horseradish, honey, and tarragon in a small serving bowl and mix until well combined. To serve, thinly slice the roast and arrange on a serving platter with the mustard sauce alongside.

Serves 6 to 8

BRINED BEEF

1 cup salt

½ cup granulated sugar

4 garlic cloves, chopped

2 Tbsp black peppercorns

6 bay leaves

4 quarts water

2 cups ice cubes

1 (3–4 pounds) eye of round roast (allow about ½ pound per person)

SEASONING

2 Tbsp garlic salt

1 Tbsp pepper

1 Tbsp sweet paprika

¼ cup vegetable oil

MUSTARD SAUCE

½ cup Dijon mustard

1 Tbsp chopped capers

1 Tbsp finely diced red onions

1 Tbsp prepared horseradish

1 Tbsp honey

1 Tbsp chopped tarragon leaves

NOTE: Start this the day before you plan to eat it.

Most people don't have a backyard smoker, so this recipe, while unconventional, allows anyone with a regular kitchen stove to produce a brisket with a natural wood-smoke flavor. Note that your house will smell like smoked meat for a couple of days afterward, but that's not the worst problem to have. (If you prefer to cook the brisket outside, follow the technique described in the Simple Hot-Smoked Pork Butt (page 109) if you have a charcoal barbecue.) A whole brisket weighs between 9 and 12 pounds on average and consists of two ends. The flat—also known as the single end, first cut, or thin end—is usually about 2 inches thick with ½ inch of fat cap. The point—also known as the double end, second cut, or fatty end—consists of two muscles separated by a layer of fat with another inch or so of fat cap on top. This thicker end is on average 4 to 5 inches high. I prefer the flat end for this recipe, as it's meatier, but the fatty end is also delicious. If you're feeding lots of people, use the whole brisket and offer your guests fatty or lean cuts piled high on rye bread.

HOUSE-SMOKED BEEF BRISKET

Mix together the salt, pepper, sugar, paprika, onion powder, and garlic powder in a small bowl. Place the brisket on a baking tray and, using your hands, massage the rub evenly into the meat. Refrigerate, covered, overnight.

Remove the brisket from the fridge and allow it to come to room temperature. Soak the wood chips in cold water for at least 30 minutes. Set one oven rack in the center of the oven and a second on the lowest setting, then preheat the oven to 250°F. Meanwhile, fill a roasting pan with 1 inch of hot tap water and place a wire cooling rack on top of the roasting pan. The rack should balance on all four sides of your roasting pan, and not be resting in the water. Have ready a 3- × 5-inch aluminum roasting pan.

Turn your extraction fan to its highest setting. Drain the wood chips and set them in a frying pan on the stovetop over medium-high heat. Shake the pan slowly back and forth until the wood chips start to smolder. When you see a good amount of smoke being created, tip the smoldering wood chips into the aluminum pan, place it on the lowest rack in the oven, and close the door.

Serves 8 to 10

3 Tbsp salt

2 Tbsp pepper

2 Tbsp packed brown sugar

2 Tbsp sweet paprika

2 Tbsp onion powder

1 Tbsp garlic powder

5 pounds brisket

3 cups wood chips

recipe continues

Place the brisket on the wire cooling rack and set the roasting pan on the center rack in the oven. You want the air to circulate all around the brisket and the water to both create steam and collect fat drippings from the brisket as it cooks. Cook the brisket for about 5 hours (or 1 hour per pound; always plan for more time rather than less), refreshing the smoke from the wood chips every hour until the brisket is cooked (see note).

After 5 hours, insert a thermometer in the thickest part of the meat to check for doneness. It is cooked when the thermometer reads 200°F. Remove the meat from the oven, cover with aluminum foil and a clean towel, and allow to rest for 30 minutes.

To serve, carve the meat as thinly as possible and arrange the slices on a serving platter.

NOTE: The smoke from the wood chips will fade after 30 to 45 minutes. To refresh it, remove the chips from the oven, return them to the frying pan over medium-high heat, and shake the pan back and forth until they begin to smolder again. Return the smoldering chips to the aluminum pan in the oven. Repeat this technique every hour until the brisket is cooked.

Start this brisket the day before you plan to serve it.

GAME

Game

I N NORTH AMERICA WE HAVE AN ODD RELATIONSHIP with game meat. On the one hand, licensed hunters bundle up in warm, waterproof gear and spend hours in the bush, waiting patiently to harvest prey such as deer and ducks. Hunting has been part of human culture since we became aware of hunger pangs, and we have developed a range of ways to kill prey, from longbows to crossbows to guns. On the other hand, most of us are now well removed from the hunting process. We no longer need to hunt to survive because we can buy animals raised and slaughtered for us in grocery store meat departments.

Our governments largely prohibit the trade of wild, hunted game because their food safety and food inspection programs allow only animals processed in an approved facility that meets specific criteria to be sold commercially. These regulations are in place to keep consumers safe from disease. If a hunter bags a deer and doesn't process it properly, anyone who eats it risks getting a foodborne illness. They are also in place to protect animal populations from extermination. If a hunter can profit from their kills, they are more likely to hunt more animals and a wider range of species.

- **Canada** As a general rule, it is illegal for hunters to sell their game, either to businesses like butcher shops and restaurants, or directly to the public. There are exceptions, like in Newfoundland, Nova Scotia, and Quebec, where a business can obtain a license to sell hunted game, but overall game is difficult to obtain if you don't hunt.
- **U.S.** Hunted game can be sold as long as it's been inspected by a state or federal agency. Most game meat companies meet this regulation by driving a mobile slaughter facility to the location of the kill and skinning and eviscerating the animal in the presence of an inspector. While this may not be the same as hunting a beast in the bush and bringing its carcass to the back door of a restaurant, it still allows people to taste meat from an animal that has only ever enjoyed foraging for food and running free.

So how are customers going to get their fix of game meats like deer and elk? For now, at least in Ontario, game animals have to be farmed just like cattle or pigs and go through the same rigorous inspection process during slaughter. That's not so bad, as farmers have learned to raise the animals in environments that closely simulate their natural wild habitat. But there is one major difference—and it affects the flavor of the meat. Farmed game gets grain and hunted game does not. In other words, farmed animals taste a little less wild, a little less like the product of their environment. I would actually like to see the regulations changed so that hunters have a maximum number of kills they can sell to grow the market. But until that happens, we'll just have to be satisfied with what we can get from game farms. Unless, of course, you know a hunter or become one.

SHOPPING FOR GAME

A few types of game meat are available in stores. I've listed the most common ones here, as well as the more domestic animal they most resemble. Wild boar, for example, is really just a pig, and you'll get the same cuts from boar that you get from pigs.

Caribou

Caribou is a type of reindeer that lives predominantly at northern latitudes and has been a staple of the Inuit diet for generations. There was a time when caribou meat was on many restaurant menus, but caribou herds have declined due to mineral development and there is now a moratorium on their harvest, which is why I haven't included a recipe for it here. Caribou is a fattier, gamey-flavored meat that resembles a rich, ruby-colored cross between beef and lamb. You can buy imported caribou meat from Greenland, but it is prohibitively expensive.
Treat like: **Beef**

Ducks

Two common breeds of duck are used for cooking. Pekin ducks are longer in the body and generally less fatty than the plumper Muscovy ducks. Pekin ducks are used in Chinese cooking, roasted whole in wood-burning ovens until lacquered and crispy. Muscovy ducks are prized by French chefs and are excellent in confit and smoking preparations. Hunted ducks are noticeably leaner and darker than farmed ones. Ducks resemble large chickens, but their meat is darker, fattier, and more strongly flavored. The females are called hens and the males are called drakes. Drakes tend to be larger than hens and could easily serve six people, so go for a drake if you're a larger group and add at least 30 minutes to the recipe cooking time. Note that ducks are notoriously difficult to defeather. At the shop, we often get birds that still have their "plugs" attached. These are casings in the duck's skin that once held the feathers. They aren't dangerous to eat, but they aren't that attractive. Simply grab them with tweezers or even a small paring knife, and pull them out.

Duck is one of my favorite birds. It's like the pork of the sky and sea combined. Super versatile, duck is used in many classic preparations around the world, especially in China and France. Since my culinary education was more European, I learned how to make duck confit (where the leg is slowly poached in its own fat), duck rillette (where the confit meat is shredded, seasoned, and made into a spreadable topping for crusty bread), and other charcuterie items like terrines and galantines. Roasting and boiling the bones makes a delicious, deeply flavored stock for all kinds of applications. And, of course, there is the breast. Duck breast needs to be cooked so the fat is rendered and the skin gets crispy; the meat is usually served slightly pink in the center.

Treat like: **Fatty chicken**

Elks

Elks are one of the largest species of the deer family—their antlers alone can weigh up to 40 pounds. An elk carcass resembles a large lamb and is butchered like venison. Elk steaks are particularly delicious and robust, offering lean meat with a rich, gamey flavor.

Treat like: **Beef**

Geese

Geese are larger than ducks and resemble large chickens. They are well known for their fat—most foie gras was originally goose liver, although duck livers have since become more popular. Their breasts are fully covered by fat, which needs to be rendered before eating. Goose isn't hugely

popular in North America but is enjoying a resurgence in Britain for
Christmastime feasts.
***Treat like:* Fatty chicken**

Guinea Fowl

These hilariously monstrous-looking creatures
resemble something from a '50s sci-fi movie.
Guinea hens have little heads with a large plumage
that covers a generally well-muscled frame. Cook
guinea fowl (male) or hens (female) like pheasants:
either braise them or separate the legs and the
breasts and cook each muscle separately.
***Treat like:* Lean chicken**

Moose

Moose meat is not legally available for sale in
Canada, except in Newfoundland (with the
right permit, of course). I have been lucky
enough to enjoy it, and I found it resembled
strongly flavored (read: gamey), very lean
beef (read: slightly tough).
***Treat like:* Lean beef**

Pheasants

Pheasants can fly but prefer running—quickly.
These beautiful birds are generally lean like
chicken and are most commonly braised or
roasted. As with many lean game birds, the
breast tends to be overcooked before the legs are
adequately tenderized, so it is common to cook
the two muscles separately: pan-roast the breasts
and braise the legs.
***Treat like:* Lean chicken**

Quail

These little birds were one of the first game birds I learned how
to cook. I've since cooked them in myriad ways, from whole
roasted, to butterflied and grilled, to deboned and stuffed with
liver. Their small size makes them popular as appetizers, and

their dark meat and tender legs and breasts make them quick to cook (and eat).
***Treat like:* Small chickens**

Rabbits

Rabbit is a super-delicious meat that most resembles a
large chicken. The meat is very lean and mildly sweet,
and can carry many different flavors. The loin makes a
great pan roast, for example, and the leg is succulent
when roasted and served in a Madeira wine sauce. I've
been cooking and selling rabbit for years but it's not as
popular as it should be—in part perhaps because it's unexpectedly expensive. Most
of the cost is due to the rabbit's small size, which makes it less cost-effective to
slaughter than other animals.
***Treat like:* Large chickens**

Venison

Venison is the common name for deer meat.
The most common breed raised for food is
the whitetail deer, which gets its name from
the fluff of white on its tail that's visible when
it's in danger. A deer carcass usually weighs
around 100 to 150 pounds and resembles a
large lamb. Look for a dark, ruby-colored
meat. Venison is very lean and makes for delicious pan-fried steaks cooked in lots
of butter, or richly flavored stews and braises.
***Treat like:* Veal or beef**

Wild Boar

Wild boar is a smaller, sleeker breed of pig than the domestic hogs we see on the
market. Boar meat is leaner and darker, and has a stronger flavor than a regular pig.
Wild boar is abundant in California, to the point where they'll tear up people's
gardens in search of food. And I thought racoons
were a menace . . . Cuts such as shoulder, loins,
ribs, shanks, and roasts are readily available at
specialty butcher shops, as are ground boar and
boar sausage meats.
***Treat like:* Pork**

Easy to cook, duck breast presents as a gourmet meal, especially with a beautiful sauce made from cherries. Pull out this recipe the next time you want to impress your in-laws. Serve with Duck Fat–Roasted Potatoes (page 343).

DUCK BREAST WITH CHERRIES

Using the tip of a sharp knife, score the skin of each duck breast in a crosshatch pattern at ¼-inch intervals. Score only the skin so the fat can escape while rendering, not the meat. Season the meat with salt and pepper. Set the duck, skin side down, in a large frying pan, place over medium-low heat, and allow the duck to warm and cook slowly for about 10 minutes.

Meanwhile, prepare the vegetables. In a separate frying pan, melt the butter over medium heat. Add the shallots and sweat until translucent. Stir in the garlic and sweat for 1 more minute, then add the Swiss chard, stirring frequently until well sautéed, about 4 minutes. Season with the nutmeg and salt and pepper to taste. Remove from the heat and set aside in the pan.

At the 10-minute point, turn the duck breasts over, turn up the heat to medium-high, and cook for 1 to 2 minutes more. Transfer the duck breasts to a plate and allow to rest.

Strain the fat into a small container (refrigerate and reserve it for future use, like roasting potatoes). Return the pan to the heat and add the cherries and stock. Using a wooden spoon, scrape any of the duck bits off the bottom of the pan. When the stock has reduced by half, about 2 minutes, add the vinegar and chives. Reduce for 1 minute before removing the sauce from the heat. Add all the cold butter, stirring until the sauce is emulsified.

To serve, divide the Swiss chard among four plates, arranging it in the center. Place the cooked breasts on a cutting board, and slice them on a slight bias into about 5 or 6 slices each. Fan each breast over the chard, then spoon the sauce evenly over the meat.

Serves 4

DUCK BREASTS

4 duck breasts (ideally from Muscovy hens)

Salt and pepper

1 Tbsp butter

1 large shallot, finely diced

1 garlic clove, minced

1 bunch Swiss chard, washed and chopped

¼ tsp freshly grated nutmeg

CHERRY SAUCE

1 cup fresh cherries, pitted and cut in half

½ cup Chicken Stock (page 360)

2 Tbsp honey vinegar or balsamic vinegar

1 Tbsp chopped chives

1 Tbsp butter, cold, cubed

A whole roast duck is special, perhaps a bit celebratory. This method is easy and is guaranteed to produce a perfect Sunday roast. If you have time, take the duck out of its wrapper and allow it to sit, uncovered, in your fridge for 6 to 12 hours before cooking. This step, while not necessary, helps dry out the duck skin, which makes it crispier. I like to serve this roast with a pan sauce made with ginger, star anise, and orange, but duck meat is very versatile and pairs well with many different sauces, so play around with a variety of flavors.

WHOLE ROAST DUCK WITH ORANGE AND GINGER SAUCE

Have a roasting pan with an elevated roasting rack ready.

Two hours before serving, remove the duck from the fridge and inspect it for small feathers and feather "plugs" (see page 239). Place the duck, breast side up, on your cutting board and remove the wishbone to make carving easier. To do this, lift the flap of fatty skin from the front of the duck and use your fingers to locate the wishbone. It runs in an inverted "V" down from where the two breasts meet. Using a paring knife, cut the meat away from each side of the wishbone, slowly exposing it. Wriggle your fingers in, grasp the wishbone, and pull it out. Save it for the pan sauce. Use the paring knife to score the duck breast in a crosshatch pattern at ¼-inch intervals, making sure that you're only cutting through the skin and not into the meat of the breast.

Roll the clementines (or mandarins) on your work surface to break up the cells of the fruit inside. Using the tip of the paring knife, poke 8 to 10 holes all around the fruit. Place the clementines and rosemary sprigs inside the cavity of the bird, then truss the duck as you would a chicken (page 22), and season it liberally with salt and pepper. Place the duck on the roasting rack and set the roasting pan on the **center rack of a cold oven.** (Yes, cold!)

Turn on the oven to 450°F. Roast the duck until the skin is a deep golden, about 15 minutes from when you turn the heat on. Turn down the oven to 300°F and roast until a thermometer inserted in the thickest part of the thigh reads 165°F, about 1 hour. Remove the duck from the oven and allow it to rest, covered, for 20 minutes before carving.

Serves 4

ROAST DUCK

1 (about 4 pounds) Muscovy duck hen

2 clementine or mandarin oranges

2 whole rosemary sprigs

Salt and pepper

ORANGE AND GINGER SAUCE

2 shallots, chopped

2 Tbsp chopped ginger

5 strips orange peel (use a vegetable peeler)

1 star anise

½ cup mirin (or dry white wine)

Juice of 1 orange

2 cups Beef Stock (page 361)

3 Tbsp cornstarch

3 Tbsp cold water

While the duck is resting, make the sauce. Drain the fat and roasting juices from the pan into a bowl and reserve. Set the roasting pan on the stovetop over medium heat and add the wishbone, shallots, and ginger, stirring well until the shallots are translucent, about 5 minutes. Add the orange peel and star anise and sweat for another minute, scraping up any bits of roast that are stuck to the bottom of the pan. Pour in the mirin, bring to a simmer, and reduce by half, 5 to 10 minutes. Add the orange juice and reduce by half again, about 5 minutes. Pour the mixture into a saucepan and bring to a simmer over medium heat.

Using a tablespoon, skim the fat from the top of the reserved roasting juices and reserve it for another use (hello, roast potatoes!). Add the roasting juices and beef stock to the saucepan, bring to a simmer, and reduce by one-quarter. Season with salt and pepper.

Make a slurry by whisking the cornstarch with the cold water in a small bowl. Slowly whisk the slurry into the sauce, bring the sauce to a simmer, and allow it to thicken—that should take a few minutes. Strain the sauce through a fine-mesh sieve into a gravy boat.

To serve, carve the duck as you would other roast poultry (see page 26) and arrange it on a platter. Serve with the gravy alongside.

If you ever fancied a holiday dinner straight out of a Dickens story, here you go. If you have time, take the goose out of its wrapper and allow it to sit uncovered in the fridge for 6 to 12 hours to help dry out the skin so it gets crispier when cooked.

ROAST GOOSE WITH PRUNES AND CHESTNUTS

Have a roasting pan with an elevated roasting rack ready.

Two hours before you plan to eat, remove the goose from the fridge and inspect it for small feathers and feather "plugs" (see page 239). Place the goose, breast side up, on your cutting board and remove the wishbone to make carving easier. To do this, lift the flap of fatty skin from the front of the goose and use your fingers to locate the wishbone. It runs in an inverted "V" down from where the two breasts meet. Using a paring knife, cut the meat away from each side of the wishbone, slowly exposing it. Wriggle your fingers in, grasp the wishbone, and pull it out. Save it for the pan sauce. Use the paring knife to score the goose breast in a crosshatch pattern at ¼-inch intervals, making sure that you're only cutting through the skin and not into the meat of the breast.

Roll the orange on your work surface to break up the cells of the fruit inside. Using the tip of the paring knife, poke 8 to 10 holes all around the fruit. Place the orange, 1 cup of the prunes, and 4 of the bay leaves inside the cavity of the bird.

Truss the goose, using the same method as for trussing a chicken (page 22). Season the goose all over with salt and pepper, place it on the roasting rack, and set the roasting pan on the **center rack of a cold oven.** (Yes, cold!)

Turn on the oven to 400°F. Roast the goose until the skin is golden, about 20 minutes from when you turned the heat on. Turn down the oven to 300°F and roast for another 2 hours.

Fifteen minutes before the goose is due to be finished roasting, heat the honey in a small saucepan over medium heat. Remove the goose from the oven, brush it all over with the honey, and return it to the oven for the final 15 minutes, or until a thermometer inserted into the thickest part of the thigh reads 165°F. Remove the goose from the oven, cover with aluminum foil, and allow to rest for at least 20 minutes.

recipe continues

Serves 6 to 10, depending on the size of the goose

1 (9–11 pounds) whole goose

1 orange

2 cups dried prunes (divided)

6 bay leaves (dried is fine, divided)

Salt and pepper

1 cup honey

4 shallots, chopped

1 cup dry red wine

1 cup Madeira

1 cup prune juice

2 cups Beef Stock (page 361)

2 Tbsp reserved rendered goose fat from the roast

2 Tbsp all-purpose flour

1 cup peeled chestnuts, roasted until golden

While the goose is resting, make the sauce. Drain the fat and roasting juices from the pan into a bowl and set aside. Set the roasting pan on the stovetop over medium heat and add the wishbone and shallots. Cook, stirring well and scraping up any bits of roast that are stuck to the bottom of the roasting pan, until the shallots are translucent, 5 to 10 minutes. Add the remaining 2 bay leaves, red wine, and Madeira, bring to a simmer, and reduce by half. Add the prune juice and reduce by half again. Pour the mixture into a saucepan and bring to a simmer over medium heat.

Using a tablespoon, skim the fat from the top of the reserved roasting juices and reserve 2 Tbsp of it (refrigerate any excess for another use—roast potatoes are ideal). Add the roasting juices and beef stock to the saucepan, bring to a simmer, and reduce by half again. Season with salt and pepper.

To thicken the sauce, mix the reserved goose fat and flour in a bowl to make a paste. Slowly whisk this paste into the sauce, bring the sauce to a simmer, and allow it to thicken, about 5 minutes. Strain the sauce through a fine-mesh sieve into a clean saucepan. Add the remaining 1 cup of prunes and the chestnuts and simmer for 5 minutes.

Carve the goose, using the same method to carve a chicken (page 26).

Pour the sauce around the goose and serve.

Pheasant has a tendency to dry out but brining helps prevent that, and stuffing helps keep it moist on the inside.

ROASTED PHEASANT STUFFED WITH WILD RICE

In a pot large enough to hold the pheasant without crowding, bring the orange zest, star anise, cinnamon, salt, ginger, peppercorns, water, and maple syrup to a boil over medium heat. Turn off the heat and allow the brine to cool completely. Submerge the pheasant in the brine and refrigerate, uncovered, for 4 hours.

To make the stuffing, cook the basmati as per the package instructions and set aside. Boil the wild rice in plenty of water until it splits and is tender. Strain the wild rice and set aside.

In a small frying pan over medium heat, melt 1 Tbsp of the butter and sweat the shallots until slightly caramelized. Add the shiitake mushrooms and sauté until soft. Add the cranberries and 3 Tbsp of the cranberry juice, turn down the heat to a simmer, and cook gently until the cranberries are plump, 3 to 5 minutes.

Place the basmati and wild rice in a bowl, then stir in the mushroom mixture, hazelnuts, parsley, and chives. Season with salt and pepper.

Preheat the oven to 450°F. Have a roasting pan with an elevated roasting rack ready. Remove the pheasant from the brine and pat dry with a towel. Stuff the cavity with the rice mixture, place the pheasant on the roasting rack, rub it all over with the oil, and season with salt and pepper.

Roast the pheasant for 10 minutes, then turn down the oven to 300°F. Add the stock to the roasting pan under the pheasant, cover the pan with aluminum foil, and steam the pheasant until a thermometer inserted into the thickest part of the thigh reads 160°F, about 1½ hours. Remove from the oven and allow to rest for 10 minutes.

To make the gravy, cook the remaining 1 Tbsp of butter with the flour in a small saucepan over medium heat. Cook this roux, stirring often, until it is a toothpaste consistency. Add the remaining 2 Tbsp cranberry juice and the wine, whisking to incorporate. Cook for another 3 minutes to evaporate the alcohol.

recipe continues

Serves 2

BRINED PHEASANT

4 slices orange zest, peeled using a vegetable peeler

1 star anise

½ cinnamon stick

3 Tbsp salt

1 tsp chopped ginger

1 tsp whole black peppercorns

4 cups water

3 Tbsp maple syrup

1 (about 4 pounds) pheasant

WILD RICE STUFFING

1 cup basmati rice

½ cup wild rice

2 Tbsp butter (divided)

2 Tbsp minced shallots

1 cup shiitake mushrooms, stems removed and caps sliced

3 Tbsp dried cranberries

5 Tbsp cranberry juice (divided)

2 Tbsp hazelnuts, roasted and crushed

2 Tbsp chopped Italian parsley

1 Tbsp sliced chives

Salt and pepper

2 Tbsp vegetable oil

3 cups Chicken Stock (page 360)

1 Tbsp all-purpose flour

2 Tbsp white wine

Strain the stock from the roasting pan, then slowly whisk it into the gravy base, starting with 1½ cups, and adding more until the sauce coats the back of a spoon. Season with salt and pepper, strain through a fine-mesh sieve into a gravy boat, and set aside.

To serve, slice the pheasant as you would a turkey or chicken (page 26) and arrange the pieces on a serving platter. Scoop the stuffing from the cavity of the bird into a bowl. Serve the stuffing and gravy alongside the pheasant.

Since most people buy a whole rabbit, here's a recipe that makes the most of it. We used to braise the whole rabbit when I worked in restaurants, and customers loved it. Added bonus: it only takes an hour to cook!

BRAISED RABBIT WITH POTATOES AND GREEN OLIVES

Preheat the oven to 350°F. Heat the oil in a large ovenproof pot over medium heat. Season the rabbit pieces with salt and pepper, add to the pan, and brown on all sides until golden, 3 to 5 minutes per side. Transfer the rabbit to a plate and set aside.

Turn down the heat to medium-low, place the onions in the pan and sweat, stirring frequently, until slightly translucent. Add the garlic, celery, carrots, thyme, and bay leaves, and cook, stirring frequently, until all the vegetables have softened. Return the rabbit to the pan, add the wine, and reduce the liquid by half, about 5 minutes. Pour in the stock, bring to a simmer, cover, and place in the oven for 30 minutes.

Meanwhile, score the tomatoes with a small "X" on the bottom end (not the core end). Fill a bowl with cold water and add a handful of ice. Bring a pot of water to a boil. Carefully drop the tomatoes into the boiling water and blanch for 10 seconds. Using a slotted spoon, transfer the tomatoes to the ice water and allow to cool completely. When cool, peel the tomatoes and discard the skins. Cut the flesh into quarters and discard the seeds. Set the tomatoes aside.

Using the side of a large flat knife, press down on each olive until it cracks and you can get at the pit. Discard the pits and set the olives aside.

At the 30-minute point, add the potatoes to the pot with the rabbit, using tongs or a spoon to submerge them. Cover the pot, return it to the oven, and let cook for 15 minutes.

At the 15-minute point, remove the pot from the oven and check the doneness of the rabbit. The meat around the legs and shoulder should have a bit of "give" from the bone. (If the joints feel too tough, cook the rabbit for another 10 minutes.) Using tongs or a slotted spoon, transfer the rabbit and potatoes to a serving platter and arrange nicely.

Serves 3 to 4

2 Tbsp olive oil

1 (3 pounds) rabbit, cut in 6 pieces (shoulders, loin, leg)

Salt and pepper

1 onion, finely diced

3 garlic cloves, minced

1 celery stalk, finely diced

1 carrot, finely diced

6 thyme sprigs

2 bay leaves

1 cup white wine

3 cups Chicken Stock (page 360)

4 plum tomatoes

12 large green olives with pits

4 medium Yukon Gold potatoes, peeled and sliced in ½-inch-thick rounds

1 Tbsp finely chopped Italian parsley

1 Tbsp unsalted butter, cold, cubed

recipe continues

Place the pot on the stovetop over medium-low heat, add the tomatoes and olives and bring to a strong simmer for about 5 minutes to reduce the sauce. Turn off the heat and add the parsley and butter, stirring until the sauce until velvety and emulsified. Season with salt and pepper. To serve, pour the sauce over the rabbit and potatoes and serve immediately.

Sauerbraten literally means "sour roast meat." It's a German pot roast that can be made with a variety of meats. The main difference between this pot roast and others is its marinating time: sauerbraten is typically marinated in red wine and vinegar for days to tenderize and add flavor to the meat before roasting. I find venison works well in this particular recipe, as its gaminess stands up to the strong flavors of the marinade. Adding juniper berries, a classic German flavoring and close friend of venison, sets this pot roast up for victory at your dinner table.

VENISON SAUERBRATEN

Serves 6 to 8

2 onions, cut in medium dice

3 garlic cloves, chopped

2 carrots, cut in medium dice

2 parsnips, cut in medium dice

1 leek, sliced

1 celery stalk, sliced

10 whole juniper berries, cracked with the side of your knife

10 whole black peppercorns

6 whole cloves

4 bay leaves

4 thyme sprigs

2 rosemary sprigs

1 Tbsp salt

1 tsp brown sugar

3 cups red wine, preferably something robust and sweet

2 cups water

1 cup red wine vinegar

1 (4 pounds) boneless venison shoulder roast, tied (page 27)

Salt and pepper

1 Tbsp butter

8 slices bacon, cut in medium dice

1 Tbsp all-purpose flour

1 Tbsp honey

1 tsp ground ginger

In a nonreactive pot large enough to hold the venison without crowding, stir together the onions, garlic, carrots, parsnips, leeks, celery, juniper berries, peppercorns, cloves, bay leaves, thyme, rosemary, salt, sugar, wine, water, and vinegar over medium heat. Bring the mixture to a boil, then turn down the heat and simmer for 10 minutes. Turn off the heat and allow the mixture to cool completely. Nestle the venison into the cooled marinade and refrigerate for 7 days. (If the meat isn't fully submerged, turn it over once a day to ensure all parts of the meat get some soaking time.)

recipe continues

Preheat the oven to 300°F. Remove the meat from the marinade, shaking off any excess, and pat dry. Strain the braising liquid through a fine-mesh sieve into a clean pot, reserving both the juice and the solids.

Season the roast with salt and pepper. Melt the butter in a large, heavy-bottomed pot over medium heat, add the roast, and brown on all sides. Transfer the roast to a plate and set aside.

Add the bacon to the pot and cook until the fat is rendered and the bacon is golden brown. Stir the strained vegetables into the pot and sweat, stirring often, until softened, about 10 minutes. Stir in the flour and cook for another 5 minutes.

Deglaze the pot with the reserved marinade juices, stir well, and bring to a simmer over medium heat. Add the honey then the ginger and stir well to incorporate. Return the venison to the pot, turning it over to coat, then cover and braise in the oven until the meat is falling apart, about 2 hours. Transfer the meat to a plate and set aside.

Strain the braising liquid through a fine-mesh sieve and discard the vegetables. Reduce the sauce until slightly thickened.

To serve, remove the twine from the roast, carve into slices, and layer the slices on a platter.

Pour the sauce over the roast and serve immediately.

NOTE: Start this dish a week before you plan to serve it.

After working in the north of Italy, I traveled for a spell, eating and drinking my way through some of the major northern cities—Genoa, Milan, Venice, and Florence. At each stop I ate the local specialties: pesto in Genoa, minestrone *semifreddo* (a cool soup) in Milan, and *sarde in saor* (sweet and sour sardines) in Venice. In Florence I ate pappardelle with wild boar ragù. Boar is commonly used in Tuscany; you'll find many hams and *salumi* (cured meats) made from its meat, usually lightly seasoned with wild fennel. This ragù is simple to make, but the aroma of orange and rosemary transforms it into something special. It's delicious as a pasta sauce, but you'll be tempted to eat it as is—like a stew. If you really can't find wild boar, pork will work as well.

WILD BOAR RAGÙ

Preheat the oven to 300°F. Have ready about 3 inches of kitchen twine.

Heat the oil in a large, heavy-bottomed ovenproof pot over medium-high heat. Place the boar in a bowl and season with salt and pepper. Working in batches, brown the meat on all sides. Using a slotted spoon, transfer the browned meat to a plate. Repeat with the remaining boar.

While the meat is browning, place the garlic and rosemary in a mortar and use the pestle to form a paste. Tie the orange peels together with the kitchen twine.

Turn down the heat to medium-low and melt 1 Tbsp of the butter. Add the onions, stir, cover, and sweat until translucent, about 10 minutes. Stir in the garlic-rosemary paste, cover, and sweat for another 10 minutes.

Place all the boar meat and the orange peel in the pot and stir well. Deglaze the pot with the wine and 1 cup of the stock, bring to a simmer, cover, and braise in the oven until the boar meat is falling apart, about 2 hours.

Return the ragù to the stovetop over low heat. Discard the orange peel, then add the ¼ cup of stock and adjust the seasoning if needed. Turn off the heat, add the remaining 1 Tbsp of butter, and stir vigorously with a wooden spoon.

To serve, add the cooked pasta to the pot of sauce and toss well. Transfer to a serving bowl and serve hot.

Serves 8 people as a sauce for pasta

2 Tbsp olive oil

1 (3½–4 pounds) boneless wild boar shoulder, cut in 1-inch cubes

Salt and pepper

6 garlic cloves

2 Tbsp rosemary leaves

2 oranges, zested into strips with a vegetable peeler

2 Tbsp butter (divided)

1 Spanish onion, cut in small dice

1 cup red wine

1 cup Chicken Stock (page 360) + ¼ cup, to finish the sauce

2 pounds hot cooked pappardelle (or other pasta)

OFFAL

Offal

OFFAL IS THE RATHER UNFORTUNATE NAME for the inner bits and bobs of animals, which really means organ meats, or some muscles like heart and tongue. Offal can be a difficult sell, especially to people who are unfamiliar with it, but I'm here to tell you that prepared the right way in the right recipe, offal can be delicious. Heck, if it weren't for offal, we wouldn't have pâté, or liver mousse, or foie gras, or hanger steak, or oxtail! Offal is also the ultimate way to pay respect to an animal. In recent years, "nose-to-tail" cooking—using every edible bit of the animal—has been popularized by iconic restaurants such as St. John in London, England, though many cultures have done this forever. If you think about it, why would you end an animal's life and then not consume as much of it as possible? It's important that we start thinking this way again: after all, the least we can do for the creature that fed us is to eat it, all of it, or as much of it as possible.

SHOPPING FOR OFFAL

Offal should be very fresh when you buy it; its shelf-life is limited. Here are the types of offal you'll find most often in a grocery store or butcher shop—and what to look for when buying them.

PORK

Liver

Great for charcuterie purposes, pork liver should be purply-red and have little to no smell. Remove the thin membrane as well as the veins and connective tissue before preparing it. Pork liver is a lean organ meat.
Good for: **charcuterie, pan-frying**

Heart

Pork heart should look ruby red and shiny when you buy it. It's a lean muscle with a rich, dense flavor that is great smoked but most commonly ground as sausage meat.
Good for: **pan-frying**

Head

Pig's head contains a lot of muscles and fat, which makes it great for charcuterie like headcheese, but it is spectacular when roasted whole. The cheeks are commonly cured for *guanciale*, a flavorful pancetta-like meat that's the essential ingredient in amatriciana pasta sauce.

Good for: **poaching for headcheese, roasting, smoking**

Tongue

Pork tongue is a tough, lean muscle that is great smoked, or thinly sliced and grilled. It should look reddish-brown when you buy it fresh.

Good for: **braising, grilling, smoking**

Ears

At the shop, we slowly dehydrate pig ears for doggie treats, but humans find them delicious when slowly poached to break down the connective tissue and then thinly sliced into salads. Look for clean, pinkish ears without too much hair or dirt (although both of those will probably be there).

Good for: **poaching**

BEEF

Liver

Fresh beef liver should be dark maroon and glisten. Remove the thin membrane, arteries, and veins before preparing it. It is commonly thinly sliced and pan-fried, and its assertive flavor stands up well to ingredients like balsamic vinegar.

Good for: **pan-frying**

Heart

Beef heart is a wonderful lean muscle that is often used as a roast or a cutlet. It is quite tender and has a mild beefy flavor. Look for heart that is deep ruby red and steak-like.

Good for: **grilling, pan-frying**

Kidney

Beef kidneys should be bright red with little smell. To prepare a kidney, cut it into smaller pieces, and soak in milk or acidulated water for at least 2 hours to neutralize some of the strong flavor, then dust with flour and pan-fry with assertive flavors like mustards and vinegars. The fat from beef kidneys, called suet, is prized for cooking and baking. It's traditionally used for Christmas puddings in England.

Good for: **pan-frying**

Tongue

Beef tongue is a large, tough muscle but it is quite versatile: it can be thinly sliced and grilled, cured like a corned beef, or slowly braised for a ragù. Look for tongue that is brown with gray and black spots.

Good for: **braising, grilling, curing**

Feet

Almost always sold frozen, feet are an extremely gelatinous, collagen-rich part of the animal and can be used to make stock or broth, or slowly simmered with beans for a lip-smacking soup. Look for pale yellow feet that are quite clean.

Good for: **poaching, roasting**

Marrow Bones

Beef marrow is the soft, fatty tissue inside large bones. It is traditionally used in a lot of sauces, but more recently it's become a superfood, popping up in bone broth or simply roasted and spread on toast as an appetizer. It is soft like butter and has a mildly beefy flavor. Look for a creamy-white marrow with splashes of pink from the blood.

Good for: **poaching, roasting**

Oxtail

Oxtail, while really a stewing cut, is commonly lumped in with other offals. It is the tail of a steer (originally an ox, hence its name) and is filled with lots of connective tissue and tough muscles that, when cooked for a long time over a low heat, yield a succulent, delicious meat. Look for bright-red meat with fat evenly distributed around a creamy-white central bone.

Good for: **braising, slow-roasting**

Hanger Steak

See page 185.

VEAL

Kidney

Veal kidney is more popular than beef because of its slightly milder flavor, but it still needs to be cut into smaller pieces and soaked in milk or acidulated water for 1 hour before cooking. Dust the kidneys with flour and pan-fry them with assertive flavors like mustards and vinegars.

Good for: **pan-frying**

Liver

Veal liver is a rich deep-red color and has a mild flavor that is highly prized. The liver from a calf that has been raised only on milk is the very mildest of veal livers.

Good for: **grilling, pan-frying**

Sweetbreads

Sweetbreads are the thymus (and less commonly the pancreas) gland of the veal calf. Their creamy texture and fairly neutral flavor pair well with many foods, and they are commonly poached before being breaded and fried.

Good for: **pan-frying, poaching**

Brain

Calf's brain is a shiny pink with plump, well-defined lobes. It can be poached and served with a piquant sauce (*tête de veau*) or ground and stuffed in ravioli, to name a few preparations. Its creamy texture makes it a delicacy in many parts of the world.

Good for: **pan-frying, poaching, used in a stuffing**

LAMB

Kidney

Fresh lamb kidneys should look dry and maroon-colored. The mildest-flavored of the kidneys commonly available, it still benefits from being soaked in milk or acidulated water for at least 2 hours. It is typically pan-fried or grilled and served as an appetizer on toast or as part of a lamb-focused mixed grill.

Good for: **grilling, pan-frying**

Liver

Lamb liver has a deep-red color and a strong lamb flavor. Remove the membrane and veins before preparing it. It's often pan-fried or ground for sausage.

Good for: **charcuterie, pan-frying**

Sweetbreads

Lamb sweetbreads are the thymus (or sometimes the pancreas) gland of the lamb. They are much smaller and less commonly used than veal sweetbreads and have a more assertive flavor. They are delicious when pan-fried or poached.

Good for: **pan-frying, poaching**

CHICKEN

Liver

Chicken livers are among the most commonly requested offal at our shop because they are so versatile. Look for smooth, shiny, deep-red livers. Chicken livers can be pan-fried and added to salad, or seasoned and puréed for a mousse.

Good for: **charcuterie, pan-frying**

Heart

Chicken hearts are beautiful smooth red muscles with a bit of external fat and lean meat. They are often grilled on skewers, as in South American *anticuchos*.

Good for: **grilling**

Gizzard

This tough muscle in the throat of birds, like chicken, helps to break down grains and other large pieces of food before they are digested. Look for fresh red meat around a creamy-white bit of cartilage. The gizzard is commonly used to build flavor in sauces and gravy, though it can be eaten on its own or as part of a mixed grill.

Good for: **grilling**

DUCK OR GOOSE

Liver (and Foie Gras)

Duck liver has a bit more flavor than chicken liver, but it is used in many of the same applications. Fatty liver (foie gras) is the liver of a duck that has been deliberately overfed. Foie gras can be sliced for pan-frying or seasoned and cooked in a terrine.

Good for: **grilling (liver), pan-frying (foie gras), roasting (foie gras)**

Heart

Duck heart looks a lot like chicken heart but it is larger. It is delicious when skewered and grilled and makes a great ragù when braised for a long time.

Good for: **braising, grilling**

I used to hate liver, probably because of a run-in I had with some that wasn't cooked very well when I was a wee lad. That all changed when I started working in restaurants and cooking liver regularly. I became much more used to the flavor and aroma, and I grew to enjoy it. Liver and onions are a classic diner dish, slightly elevated here with the addition of balsamic vinegar.

BEEF LIVER AND ONIONS

Before you begin, be sure the membrane and any traces of the arteries have been removed from the liver. Place the liver in a bowl with the milk and refrigerate for 1 hour. Discard the milk and pat dry the liver on a towel.

Melt 2 Tbsp of the butter in a large pot over medium-low heat. Add the onions and bacon, cover, and simmer, stirring frequently, until the bacon is brown and the onions caramelized, at least 1 hour. Season with salt and pepper, remove from the pot, and set aside.

Place the flour in a shallow bowl. Season the liver with salt and pepper, then dredge the slices in the flour, shaking off any excess, and place them on a plate. Melt the remaining 2 Tbsp butter in a large frying pan over medium-high heat. Add a few slices of liver, brown them on the outside, and transfer to a clean plate. Repeat with the remaining liver.

Add the onion and bacon mixture and the sage to the frying pan. Pour in the vinegar and Worcestershire sauce and bring to a simmer. Add the browned liver and stir until well combined.

To serve, divide the liver and onions among individual plates and serve immediately with the mashed potatoes.

NOTE: One of the reasons most people don't like liver is because it has been cooked to death. Liver, whether beef, veal, or poultry, can be served slightly pink, but I prefer when it's been just cooked through (160°F internal temperature). Overcooked liver develops a mealy texture. When thinly sliced, liver just needs a quick sear, followed by a minute of reheating in the sauce.

Serves 4

1½ pounds beef liver, well cleaned and thinly sliced

1 cup milk

4 Tbsp butter (divided)

2 onions, thinly sliced

8 slices bacon, cut in medium dice

Salt and pepper

¼ cup all-purpose flour

2 Tbsp chopped sage leaves

2 Tbsp balsamic vinegar

1 Tbsp Worcestershire sauce

1 batch Creamy Mashed Potatoes (page 342)

Lamb kidneys are pretty easy to find and are less assertive in flavor than beef kidneys. The term "deviled" comes from the use of spicy mustard in the dish—'cause, you know, the Devil likes his food spicy!

DEVILED LAMB KIDNEYS ON TOAST

Slice through the kidneys, as if you were opening a book, to cut them into two thin pieces. Cut out and discard the gristly white core of the kidney, then cut the meat into 1½-inch cubes. Place in a bowl with the milk and refrigerate for about 1 hour. Discard the milk and pat dry the kidneys.

Place the flour in a shallow bowl. Dredge the kidney pieces in the flour, shaking off any excess, season with salt and pepper, and place them on a plate.

Melt 2 Tbsp of the butter in a large frying pan over medium heat. Add the kidneys and cook until golden all over: about 1½ minutes per side. Transfer to a clean plate and set aside.

Add the remaining 1 Tbsp of butter to the pan, stir in the shallots, and sweat until translucent. Deglaze the pan with the sherry, then add the mustard, Worcestershire sauce, tomato paste, and finally the cayenne. Turn down the heat and stir well, bringing the mixture to a simmer. Return the kidneys to the pan, add the parsley, and toss well, cooking until the kidneys are firm to the touch, about 3 minutes.

To serve, arrange a piece of grilled bread on each plate, top with one-quarter of the kidney mixture, and serve hot.

Serves 4

6 lamb kidneys

1 cup milk

¼ cup all-purpose flour

Salt and pepper

3 Tbsp butter (divided)

2 Tbsp minced shallots

2 Tbsp sherry

2 Tbsp strong English or Dijon mustard

2 Tbsp Worcestershire sauce

1 Tbsp tomato paste

½ tsp cayenne powder

1 Tbsp chopped Italian parsley

4 slices country bread, toasted

I would hazard a guess that sweetbreads are the most popular offal on restaurant menus—outside of foie gras. Sweetbreads are remarkably easy to prepare, and because they are mild-tasting they are a great vessel for other flavors, such as sweet fortified Madeira wine. If you don't have Madeira, port also works well here.

FRIED SWEETBREADS WITH MADEIRA

Place the onions, 6 half-cloves of garlic, carrots, celery, lemon, peppercorns, thyme, and bay leaves in a large pot with the water and wine. Bring to a simmer over medium-high heat, then turn down the heat to low. Simmer, uncovered, for 30 minutes to allow the liquid to develop a good flavor.

Fill a large bowl with ice water. Add the sweetbreads to the simmering liquid and poach for 11 minutes. Using a slotted spoon, immediately transfer them to the ice water and allow them to cool. Discard the poaching liquid.

When the sweetbreads are cool enough to handle, use a sharp knife to clean them of any excess fat and pieces of membrane clinging to the glands. Slice the sweetbreads into ½-inch disks and dry well on a towel.

Place the flour in a large shallow bowl. Season the sweetbreads with salt and pepper, dredge them in the flour, shake off any excess, and set them on a plate.

In a large frying pan over medium-high heat, melt 2 Tbsp of the butter. Add the sweetbreads in batches, browning them on both sides, then set them aside on a clean plate.

Add 1 Tbsp of butter to the pan, followed by the minced garlic and shiitake mushrooms. Turn down the heat to medium-low, season with salt and pepper, and stir until the mushrooms are soft and the garlic is aromatic, about 5 to 10 minutes. Deglaze the pan with the Madeira, allow it to reduce slightly, then add the stock. Reduce until the sauce coats the back of a spoon, about 5 minutes, and then return the sweetbreads to the pan. Remove the pan from the heat, add the remaining 1 Tbsp butter and the thyme and stir well to combine.

To serve, divide the sweetbreads between individual plates and serve immediately.

Serves 4

1 onion, chopped

4 garlic cloves; 3 cut in half + 1 whole clove, minced

1 carrot, chopped

1 celery stalk, chopped

½ lemon

1 Tbsp peppercorns

4 thyme sprigs

4 bay leaves

4 quarts water

½ cup white wine

1½ pounds veal sweetbreads

¼ cup all-purpose flour

4 Tbsp butter (divided)

1 cup shiitake mushrooms, stems removed and caps sliced

½ cup Madeira

½ cup Beef Stock (page 361)

1 Tbsp finely chopped thyme

The next time you're craving beef but you feel like saving a few bucks, why not try beef heart? Heart is a muscle, not an organ, so it has a steak-like quality that people who are squeamish about organs will be cool with. I developed this recipe years ago when I was at Mistura; it's a cross between a steak dish and a carpaccio. Serve it as an appetizer at your next party and see if anyone notices what cut it is. This recipe calls for the heart to be barbecued, but you can absolutely sear it in a hot frying pan instead.

GRILLED BEEF HEART

Preheat the barbecue to high.

Using a sharp knife, clean the beef heart thoroughly of all its connective tissue, fat, and veins. Set the heart flat on a cutting board and cut it evenly on a bias into ¼-inch slices. Season with the vinegar, salt, and pepper, then rub in 2 Tbsp of the oil. Set aside.

In a medium frying pan, heat 2 Tbsp of the oil over medium heat. Add the garlic, lemon zest, and chili flakes and sweat. When the garlic starts to toast, add the celery, capers, and anchovy paste. Sauté for another 2 minutes, then add the bread crumbs. Stir frequently until the bread crumbs are toasted, then remove from the heat and set aside.

In a medium bowl, mix the fennel and arugula with 2 Tbsp of the oil and the lemon juice. Season with salt and pepper. Toss well and set aside.

Place the heart on the grill over very high heat, turning the slices once to get a good char on each side. Try to keep it slightly pink in the center. Remove from the grill and keep warm.

To serve, arrange slices of heart in a circle like a carpaccio on four plates. Scatter the bread crumbs evenly over top. Arrange the salad on top, then scatter the cheese over each plate. Serve immediately.

Serves 4

1 beef heart, whole

2 Tbsp balsamic vinegar

Salt and pepper

6 Tbsp olive oil (divided)

1 Tbsp minced garlic

1 Tbsp grated lemon zest

1 tsp chili flakes

3 Tbsp finely chopped celery

1 Tbsp capers

1 tsp anchovy paste

1 cup bread crumbs

2 cups thinly sliced fennel (preferably on a mandoline)

2 cups arugula

2 Tbsp lemon juice

1 cup shaved Parmigiano-Reggiano cheese

NOTE: Beef heart, when sold whole, is usually butterflied open, exposing the veins and connective tissue. You can easily remove these yourself, but feel free to ask your butcher to do it for you.

As a cook, I was trained in the tradition of modern French and Italian chefs who season primarily with salt, pepper, lemon juice, and fresh herbs. So imagine my reaction the first time I cooked with Alia's Jamaican family. It was Christmas dinner, and I had a beautiful grass-fed prime rib that I wanted to roast with, obviously, just a little salt and pepper. But my mother-in-law-to-be looked at me sideways, and said delicately, "Well, maybe we should just give it a little more flavor." Who was I to disagree with her in her own kitchen? I watched aghast as she crushed up allspice berries with salt, pepper, fresh thyme, garlic, green onions, shallots, and a *tups*—Jamaican patois for "just a wee amount"—of Scotch bonnet. She then poked holes in the rib and smeared the marinade all over the roast, shoving it into those holes, before wrapping up the roast and refrigerating it overnight. That Christmas roast was a revelation for me! Not only was it spiced perfectly, but the flavor of the beef was still very much present. Traditionally served with spinners, simple flour dumplings that you "spin" in your hands to shape.

OXTAIL STEW AND SPINNERS

Serves 8 to 10

OXTAIL STEW

5 pounds oxtail, cut by your butcher in 2-inch cubes or through the joints

Salt and pepper

4–5 Tbsp vegetable oil (divided)

2 onions, diced

4 shallots, diced

4 garlic cloves, chopped

2 carrots, diced

2 celery stalks, diced

1 bunch green onions, chopped + 4 Tbsp for garnish

½–1 small Scotch bonnet, seeded and minced, or 1 Tbsp hot sauce made with Scotch bonnets

10 thyme sprigs or 2 Tbsp dried thyme

4 dried bay leaves

1 cup red wine

4 cups Chicken Stock (page 360)

3 Tbsp oxtail seasoning (see note)

1 Tbsp ground allspice

SPINNERS

1 cup all-purpose flour

½ tsp salt

Cold water

recipe continues

Preheat the oven to 425°F. Have a roasting pan with an elevated roasting rack ready.

In a large bowl, toss the oxtail with the salt, pepper, and 4 Tbsp of the oil. Place the oxtail in the roasting pan and roast in the oven, stirring once halfway through, until browned all over, about 20 minutes.

While the oxtail is roasting, heat 1 Tbsp of the oil in a large ovenproof pot over medium heat, and add the onions, shallots, and garlic. Turn down the heat to medium-low, cover the pot, and allow the onion to sweat, stirring every few minutes with a wooden spoon. When the onion is translucent, turn up the heat to medium.

Add the carrots, celery, green onions, Scotch bonnet, thyme, and bay leaves. Cook, stirring frequently, until the vegetables are beginning to brown. Deglaze the pot with the wine and reduce by half, about 10 minutes. Add the stock, oxtail seasoning, and allspice. Stir well and bring to a simmer.

Add the browned oxtail to the pot and stir well. (If the meat isn't fully submerged, add more stock or water.) Bring the stew to a simmer, cover the pot, and place in the oven. Cook until the oxtail is starting to fall away from the bone, 3 to 4 hours. Remove the stew from the oven, taste, and adjust the seasonings, if needed. Remove the lid, allow the oxtail to cool completely, and refrigerate, uncovered, overnight.

About 30 minutes before you plan to serve the stew, use a spoon to scrape off and discard as much solidified fat as you can from the top of the stew. Set the stew on the stovetop over medium heat and bring to a simmer.

While the stew is reheating, make the spinners. In a mixing bowl, combine the flour and salt. Slowly add cold water (starting with ¼ cup, then adding 1 Tbsp more at a time as needed) to the flour, mixing constantly with your hands, until a tacky dough forms. You don't want the dough to be too wet or you won't be able to spin it, but if it's too dry the dumplings will be floury. You want enough cold water to make the flour malleable. Form small dumpling balls, slightly larger than big marbles.

Spin the dumplings between your palms, drop them in the simmering stew, and cook for 20 minutes. Test the doneness by removing a dumpling and cutting it in half. A fully cooked spinner will be soft in the center. If not soft, cook for another 5 minutes.

To serve, ladle the stew into a serving bowl, sprinkle with a few more green onions, and enjoy!

NOTE: Brown your braising cuts in the oven before putting them in a pot. You get overall caramelization in an easy-to-control technique.

Oxtail seasoning is widely available wherever you find Jamaican specialty foods. If you can't find it, mix together 1½ tsp ground allspice, 1½ tsp dried thyme, 1 Tbsp garlic salt, and 1 Tbsp salt.

Start this the night before you plan to eat it to give the oxtail time to develop flavor and give you time to skim off any excess fat before reheating.

This simple recipe plays off the classic Salade Lyonnaise, which is made with bitter greens and a poached egg. I like the creaminess of the chicken livers against the strongly flavored frisée.

PAN-FRIED CHICKEN LIVER SALAD

Using a sharp knife, clean the chicken livers of any excess connective tissue and fat. Trim away any green areas, a possible sign the liver has been tainted by the gall bladder, which, while not inedible, can prove to be very bitter. Place the livers in a bowl, add the milk, and refrigerate for 1 hour. Discard the milk and dry the livers well on a kitchen towel.

Fill a bowl with cold water. Half-fill a medium pot with water, add the vinegar, and bring to a simmer over medium-low heat. Crack each egg into a small bowl. When the water is simmering, stir it to create a slow "cyclone" effect. Drop the eggs in, one by one, maintaining the "cyclone" effect. Poach the eggs for 4 minutes, then remove with a slotted spoon and gently place in the cold water to cool.

Place the bacon in a frying pan over medium heat and fry until crispy. Drain off the fat and set the bacon aside. Wipe out the pan, add 1 Tbsp of the butter, and melt it over medium heat. Add the bread cubes and sauté until golden all over. Set aside.

To prepare the vinaigrette, whisk together the vinegar, oil, shallots, mustard, and thyme. Set aside.

Place the flour in a shallow bowl. Season the chicken livers with salt and pepper, then dredge them in the flour, shaking off any excess, and set them on a plate. Melt 1 Tbsp of butter in a large frying pan over medium-high heat. Add half of the livers and brown until just cooked through, about 3 minutes per side. Transfer the cooked livers to a clean plate and repeat with the rest of the livers.

Deglaze the pan with the brandy, then return the livers to the pan and turn off the heat. Sprinkle the chives over top and keep warm.

In a mixing bowl, toss the frisée with the bacon, croutons, and vinaigrette.

To serve, divide the salad between four plates. Place a poached egg in the center of each salad, then spoon the chicken livers artfully around the egg. Eat immediately.

Serves 4

CHICKEN LIVER SALAD

1 pound chicken livers

1 cup milk

1 Tbsp white vinegar

4 eggs

6–8 slices bacon, cut in small dice

3 Tbsp butter (divided)

6 slices white bread, crusts removed, cut in 1-inch cubes

2 Tbsp all-purpose flour

Salt and pepper

¼ cup brandy

1 Tbsp chopped chives

2 heads frisée lettuce

VINAIGRETTE

2 Tbsp sherry vinegar

3 Tbsp olive oil

1 Tbsp minced shallots

2 tsp Dijon mustard

1 tsp chopped thyme

London's St. John was by no means the first restaurant to serve roasted bone marrow, but since it popularized it, restaurants all over the world have put their spin on this rustic classic. This is my version, which pairs creamy marrow with a punchy fresh herb salsa. Ask your butcher to cut the marrow bones so that they resemble canoes.

ROASTED BONE MARROW WITH SALSA VERDE

Preheat the oven to 450°F. Line a baking tray with parchment paper.

Arrange the bone marrow, cut side up, on the baking tray. Season lightly with salt and pepper and roast until the marrow is translucent and the bone is caramelized, about 20 minutes.

While the marrow is cooking, make the salsa verde. In a small bowl, mix together the parsley, chives, mint, shallots, zest, vinegar, and mustard. Season with salt and pepper.

To serve, place the marrow bones hot from the oven on individual plates, with the salsa and toasted baguettes on the side.

Serves 4 as an appetizer

2 beef marrow bones, cut lengthwise on a band saw

Salt and pepper

3 Tbsp finely chopped Italian parsley

2 Tbsp finely chopped chives

1 Tbsp finely chopped mint

1 Tbsp minced shallots

1 tsp minced lemon zest

2 Tbsp sherry vinegar

1 Tbsp Dijon mustard

12 slices baguette, toasted on a grill or in an oven

SAUSAGES, CHARCUTERIE, AND MEAT PIES

Sausages, Charcuterie, and Meat Pies

MANY PEOPLE HEAR THE WORD "CHARCUTERIE" and imagine expensive specialty meats. In fact, charcuterie is just preserved meat (as the word itself suggests—it comes from the French words *chair*, "meat," and *cuite*, "cooked"). At one time, household cooks regularly preserved meat for their families as pâté, salami, or sausage. Today, any deli meat is a form of charcuterie, whether it's bologna or Black Forest ham, pâté en croûte or prosciutto. Charcuterie is also the banner under which sausages and bacon live; you know, part of a full English breakfast (and full Irish, and full American . . .). If you eat the good stuff and only enough to satisfy you—just like good bread, cheese, or wine—you can't go wrong. My staff and I have been making charcuterie since I opened my second shop, which has a kitchen to fool around in. At first we developed a couple of terrine recipes and a couple of meat pies, but Scott Draper, our charcutier, now offers a full range of products, from headcheese to rillettes. Scott's passion is for using every part of the animal—especially the ones consumers don't want or don't know what to do with. He transforms pig heads, for example. And feet. And hocks. Our charcuterie program has flourished under his watch. Our goal now is to make more people aware of charcuterie and the type of products we sell—and hopefully to make them more mainstream, one mousse at a time.

CHARCUTERIE 101

Ballotine

Traditionally, a ballotine is poultry that has been deboned and stuffed with seasoned ground meat known as forcemeat (historically, pâté). It is served either hot or cold and is usually made as a single-serving portion.

Confit

Confit involves slowly cooking seasoned meat in its own fat. This classic method of preserving meat uses the cooked fat to keep oxygen from the meat; confit can last for quite a while in a root cellar (or a fridge).

Galantine

Similar to a ballotine, a galantine is poultry (or fish) that has been deboned and stuffed, then poached and served cold, often covered with a gelée. A galantine is larger than a ballotine and is a common feature at a charcuterie counter.

Mousse

Usually made with pork, chicken, or duck liver, a mousse is an emulsification of liver, cream, and eggs. It is super light and spreadable, and very easy to both cook and eat. It is also commonly made with fish, fruits, or chocolate.

Pâté

When most people think about pâté, they think about the pork liver mousse that's seasoned with brandy and peppercorns and sold in little packages at the grocery store. I grew up spreading this stuff on crackers, especially around Christmastime. The word *pâté* is an old French word that means "paste," as in the paste of meat that you fill a pie with. It is a generic term referring to the mixture of meat and fat used in a recipe, sometimes, but not commonly, also known as forcemeat or farce.

Pâté en Croûte

Croûte, or "crust," is a savory pie dough. When a pâté mixture is baked in a crust, the final product is called a pâté en croûte. It is sliced, with the pastry wrapped all around the pâté, and usually served on its own as a first course, perhaps with some pickled vegetables, jam, or a salad. English pork pies are worth mentioning here, as they are England's take on a round pâté en croûte.

Pâté en Terrine

When the pâté mixture is baked on its own in a rectangular mold, the result is a pâté en terrine. This is the phrase that got shortened to "pâté" in North America and Britain and to "terrine" in France and culinary schools. A terrine is the name of the mold, so pâté en terrine is a pretty literal description.

Rillette

Rillette is cooked confit meat—usually pork, duck, or goose—that is pounded with the fat until it becomes spreadable. It's lovely on a bit of grilled toast.

Sausage

A sausage is basically seasoned ground meat that has been stuffed into a casing. The casing can be natural—the salted intestines of hogs and sheep—or artificial. Artificial casings are either edible, as in the case of some collagen-based ones, or inedible, as in the case of plastic casings. There are too many kinds of sausages to list them all here, but here are a few types to whet your appetite:

- **Fresh**: Meat mixed with spices and stuffed into a casing. These sausages need to be cooked before eating.
- **Emulsified**: A sausage that is stuffed with meat and fat that has been mixed together so well that the different grains of meat are indistinguishable from one another. They are usually either poached (boudin blanc) or smoked (kielbasa).
- **Smoked:** A fresh sausage that is hot-smoked or cold-smoked. These sausages are cooked, but need to be heated through to be enjoyed.
- **Dry-cured**: A sausage that is mixed with a predefined proportion of salt and sodium nitrite, then fermented before being hung to dry in a temperature-controlled environment. Think salami and pepperettes.

There are definitely crossover sausages, where perhaps the links are smoked before being dried out, but if you have a good grasp on the ones listed above, you'll be fine out there in sausage-land.

Terrine
A cooking vessel, often rectangular in shape, that is used to cook and mold pâté. It is sometimes made of aluminum or stainless steel, but most commonly it is stoneware or enameled cookware.

Whole Muscle
Whole muscles—like hams, capicollo, and loins—can be prepared in a variety of ways. Here are some of the most common:

- **Dried**: A muscle that is salted and left to dry in a temperature-controlled environment. Prosciutto is a perfect example; look for hams that have cured for a minimum of 24 months. There are knockoffs that cure within 6 months, but they are too salty and rubbery.
- **Smoked**: A whole muscle that has been cured and smoked. In Germany, Kassler chops are cut from a whole pork loin that has been cured and smoked. Also, bacon!
- **Brined**: A whole muscle that is sold as a brined item. Think of corned beef, before it is cooked by poaching.
- **Poached**: A whole muscle that has been brined for days before being poached in flavored water. Jambon de Paris, made from a whole ham, is a perfect example.

If you travel, you might find regional specialties. Quebec, for example, has cretons (pork simmered in milk and spices to make a spread). I urge you to become more familiar with charcuterie; it's a great way to support local producers and it really does make life that much sweeter.

Preservatives: The Nitrate Debate

A question I get asked often in the shop is "Does your deli meat have nitrates in it, and if so, why?" The short answer is yes, and to make sure the meat doesn't spoil. Let me explain.

All deli meats, charcuterie, confit, terrines, bacon, smoked meats, etc., are preserved proteins. By definition, they contain some sort of preservative—whether it's plain old sea salt, nitrite-cures, or nitrates. Remember this when you ask for deli meats with no preservatives or when you read these words on pre-packaged deli products. If you want to eat meat, it's going to come from an animal. If you want to eat preserved meat, it's going to contain preservatives. But what are these preservatives?

Sodium Nitrate A lot of people have heard about nitrates and the studies in the '70s and '80s that linked them to Alzheimer's disease and cancer. They picture a food additive cooked up in a lab. In fact, nitrates are naturally occurring minerals that are present in a lot of vegetables, fruits, and grains. They can also be synthesized. Sodium nitrate—both naturally occurring and synthetic—is used in meat preservation for four main reasons: it inhibits the growth of bacteria that cause botulism; it prevents fat from going rancid, thus extending the shelf-life of meat; it gives meat an appetizing rosy color; and it adds a tangy depth of flavor to cured meats. Governments regulate the amount of nitrates that are used in food production. On the one hand, they want to make sure no one dies from botulism after eating a bad batch of salami. On the other hand, they want to make sure no one gets ill from consuming too many nitrates. Most people who eat meat get 85%–90% of their daily sodium nitrate intake from vegetables such as beets, lettuce, and celery—and the balance of around 10% from cured meats.

Sodium Nitrite Many people use the words "sodium nitrite" and "sodium nitrate" interchangeably, but they're not the same thing. Both are food additives, but sodium nitrite has two oxygen atoms whereas sodium nitrate has three. So what? When sodium nitrate is used to cure meats, time and/or the digestive process converts the nitrate into nitrite. Food scientists can isolate nitrite and use that ingredient to preserve meats in the same way they use nitrates, but in much smaller amounts. Sodium nitrite—mixed with salt and sold as Insta Cure or Prague powder—is therefore a more common ingredient in cured meats. Governments also regulate the amount of nitrites that are used in food production for the same reasons as they regulate nitrates.

Nitrosamines When nitrites combine with amino acids under highly acidic conditions in our stomachs, or when meat cured with nitrite is cooked at too high a heat and gets charred, nitrosamines can form. Some nitrosamines are carcinogens. Although they are often associated with bacon, they are also found in significant levels in other foods with naturally occurring nitrite, including beer and salted fish. So should you avoid nitrosamines, and if so, how? You can buy products like dark brown frozen hot dogs that are labeled "nitrate-free" or "nitrite-free." These meats can legally be labeled this way because they contain no *synthesized* sodium nitrate or sodium nitrite. Instead, they use celery powder or another naturally occurring nitrate, which will still convert to sodium nitrite. It is possible to preserve meats using salt alone, but most end up gray and not as tasty. Instead of completely avoiding nitrates, many meat producers add vitamin C (ascorbic acid) to their recipes because it inhibits the transformation of nitrites into nitrosamines and can therefore help to prevent carcinogens from forming.

Riveting stuff, eh? Truthfully, the research concerning the use of nitrates/nitrites is split. That said, preserved meat needs an ingredient that will allow it to last longer than fresh meat. There's really no way around it—and for as long as humans have been on this planet we have been trying to save meat from going bad. These days, with proper refrigeration and freezers, we don't really even have to worry about curing, fermenting, or smoking to preserve our meat. Except for one little thing . . . *charcuterie is delicious*. But just as with coffee, wine, donuts, pasta, apples, and pretty much everything else under the sun, I will consume my nitrates/nitrites in moderation.

THE JOY OF MEAT PIES

Meat encased in pastry has been a staple in every culture's cuisine for centuries. In every country I have traveled to, I have always found some kind of meat pie on display at the local bakery or butcher. From Croatian burek to Jamaican beef patties, people love meat in pastry. And why shouldn't they? Meat pies are made to be eaten on the go or enjoyed around a table with loved ones. However they are consumed, meat pies are delicious to eat, and relatively easy to make by hand. Unless you have to make hundreds of them, then you should let a machine help you when it can. I'm all for artisanal, handcrafted food and other goods. But machines, when made well and functional, can be an artisan's best friend.

Making Perfect Sausages

Follow these tips closely and you'll have homemade sausages any time you want.

USE THE RIGHT TYPE OF MEAT. Pork is a perfect sausage meat. Well-raised hogs have a good amount of fat, which you want for a juicy sausage. We make our pork sausage fillings from primarily shoulder and belly meat, with added back fat if necessary. We also use trim from the loins and leg cuts, as long as we keep a good 25%–30% fat content, which is needed for a moist sausage. Lamb also makes a great sausage; if you get an older lamb, it will have more fat and a more pronounced flavor. Beef can make a decent sausage, but in my experience, you need a little pork fat to make it more succulent. I generally save the beef trim for grinds and hamburger patties.

AIM FOR 25%–30% FAT. For a juicy sausage, you want the meat mixture to be 25%–30% fat. For a pork sausage, use about 75% shoulder meat and 25% belly meat to put you in that ballpark. Grind the meat yourself or ask your butcher to do it. If you're buying pre-ground meat, ask for "fatty" ground pork. Most regular ground pork contains 15%–20% fat, which is too lean for sausage.

GRIND MEAT ONLY WHEN IT'S COLD. When you grind meat in a machine, the grinder often gets a little warm due to friction. If the meat is already warm, it can emulsify while it grinds, which causes what is called "smearing" and gives sausages a greasy mouthfeel once they're cooked. To prevent this, cut the meat into pieces that will fit through your machine. Arrange the meat on a plate and place it in the freezer for 30 minutes so it's really cold (but not frozen) when you grind it.

HAVE FUN WITH FLAVORS. There are a million and one spices and flavors out there, and sausages can be the best way to experiment with them. Do you have seasonal fresh fruit or some weird wine you were gifted once? It's sausage time, baby!

MAKE A SLURRY FOR THE SEASONING. Whatever seasoning you're using for the sausage, mix it with enough water to create a slurry before combining it with the meat. This will help evenly distribute the spice throughout the mix so you don't end up with unpleasant clumps of spice in your finished sausage. If your seasoning contains fresh garlic and you're grinding your own meat, mince the garlic and then grind it with the meat first.

DON'T OVERMIX THE SAUSAGE MEAT. If you use an electric mixer to combine the meat and seasonings, watch it carefully. You want to mix the sausage just enough to both distribute the seasonings and have the small pieces of ground meat stick to each other. If the meat gets overmixed, it can emulsify, which gives the cooked sausage an undesirable texture.

CHOOSE YOUR CASING CAREFULLY. *We use only all-natural casings from hogs and sheep.* These are intestines that have been washed out and packed in salt. Most commercially prepared sausages are made with collagen casings, which are processed from cattle hide. They're thinner and stronger than natural casings, which means they don't break as easily. But they also don't have the same "bite" as the natural casings. We use hog and lamb casings because I want to produce a sausage that is made with the fewest possible processed ingredients.

SOAK THE CASINGS IN WATER. Natural sheep and hog casings are stored in salt, so rinse them well before stuffing them to improve their flavor and prevent them from drying out. Place the casings in a bowl, add enough cold water to cover them completely, and allow them to soak for 10 minutes. Repeat this process, changing the water until it doesn't taste salty. Casings that aren't soaked sufficiently can break when cooked, as the salt dries them out.

USE A SAUSAGE STUFFER. We stuff our sausages by feeding the casings onto a cylinder that is attached to the stuffer. The sausage mix, or farce, goes into that sausage stuffer. Then we use a hand crank to coax the farce from the stuffer into the casings. If you plan to make a lot of sausage, I recommend you purchase one, but a few hacks (see below) will help you get by with limited equipment.

OR USE PARCHMENT PAPER TO FORM YOUR SAUSAGES. If you don't have a sausage stuffer, shape your sausage meat on a sheet of parchment paper. Set about 5 cups of the meat on a sheet of parchment, tightly roll the edge of the paper around the meat, and keep rolling the paper to tighten the sausage. Seal both ends with kitchen twine. Remove the parchment before baking the sausage log in a 350°F oven for 10 minutes to set it, then cutting it into smaller pieces and frying it to brown the outside.

OR USE A FREEZER BAG TO PIPE YOUR SAUSAGES. If you don't have a sausage stuffer, you can place your sausage meat in a heavy-duty freezer bag and cut off one of the corners to create a makeshift piping bag. Squeeze the meat out of the bag to fill a natural casing.

DON'T OVERSTUFF YOUR SAUSAGES. A well-stuffed sausage should feel like a very ripe banana still in the peel. It should definitely have some give to it when gently squeezed. Overstuffed sausages can burst while cooking because the meat inside the casing expands as it cooks. Understuffed sausages can easily be fixed with a few more twists of the casing. A good method is to pinch the coil at the 6-inch mark and spin it forward a few times. Skip the next 6 inches, then repeat the double-pinch-and-forward-spin. This naturally creates a sausage in between. Many sausage makers suggest alternating between spinning the casing forward with one link and backward with the next, but this method avoids that added step.

PRICK YOUR CASING. If you're using fresh casing, fill it evenly to avoid air holes. To do this, simply ensure you have a steady stream of farce entering your casing. Most air holes occur when there are gaps in the flow. No matter what you do, you will get some air holes, though. The easiest way to get rid of them is by pricking holes in the piped sausage with a specialized tool or the tip of a sharp paring knife.

BE CAREFUL HOW YOU COOK THEM. Several years ago I received the following tweet: FOR THE 4th TIME IN A ROW ALL YOUR GODDAMN SAUSAGE CASINGS BUSTED 3 MINUTES AFTER PUTTING THE GODDAMN SAUSAGES ON THE GODDAMN BBQ! @sanagans Wow! All caps means I'm being yelled at. I get the dude's mad. I would be too. I wouldn't want to pay for a perfectly good, well-seasoned sausage and have it blow up like an overpumped bike tire when cooked. The most common reasons for this are a) the stuffing is packed too tightly and b) the chosen cooking method hasn't been the best option. Cook sausages slowly and evenly and then the chances of splitting are minimal.

When I opened my butcher shop, I had to quickly learn how to deal with a lot of trim from whole animals. We were bringing in a few whole pigs and lambs every week, and those animals, especially the pigs, produced enough trim to make hundreds of sausages per week. After a bit of trial and error, I figured out the best methods and techniques for making delicious fresh sausages. These are the easiest links to make at home as well.

Note that we don't use nitrite in our fresh sausages. While nitrites are almost essential in cooked charcuterie (for shelf-life stability and color), fresh sausages that will be immediately consumed don't need them.

I'm giving you a bunch of Sanagan's "secret" recipes here—variations of flavor combinations borrowed from chefs and butchers before me—but once you get the hang of it, trust your instincts and make your own unique flavor combinations.

FRESH SAUSAGES

Each recipe makes 40 to 50 sausages, each one around 3½ ounces. Additionally, each recipe will fill 2 to 3 lengths of hog casing, or 4 to 5 lengths of lamb casing.

Hog or lamb casings (see Making Perfect Sausages, page 286)

MILD ITALIAN SAUSAGE

11 pounds pork

2½ Tbsp garlic cloves, minced

4 Tbsp salt

1½ Tbsp pepper

3 Tbsp toasted fennel seeds (we use whole seeds, but grind them after toasting if you prefer)

Variation: Add 2 tsp of dried chili flakes to make these Hot Italian Sausages

BREAKFAST SAUSAGE

11 pounds pork

4 Tbsp salt

1 Tbsp pepper

1 Tbsp onion powder

2 tsp garlic powder

1 tsp dried thyme

1 tsp dried sage

LAMB MERGUEZ

11 pounds lamb

4 Tbsp salt

2 Tbsp pepper

4 Tbsp ground fennel seeds

1¼ cups harissa paste

BRATWURST

11 pounds pork

4 Tbsp salt

2½ tsp ground coriander

2½ tsp onion powder

1½ tsp ground white pepper

Pinch dried marjoram

Pinch ground cloves

Pinch ground cumin

Pinch ground nutmeg

Pinch ground cinnamon

1¼ cups heavy (35%) cream

recipe continues

HONEY GARLIC SAUSAGE

11 pounds pork

4 Tbsp garlic cloves, minced

4 Tbsp salt

2 Tbsp pepper

1 tsp garlic powder

2 cups honey

LOUKANIKO SAUSAGE

11 pounds pork

4 Tbsp garlic cloves, minced

1½ Tbsp orange zest

4 Tbsp salt

1¼ Tbsp pepper

1 Tbsp dried thyme

1 Tbsp dried oregano

1 Tbsp ground coriander

2 cups white wine

BEEF, BACON, AND SRIRACHA SAUSAGE

6½ pounds beef

3½ pounds pork

1 pound bacon

1 cup sliced green onions

1 Tbsp lime zest

3½ Tbsp salt

1½ Tbsp pepper

1¼ cups Sriracha

MAPLE FIVE-SPICE SAUSAGE

11 pounds pork

4 Tbsp salt

1½ Tbsp pepper

1½ Tbsp Chinese five-spice powder

1½ cups maple syrup

PORK TACO SAUSAGE

11 pounds pork

½ cup (½ can) chipotle in adobo sauce

1½ cups cilantro, finely chopped

1½ cups green onions, finely chopped

4 Tbsp salt

2 Tbsp ground cumin

1¼ Tbsp paprika

1 Tbsp Mexican chili powder

1 cup water

TOULOUSE SAUSAGE

11 pounds pork

4 Tbsp salt

1 Tbsp pepper

½ Tbsp ground clove

1 tsp ground nutmeg

1½ cups white wine

Prepare the sausages according to the method in Making Perfect Sausages (page 286). Once the sausages have been prepared, you can cook them in a variety of ways. Four of the most popular methods are oven roasted, grilled, pan-fried, and poached.

To oven roast, preheat the oven to 350°F. Place the sausages on a parchment-lined pan and roast in the oven for 20 minutes, flipping once at the 10-minute mark.

To grill, preheat the barbecue to 350°F. Once preheated, put the sausages on the grill, leaving the lid open. Grill the sausages, turning every 5 minutes, until fully cooked, about 20 minutes.

To pan-fry, place a pan on a low heat and add 1 Tbsp or so of olive oil. Add the sausages and cook for 20 minutes, turning once at the 10-minute mark.

To poach, bring a pot of water to a simmer on low heat. Add the sausages and simmer for 20 minutes, turning once in the pot at the 10-minute mark.

For centuries, British people stretched out their leftover meat by cooking it in a Yorkshire pudding batter and feeding their large families on a budget. Families may have gotten smaller over the decades, but this recipe still makes a killer brunch dish. You can use any sausage, but stick to ones with the traditional "English" flavorings of sage, onion, and nutmeg to guarantee that authentic experience. Serve with English mustard or HP Sauce.

TOAD IN THE HOLE

First, make your batter. Place the flour in a large mixing bowl and make a well in the center. Crack the eggs into the well, beat them with a whisk, and then gradually incorporate the flour, whisking it into the egg mixture bit by bit to make a thick batter. Slowly whisk in the milk, then the butter and salt. The batter should have the consistency of a smooth custard. If it seems too thin, add a bit of flour; if it's too thick, add a bit more milk. Refrigerate the batter for at least 20 minutes, and up to 1 hour.

Preheat the oven to 400°F. When the oven reaches temperature, place an ungreased 10-inch square or round baking pan in the oven for about 3 minutes to heat up. (This step helps brown the sausages.) Carefully remove the pan from the oven.

Arrange the sausages in a single layer in the hot pan, leaving at least 1 inch between each one. Add the oil over the sausages and brown in the oven for about 8 minutes. Remove the pan from the oven and turn up the heat to 425°F.

Carefully pour the cold batter into the hot pan, making sure you get it over and in between the sausages. Return the pan to the oven and bake until the edges and top of the batter are golden, about 20 minutes.

To serve, cut the toad in the hole into wedges or squares and serve on individual plates.

Serves 4

1 cup less 2 Tbsp all-purpose flour

2 large eggs

1 cup milk

1 Tbsp melted butter

½ tsp salt

10–12 breakfast sausages (page 289 or store-bought)

1 Tbsp vegetable oil

Boudin blanc is an emulsified sausage made with lean meat (pork, chicken, or veal are common), cream, milk, and eggs and poached to set all of the ingredients. Popular in France and Belgium at Christmastime, slightly browned and served with buttered cabbage and potatoes, and, if you can find them, freshly shaved black truffles.

BOUDIN BLANC

In a pot over medium-high heat, combine the celery, leeks, onions, garlic, thyme, bay leaf, salt, pepper, nutmeg, milk, cream, and port. Bring to a boil, turn down the heat, and allow to simmer for 5 minutes. Remove from the heat and set aside to infuse for 30 minutes.

Grind the pork belly and shoulder twice through a grinder with a fine plate.

Strain the milk mixture through a fine-mesh sieve into a bowl. Place the meat in a food processor and purée on high speed. With the machine running, drizzle in half the warm milk mixture.

In a medium bowl, whisk together the egg whites and egg until slightly thickened. With the food processor on the pulse setting, slowly add the eggs to the meat purée, a couple of tablespoons at a time, ensuring each addition is fully incorporated before adding more.

When all the egg has been added, switch the food processor to low speed and drizzle in the remaining milk mixture, ensuring it is well combined. Scoop the meat into a bowl and refrigerate, covered, until ready to use.

Make the sausage as you would any other (page 286), but know this will be a wetter farce. Fill the casings and tie them off.

To cook the sausages, have a large bowl of ice water ready. Bring a large pot of water to a low simmer over low heat. Place half of the sausages in the water and poach until fully set, about 25 minutes.

Place the cooked sausages in the ice water and allow to cool. Repeat the poaching and cooling with the remaining boudin. Tightly wrap the boudin in plastic when cool and refrigerate until you're ready to use them. In France, these are eaten the day they are made, but they can last in your fridge for 3 to 4 days. To serve, brown the boudin slightly in a pan with the butter and warm right through.

Makes about 20 sausages

2 celery stalks, chopped

1 leek, white part only, chopped

1 onion, sliced

8 garlic cloves, sliced

10 thyme sprigs

1 bay leaf

6 Tbsp salt

1 Tbsp white pepper

½ tsp grated nutmeg

3 quarts milk

Scant 2 cups heavy (35%) cream

¼ cup port

1 (4½ pounds) pork belly

2¼ pounds pork shoulder

2 egg whites

1 egg

4 Tbsp butter

NOTE: This farce is very wet and can be messy when piped. When you set up your piping station (page 286), place a baking sheet directly under the sausage stuffer. This will catch any loose farce, and help keep you clean and organized.

Making your own bacon seems like a daunting task, perhaps, but if you have a charcoal or propane barbecue, I highly recommend trying it out. First off, the meat won't break the bank. Pork belly, even if you're using a heritage breed of pig, is one of the least expensive cuts of hog. Second, everyone loves bacon. I even know cheating "vegans" who will slip a crispy rasher in their mouths at holiday times. Finally, it's actually pretty simple. This recipe is a basic one, but once you've tried it, experiment with different cures for flavor, like Orange and Earl Grey Tea, or Espresso and Cocoa. This recipe makes a lot of bacon. I would freeze some and keep the rest in the fridge, ready to go when company comes a-calling.

BACON

Combine the sugar, salt, pepper, and curing salt in a medium bowl.

Using a sharp knife, score the skin of the pork belly in a crosshatch pattern at ½-inch intervals. Place the belly in a glass casserole dish or other nonreactive dish. Using very clean hands (or latex gloves if you have them), massage the cure into the pork belly, using a bit of force. You want the cure to really get into the meat. Make sure it gets into both the top and bottom of the belly. (I recommend gloves for this part due to the curing time of a few days; you don't want to risk passing on any extra bacteria from your hands on to the belly.)

At this point you can either leave the belly in the dish and wrap it tightly in plastic, or put it into a large freezer bag. Either way, refrigerate it for 10 days, turning it once a day.

After 10 days, remove the pork belly from the dish (or the bag) and rinse it well under cold, running water, then pat dry. Place it on a wire rack over a roasting pan that will fit on your barbecue. Allow the belly to rest at room temperature for 2 hours so it forms a *pellicle*, a layer of sticky proteins that rise to the surface of the belly.

Soak 2 cups of wood chips in cold water for 30 minutes. If you're using a propane barbecue, you'll need a smoke box. If you don't have one, wrap the soaked wood chips completely in aluminum foil and poke this parcel with a few holes. Preheat the barbecue to 200°F on one side of the grill, and place your smoke box/parcel under the grate on this heated side. If you're using a charcoal barbecue, light the charcoal and place it to one side of the barbecue. Liberally sprinkle the wood chips onto the charcoal. Close the lid of your barbecue.

Serves 10 to 12

1 cup packed brown sugar

6 Tbsp salt

3 tsp freshly cracked black pepper

1 tsp curing salt (sodium nitrite, sometimes sold as "pink salt," see note)

5 pounds pork belly, skin-on

2 cups wood chips

NOTE: Curing salt goes by a few different names and can have different levels of nitrite by volume. Make sure you follow the package instructions when you're using it. Also, it can be hard to find in stores. Ask a butcher shop if they have any; otherwise you should be able to find it online.

The bacon needs to cure for 10 days, so give yourself some time when starting this recipe.

When the barbecue reaches 200°F, check to be sure the smoke is billowing. Place the roasting pan with the bacon on the cooler side of the grill or away from the charcoal and smoke until a paring knife plunged directly into the center of the bacon goes in and out easily, about 2 hours. Remove from the heat and allow the bacon to cool.

Using a sharp knife, trim and remove the rind (save it for snacks!), then slice the bacon into thin strips. Tightly wrap the bacon in plastic wrap and refrigerate for up to 1 week, or freeze for up to 3 months, or cook it right away.

Chicken liver mousse is delicious. I think of it like meat butter, and if I owned a restaurant, I would serve liver mousse with bread before a meal. Hopefully, you enjoy butter as much as I do, as there is a ton of it in this recipe. Serve this mousse with some gherkins and crusty French bread.

CHICKEN LIVER MOUSSE

Clean the livers by trimming them of any visible fat, green bits (which would be from the connected gall bladder), or excess membrane. Place the livers in a bowl, cover with the milk, and allow to soak for 1 hour. Discard the milk, rinse the livers well, and dry them completely using a towel. Remove as much moisture as possible so they fry well.

Season the livers liberally with salt and pepper. Heat the oil in a large frying pan over medium-high heat. Once it's hot, add half the livers to the pan and cook until browned on both sides, about 3 minutes per side. Transfer the cooked livers to a plate to cool. Repeat with the remaining livers. Turn down the heat to medium.

Melt 1 Tbsp of butter in the pan, then add the shallots, garlic, thyme, bay leaf, and espelette pepper (or paprika) and sweat until the shallots are translucent. Deglaze the pan with the brandy, scraping all the bits off the bottom of the pan, and cook until the brandy is reduced by half, 5 to 10 minutes. Remove from the heat.

Place the chicken livers and shallot mixture in a blender and purée on high speed. Gradually add the remaining 1 cup of cold butter, stirring until fully emulsified. Season, if needed. Strain the purée through a fine-mesh sieve into a clean measuring jug.

Have ready four sterilized 1-cup jars with lids. Melt the schmaltz (or duck fat) in a pot over low heat.

Fill each jar three-quarters full with liver mixture, then spoon 1 Tbsp of the hot fat over each mousse to prevent it from oxidizing. Tightly seal the lids and refrigerate overnight to allow the flavors to develop. The mousse will keep, refrigerated, for up to 2 weeks.

Makes about four 1-cup jars

1 pound chicken livers

½ cup milk

Salt and pepper

3 Tbsp vegetable oil

1 cup cold butter, diced + 1 Tbsp butter for cooking

1 cup minced shallots

2 Tbsp minced garlic

1 Tbsp chopped thyme

1 bay leaf

½ tsp ground espelette pepper or paprika

½ cup brandy

¼ cup rendered chicken schmaltz or duck fat

NOTE: I prefer to pot my mousse in little jars and top it with melted chicken fat so it doesn't oxidize. Prepared this way, it makes a great host gift! Alternatively, you can set the mousse in a small 16 ounce terrine mold.

Rillettes are a simple preparation of cooked meat, normally fatty pork, that has been shredded and thoroughly mixed to produce a spread-like quality. One day we had a huge order for chicken thighs to go out to a restaurant. That meant we were sitting on a few hundred pounds of chicken drumsticks. Well, necessity being the mother of invention and all that, I came up with this recipe to turn the drumstick meat into a terrine—delicious when spread on grilled baguette. The herb gelée is not essential, but it does make for a pretty topping to the meat. Serve with toasted baguette and plenty of good wine.

CHICKEN RILLETTES WITH TARRAGON

NOTE: Start the rillettes 2 to 3 days before you plan to serve them so their flavor develops and the gelatin sets completely.

In a large bowl, toss together the drumsticks, salt, sugar, chopped garlic, bay leaves, and thyme. Cover and refrigerate overnight.

Preheat the oven to 300°F.

In a large ovenproof pot over medium-low heat, melt the schmaltz (or duck fat). Using dry hands, rub the excess cure off the drumsticks. Carefully lower the drumsticks into the fat to submerge (if not submerged, add more schmaltz or duck fat) and bring them to a simmer. Cover, place the pot in the oven, and cook until the meat is falling from the bone, 2½ to 3 hours. Remove from the oven, carefully strain the fat into a bowl, and allow the chicken and fat to cool.

Use a spoon to separate the fat from the natural jelly that will form underneath it. Set aside.

Add a small amount of the fat to a frying pan, add the shallots and minced garlic, and sweat over medium heat until translucent. Add the wine and reduce by half.

When the chicken is cool enough to handle, shred the meat from the bone and place it in a mixing bowl. Finely chop any of the skin and add to the meat. Discard the bones and cartilage.

Makes a regular-sized terrine (about 2 pounds) or eight 4-ounce jars

CHICKEN RILLETTE

10 pounds chicken drumsticks

¼ cup salt

¼ cup granulated sugar

½ cup chopped garlic + 2 Tbsp finely minced garlic

5 bay leaves

½ bunch thyme

5–6 quarts chicken schmaltz or rendered duck fat

1 cup finely minced shallot

1 cup white wine

1 bunch fresh tarragon, leaves picked and finely chopped

½ bunch fresh chives, finely chopped

Pepper

TARRAGON GELÉE

1 bunch Italian parsley, leaves picked

1 bunch tarragon, leaves picked (reserve a few leaves for garnish)

¼ cup powdered gelatin

1 cup cold water

1 cup hot water

recipe continues

Place the meat in the bowl of a stand mixer fitted with the paddle attachment. Add 2 cups of the natural jelly, shallot-wine mixture, and chopped tarragon and chives, and mix at low speed to combine the ingredients, about 1 minute. Turn the mixer to full speed and beat the meat. Season with salt and pepper.

Line a 3- × 12-inch terrine mold with a very large sheet of plastic wrap, making sure it extends beyond the edges of the mold. (You can also use eight 4-ounce ramekins lined with plastic wrap.) Spoon the chicken mixture into the terrine, packing it down tightly. Fold the plastic wrap over top of the terrine to enclose the meat mixture, set a weight on top of the terrine, and refrigerate for at least 6 hours to set.

Meanwhile, make the gelée. First make chlorophyll (green) water. Fill a large bowl with ice water. Bring a large pot of water to a boil over high heat, add the parsley and tarragon, and blanch for 10 seconds. Using a slotted spoon, transfer them immediately to the ice water so they retain their color, and allow to sit for a few seconds. Drain and set aside.

In a bowl, whisk the gelatin into the 1 cup of cold water and allow to sit for 3 minutes to bloom. Whisk in the 1 cup of hot water, then place the mixture in a blender with the herbs. Purée on high speed until the water is bright green. Strain the mixture through cheesecloth or a fine-mesh sieve into a clean bowl.

Remove the weight from the terrine. Decorate the top of the rillette with the reserved tarragon leaves, then ladle 2 inches of herb gelée over the rillette. Allow the gelée to set (about 30 minutes) before wrapping the terrine in plastic again. Refrigerate for 24 hours.

To serve, unwrap the terrine. Using the plastic lining as assistance, lift the meat out of the terrine. Discard the plastic wrap and arrange the rillette on a platter.

I read somewhere that corned beef—beef brisket cured in brine and boiled—was invented by Irish immigrants who landed in New York and couldn't find the cured pork bacon they remembered from home, so they cured beef instead. That theory is kind of ridiculous, given that cured and smoked pork were popular among the new Americans of European descent, particularly those from Poland or Hungary. And that Ireland has a rich history of corning beef going back to the 1600s. And that pigs were surely available in 19th-century New York. But for whatever reason, cured Irish bacon (cut from the loin) never gained popularity. Corned beef, however, was hugely popular, and to this day is thought of as the national food of Ireland.

CORNED BEEF AND PARSLEY SAUCE

Serves 8

CORNED BEEF

4 quarts water

4 whole garlic cloves

1¼ cups salt

½ cup granulated sugar

3 Tbsp curing salt

3 Tbsp pickling spice (divided, see note)

1 (4–5 pounds) beef brisket, flat cut end (ask your butcher)

1 medium onion, cut in small dice

1 large carrot, cut in small dice

1 celery stalk, cut in small dice

2 garlic cloves

1 tsp whole black peppercorns

2 bay leaves

PARSLEY SAUCE

1 cup milk

¼ onion, thinly sliced

3 whole cloves

2 dried bay leaves

1 Tbsp butter, cold

2 Tbsp all-purpose flour

1 cup hot braising liquid from the corned beef

1 cup finely chopped curly parsley

2 tsp English mustard powder

In a medium pot, bring the water to a boil over high heat. Add the garlic, salt, sugar, curing salt, and 2 Tbsp of the pickling spice, whisking to dissolve the salts and sugar. Remove from the heat and allow to cool to room temperature.

recipe continues

Place the brisket in a nonreactive container and cover with the brine. Set a small plate on the brisket to weigh it down and keep it submerged. Cover and refrigerate for 7 days, checking periodically to make sure it's still submerged. If needed, place another plate on top to weigh it down further.

After a week, discard the brine and soak the brisket in cold water for about 2 hours, changing the water every 20 minutes to rinse off the excess salt.

Place the brined beef in a pot large enough to hold it without crowding, cover with cold water, and add the remaining 1 Tbsp pickling spice, the onions, carrot, celery, garlic, peppercorns, and bay leaves. *Do not add salt.* Bring the brine to a gentle simmer over medium-low heat, cover, and allow to gently simmer until the meat yields when pricked with a fork, about 4 hours. Remove from the heat, cover, and allow to rest for 20 minutes before carving.

While the beef is simmering, prepare the parsley sauce. In a medium saucepan over medium heat, warm the milk with the onions, cloves, and bay leaves. When the milk begins to simmer, remove it from the heat and allow to sit for 15 minutes to infuse.

Melt the butter in a separate pot over medium heat. Add the flour and stir vigorously to blend. Allow this roux to cook just until golden, about 5 minutes. Strain the milk through a fine-mesh sieve into a bowl, then very slowly and gradually whisk it into the roux, until the sauce is emulsified.

When all the milk has been added, whisk in the hot braising liquid. Add the parsley and mustard powder, and simmer for about 10 minutes. Remove the sauce from the heat and purée in a blender (or use an immersion blender). Pour the lovely green sauce into a gravy boat.

To serve, slice the corned beef and arrange on a serving platter. Serve hot with the parsley sauce alongside.

NOTE: To make your own pickling spice at home, combine 2 Tbsp yellow mustard seeds, 1 Tbsp whole allspice, 2 tsp coriander seeds, 2 whole cloves, 1 tsp ground ginger, 1 tsp chili flakes, 2 bay leaves, and 1 cinnamon stick.

Start this recipe a week before you plan to serve it and it's important to note that you have to *weigh* some ingredients to ensure success with this.

At the shop, our charcutier Scott Draper makes a version of duck confit with pink peppercorns. Here is a very simplified version that anyone can build different flavors on. Serve with Sautéed Potatoes (page 346) and a leafy green salad.

Be sure to give the duck at least 12 hours to cure.

DUCK CONFIT

In a large nonreactive mixing bowl, toss together the salt, sugar, garlic, peppercorns, thyme, and bay leaves. Add the duck legs and toss well to coat them completely. Cover and refrigerate overnight.

Preheat the oven to 275°F.

Melt the duck fat in a large ovenproof pot over low heat. Rinse the duck legs under cold, running water to remove the surface cure, add them to the pot, and bring to a simmer. Cover and braise in the oven until the duck meat is pulling away from the bone, 2½ to 3 hours. Remove from the oven and allow to cool in the fat.

About 20 minutes before you plan to serve the confit, preheat the oven to 450°F. Place a sheet of parchment paper in the bottom of a frying pan large enough to hold all the duck legs (or use two pans). Have ready some paper towels or a kitchen towel.

Arrange the duck legs, skin side down, in the pan, add a few tablespoons of duck fat, then set on the lower rack of the oven and roast until the skin is golden brown, about 15 minutes. Remove the duck legs from the oven and allow to cool on the towel.

Arrange the duck legs on a serving platter and serve hot.

Serves 6

1 cup salt

1 cup granulated sugar

6 garlic cloves, crushed with the side of your knife

2 Tbsp whole peppercorns

15 thyme sprigs

4 bay leaves

6 duck legs, preferably from smaller hens

1 quart rendered duck fat

Ever sit around late at night thinking to yourself, "Now, what am I to do with those pig heads?" If so, you're probably a butcher. Headcheese was born from a desire to use the whole hog. I mean, you're paying for all the parts, so it doesn't make sense to just throw any of them away, does it? Why not make a delicious deli meat out of it? And by calling it headcheese, which is marginally more palatable than "poached pig face," you'll actually be able to sell it!

HEADCHEESE

Place the pig parts, onions, carrots, celery, garlic, bay leaves, water, and wine in a very large stockpot. All the ingredients should be completely covered with liquid, so you may need slightly more water. Place over medium heat, and simmer, uncovered, until the meat is falling from the bone, about 5 hours. Remove from the heat and allow to cool in the poaching liquid until you can comfortably handle the meat.

Line a 3- × 12-inch terrine mold with plastic wrap (or cut a very large sheet of plastic wrap).

Remove the head and feet from the liquid and pick off all the meat (including the tongue). Place the meat in a mixing bowl. Finely slice the ears and add to the bowl. Finely slice some skin and add it to the meat (aim for a ratio of 70% meat to 30% skin). Discard the fat, brains, and bone. Weigh the bits in the bowl.

Add the seasonings to the bowl and mix well, but not too vigorously, to avoid emulsification. Press the mixture into the terrine mold (or mound it in the center of the plastic wrap, twist in the ends, and roll it very tightly in the plastic, removing all air bubbles). Refrigerate and allow to set overnight.

To serve, unmold the terrine (or unwrap the headcheese), slice, and serve.

NOTE: Rolling the headcheese in plastic wrap makes for a great presentation, but if you're worried about it getting too messy, by all means allow it to set in a terrine mold lined with plastic wrap. Once the terrine has set, you just have to turn it out and peel off the plastic wrap.

Start this the night before you plan to eat it.

Makes one 3- × 12-inch terrine or 1 roulade

POACHED PIG

1 pig head, split (ask your butcher to do this)

4 pig feet, split (ask your butcher to do this)

3 large onions, cut in small dice

3 large carrots, cut in small dice

6 celery stalks, cut in small dice

1 cup whole garlic cloves

1 cup whole dried bay leaves

12 quarts (or so) water

2 cups white wine

SEASONINGS

For every 2 pounds of cooked head meat, add:

Grated zest of 4 oranges

1 Tbsp salt

½ tsp ground cinnamon

½ tsp ground coriander

½ tsp pepper

¼ tsp ground cloves

¼ tsp ground nutmeg

3 Tbsp brandy

This is the classic pâté en terrine. Served with gherkins, mustard, and a loaf of country bread, it makes a perfect lunch with a leafy green salad, or a great addition to a charcuterie board. It is one of the easiest ways to start making your own charcuterie at home, and I encourage everyone to try it at least once.

PÂTÉ DE CAMPAGNE

Preheat the oven to 350°F. Line a terrine mold with parchment paper, making sure the paper extends beyond the edges of the mold.

Line the mold with the bacon, overlapping the slices.

In a food processor, purée the duck liver and pour it into a large clean bowl. Place the prunes, garlic, and brandy in the food processor (no need to clean it first). Purée, and add to the bowl with the liver. Fold in the pork, bread crumbs, pistachios, eggs, quatre épices, paprika, salt, and curing salt.

Pour this farce into the bacon-lined terrine mold. Tap the terrine a few times on your work surface to encourage air bubbles to rise to the top. Cover the terrine with aluminum foil and place it in a roasting pan. Fill the pan with hot water until it comes halfway up the side of the terrine mold. Place in the oven and cook until a thermometer inserted in the center of the meat reads 155°F, about 1½ hours. Remove the terrine from the roasting pan.

Weight the terrine overnight. To do this, wrap a piece of stiff cardboard in plastic wrap, set it on top of the foil, and balance a few cans of beans on top, then refrigerate the terrine.

To serve, unweight and unmold the terrine. Use a sharp knife to slice the terrine into individual portions and and serve.

Makes one 3- × 12-inch terrine

⅔ pound smoked bacon, thinly sliced

¾ pound duck liver

⅓ cup pitted prunes, chopped

1½ Tbsp minced garlic

⅓ cup brandy

2 pounds ground pork

2¼ cups bread crumbs

⅓ cup pistachios, shelled

4 whole eggs, whisked

1½ Tbsp quatre épices (see note)

½ tsp smoked paprika

1½ tsp salt

½ tsp curing salt

NOTE: Quatre épices is a spice blend used in baking and charcuterie when warm flavors are desired. Although the name of this spice blend seemingly calls for only four spices, most recipes list at least five, and some I've seen have even more. Oh, the French! You can make your own using 2½ Tbsp black pepper, 1½ tsp ground nutmeg, 1 tsp ground cloves, 1 tsp ground ginger, and ½ tsp ground allspice.

Start this the day before you plan to eat it.

Pork and Dried Fruit Terrine, top; Wild Boar Terrine with Armagnac and Prunes, bottom right; Pâté de Campagne, bottom left.

The pairing of Armagnac and prune is absolutely classic. I first encountered it as an ice cream flavor when I worked at Le Sélect Bistro many years ago. Armagnac is a special type of brandy made in the southwest of France—I find it to be a bit gutsier than cognac. Because of this, it pairs exceptionally well with game meats such as duck and, in this case, wild boar. See photo on page 309.

Start this the day before you plan to eat it.

WILD BOAR TERRINE WITH ARMAGNAC AND PRUNES

Place the prunes in a medium bowl, add the orange juice, prune juice, and wine, and soak until soft, about 4 hours. Strain through a fine-mesh sieve, reserving the fruit and the excess liqueur separately.

Preheat the oven to 325°F.

Fill a bowl with ice water. Bring a pot of water to a boil over high heat, add the diced back fat, and blanch for 30 seconds. Drain the boiling water and add the back fat to ice water. Strain through a fine-mesh sieve and set aside.

In a food processor, purée the boar liver and pour it into a large clean bowl. Fold in the diced back fat, ground boar and pork, orange zest, thyme, curing salt, pepper, cocoa, nutmeg, and cinnamon.

Heat the butter in a frying pan over medium heat. Add the shallots and garlic and sweat until translucent. Add the reserved liqueur, the bay leaf, and Armagnac, and reduce by half, 5 to 10 minutes. Allow to cool slightly, then fold into the meat mixture.

Line a terrine mold with overlapping strips of back fat, allowing the ends to hang over the edges of the terrine. Pour half of the meat mixture into the terrine, strategically place the soaked prunes throughout the meat, and pour the remaining meat mixture over top. Tap the terrine gently on your work surface to encourage air bubbles to rise to the top. Fold the ends of the back fat over the top of the terrine.

Makes one 3- × 12-inch terrine

25–30 prunes

1 cup orange juice

½ cup prune juice

½ cup red wine

½ pound pork back fat, cut in medium dice + 20 thin slices of pork back fat, cut into 10–12 inch strips

½ pound wild boar liver, cleaned

1 pound wild boar shoulder, twice ground

1 pound pork shoulder, twice ground

Grated zest of 1 orange

¼ bunch thyme, leaves picked and chopped

1 Tbsp curing salt

2 tsp ground pepper

¾ tsp cocoa powder

¼ tsp ground nutmeg

¼ tsp ground cinnamon

2 Tbsp butter

½ cup finely minced shallots

1 Tbsp minced garlic

1 bay leaf

½ cup Armagnac

Cover the terrine with aluminum foil and set it into a roasting pan. Fill the pan with enough hot water to come halfway up the side of the terrine mold. Cook in the oven until a thermometer inserted in the center of the meat reads 155°F, about 1½ hours. Remove the terrine from the roasting pan.

Weight the terrine overnight. To do this, wrap a piece of stiff cardboard in plastic wrap, set it on top of the foil, and balance a few cans of beans on top, then refrigerate the terrine.

To serve, unweight and unmold the terrine. Use a sharp knife to slice the terrine into individual portions and serve.

This terrine is particularly beautiful, as the dried fruit forms a mosaic in each slice of terrine—almost a stained glass of charcuterie. This terrine goes well with cheese on a mixed board to start a meal. See photo on page 309.

PORK AND DRIED FRUIT TERRINE

Preheat the oven to 350°F. Line a terrine mold with parchment paper, making sure the paper extends beyond the edges of the mold.

Line the terrine mold with the ham, overlapping the slices.

Fill a bowl with ice water. Bring a pot of water to a boil over high heat, add the back fat, and blanch for about 30 seconds. Drain off the boiling water and place the back fat in the ice water. Strain through a fine-mesh sieve and place in a large mixing bowl.

Add the ground pork, apricots, cranberries, figs, chives, salt, quatre épices, egg, cream, and sherry to the bowl, and mix until thoroughly combined. Pour this farce into the ham-lined terrine mold. Tap the terrine a few times on your work surface to encourage air bubbles to rise to the top. Cover the terrine with aluminum foil and set it in a roasting pan. Fill the pan with hot water until it comes halfway up the side of the terrine mold. Cook in the oven until a thermometer inserted in the center of the meat reads 155°F, about 1½ hours. Remove the terrine from the roasting pan.

Weight the terrine overnight. To do this, wrap a piece of stiff cardboard in plastic wrap, set it on top of the foil, and balance a few cans of beans on top, then refrigerate the terrine.

To serve, unweight and unmold the terrine. Use a sharp knife to slice the terrine into individual portions and serve.

Makes one 3- × 12-inch terrine

18 thin slices smoked ham

¾ pound pork back fat, cut in medium cubes

2 pounds ground pork

½ pound dried apricots, quartered

½ pound dried cranberries

¼ pound dried figs, cut in medium dice

¼ cup finely minced chives

2 Tbsp salt

2 Tbsp quatre épices (see note, page 308)

1 egg, beaten

1½ cups heavy (35%) cream

2 Tbsp sherry

This is a basic short-crust pie dough that we use for all of our meat pies. Short crust is a type of pastry defined by the ratio of two parts flour to one part fat. We like to use a mix of butter and lard in our pastry because the butter gives it a deliciously sweet flavor and the lard gives it a smooth texture. Also, being a butcher shop, we tend to have a lot of lard lying around. You can make this recipe without an electric mixer, but it's much easier with one. When you make and fill your pie, use any extra dough bits to decorate the top of the pie crust. We have little animal cookie cutouts that we use to differentiate each pie— believe me, when you have 300 pies ready to bake, you want to know what's in each one!

SAVORY PIE DOUGH

Place the flour, salt, and sugar in the bowl of a stand mixer fitted with the paddle attachment and mix to combine. Add the butter and lard and mix at low speed until it looks coarse and mealy.

With the motor running, pour the water into the dough and allow the dough to gather around the paddle. Turn off the mixer.

Turn out the dough onto a floured work surface and gather it together in a pile. Cut the dough in half, place each piece on top of each other, and press together, using a decent amount of force. Repeat this step three more times.

Cut the dough in half again, wrap each half in plastic wrap, and refrigerate for 30 minutes.

Remove the plastic wrap from the dough and place each piece on a floured work surface. Roll each piece of dough into a disk about ⅛ inch thick. At this point you can refrigerate (or freeze) the pie shells until you're ready to fill them. They'll keep refrigerated for 5 days or frozen for 3 months. Let frozen dough thaw overnight in the fridge before using.

Roll out each piece of dough to just larger than your pie plate. Invert your pie plate onto one of the circles. Using a paring knife, cut around the circumference of the dish. Set this top piece aside.

Line a pie plate with the other dough disk, pressing it into the corners and up the sides. Use a pair of scissors or a paring knife to cut away any overlapping pieces of dough.

Makes enough dough for one double-crust 10-inch pie

4 cups all-purpose flour
1 Tbsp salt
1 tsp granulated sugar
¾ cup butter, cold, cubed
⅓ cup cold, rendered lard
Scant ½ cup ice-cold water

NOTE: Lard really gives this dough its *quatre épices*, but if you don't have lard, use 1 full cup of butter instead.

Tourtière has a special place in the hearts of all Canadians, but especially the Québécois, from whose province the dish originates. For many of our customers, Christmas Eve just isn't right until one of our pies hits the dinner table. I've had tourtières stuffed with vegetables or potatoes, but we prefer a meat-only version. It's slightly costlier, but vastly more satisfying. Save the vegetables for the salad.

TOURTIÈRE

In a large pot over medium heat, brown the bacon. Add the onions and sweat until slightly caramelized and fragrant. Add the pork, quatre épices and salt and pepper to taste and brown well, stirring regularly. Using a ladle or large spoon, remove and discard about half of the rendered fat.

Turn down the heat to low, add the milk, and bring to a low simmer. Cover, and cook for about 1 hour, stirring every 10 minutes or so, until the meat is tender.

Add the bread crumbs and thyme, stir well, and add salt to taste if necessary. Remove from the heat and allow to cool completely at room temperature.

Preheat the oven to 375°F.

Fill the prepared pie dough with the pork mixture to just under the top of the pie plate.

Make an egg wash by whisking the egg together with a splash of water. Using a pastry brush, brush the egg wash around the lip of the pie shell. Place the top piece over the filling, press down gently, and crimp the edges of the pie to seal the top to the bottom. Use the leftover bits of dough to make designs, if you like, then brush the egg wash over the whole pie crust. Bake until the crust is deep golden brown, 40 to 45 minutes.

To serve, allow to cool slightly and cut into individual servings.

Makes one 10-inch pie

¼ pound bacon, cut in small dice

1 onion, finely minced

1 pound ground pork, not too lean

1½ tsp quatre épices (see note, page 308)

Salt and pepper

1 cup milk

¼ cup bread crumbs

1 Tbsp finely chopped thyme

1 batch Savory Pie Dough (page 313)

1 egg

This recipe was originally conceived to use up our leftover rotisserie chickens. It became so popular that we now use chicken breast meat, but it's still a brilliant way of using leftovers. After Thanksgiving, for example, mix your turkey leftovers with your leftover gravy.

CHICKEN, LEEK, AND BACON PIE

Makes one 10-inch pie

Preheat the oven to 400°F. Line a baking tray with parchment paper.

In a frying pan over medium heat, cook the bacon until golden and fragrant. Add the chicken and leeks, turn down the heat to medium-low, and sweat until the chicken is fully cooked and the leeks are translucent. Turn off the heat and set aside.

In a bowl, toss the potatoes in the oil and season with salt and pepper. Arrange them in a single layer on the baking tray and roast in the oven for 10 minutes. Stir the potatoes, then roast until golden brown and crisp, about 10 minutes. Remove from the oven and set aside to cool.

Heat the milk with the thyme in a small saucepan over low heat. Do not allow it to simmer.

Melt the butter in a large saucepan over medium heat. Add the flour and stir well to form a roux. Slowly whisk the hot milk into the roux, whisking continuously until the mixture is smooth. Allow the sauce to come to a simmer and cook for 5 minutes. Season with salt, pepper, and a squeeze of lemon juice. Remove the pot from the heat and add the bacon, chicken, and leek mixture. Stir well, and season with salt and pepper. Allow the filling to cool completely at room temperature.

Preheat the oven to 375°F.

Fill the prepared pie dough with the chicken mixture to just under the top of the pie plate.

Make an egg wash by whisking the egg with a splash of water. Using a pastry brush, brush the egg wash around the lip of the pie shell. Place the top piece over the filling, press down gently, and crimp the edges of the pie to seal the top to the bottom. Brush the egg wash over the whole pie crust. Bake until the crust is deep golden brown, 40 to 45 minutes. To serve, cool slightly and cut into individual servings.

¼ pound bacon, cut in medium dice

1 pound skinless, boneless chicken breast, cut in 1-inch cubes

1 leek, washed, trimmed, and sliced in ½-inch rounds

½ cup potatoes (I like Yukon Gold), peeled and cut in medium dice

2 Tbsp vegetable oil

Salt and pepper

1½ cups milk

1 Tbsp chopped thyme

2 Tbsp butter

¼ cup all-purpose flour

Lemon juice

1 batch Savory Pie Dough (page 313)

1 egg

This recipe is traditionally made with beef kidney, but I'm sorry, I don't like kidneys. I know as a foodie-cheffy-butchery guy I'm supposed to, but I don't. But if you like kidney, use ¼ pound of kidney to ¾ pound of stewing beef.

STEAK AND ALE PIE

Preheat the oven to 350°F.

Place the beef in a bowl and season liberally with salt and pepper. Heat the oil in a large ovenproof pot over medium heat and, working in batches, brown the beef on all sides. Transfer the beef to a plate and set aside.

Add the onions, carrots, and celery to the pot and sweat, stirring often, until slightly caramelized. Add the garlic, and sweat until fragrant. Add the tomato paste and cook for another 2 minutes. Return the browned beef to the pot, dust with the flour, stir well to incorporate, and continue cooking for another 3 minutes.

Deglaze the pot with the beer, scraping up any cooked bits stuck to the bottom of the pot. Bring to a simmer and reduce slightly, about 5 minutes. Add the bay leaf, stock, and Worcestershire sauce. Bring to a simmer, cover, then set the pot on a center rack in the oven and stew for 30 minutes. Turn down the heat to 325°F and cook for 1½ hours more.

Add the potatoes to the stew, stir well, and cook in the oven until the potatoes are cooked through, about 25 minutes. Remove the pot from the oven and stir in the thyme and rosemary, then season with salt, pepper, and a squeeze of lemon juice. Allow to cool completely at room temperature.

Preheat the oven to 375°F.

Fill the prepared pie dough with the beef mixture to just under the top of the pie plate.

Make an egg wash by whisking the egg with a splash of water. Using a pastry brush, brush the egg wash around the lip of the pie shell. Place the top piece over the filling, press down gently, and crimp the edges of the pie to seal the top to the bottom. Brush the egg wash over the whole pie crust. Bake until the crust is deep golden brown, 40 to 45 minutes. To serve, allow to cool slightly and cut into individual servings.

Makes one 10-inch pie

1 pound stewing beef, preferably from the blade, in 1½-inch cubes

Salt and pepper

2 Tbsp vegetable oil

1 medium onion, cut in small dice

1 medium carrot, cut in small dice

1 celery stalk, cut in small dice

2 garlic cloves, minced

2 Tbsp tomato paste

2 Tbsp all-purpose flour

½ cup dark and tasty ale

1 bay leaf

1 cup Beef Stock (page 361)

2 tsp Worcestershire sauce

½ cup medium-diced potatoes

1 Tbsp chopped thyme

1 Tbsp chopped rosemary

Lemon juice

1 batch Savory Pie Dough (page 313)

1 egg

Family Feasts

THE TERM FAMILY MEANS A FEW THINGS TO ME. Of course, there is my immediate family. Alia, my wife, Desmond, and I make the best memories and dinners together regularly; ones I will cherish and ones I will recall at my son's wedding. And then my extended family, including my mom and dad, my sisters, brother, and their kin, and now my in-laws and nieces and nephews; so many people with whom I get to share meals, stories, and belly laughs. Finally, I have always had a "work family." In the restaurant and butcher shop business you end up spending a lot of time with the people you work with. And if you're lucky, you get to share a meal together from time to time. This chapter showcases recipes that work well with large groups, and I have a particular soft spot in my heart for these dishes, as they all remind me of time with family.

If you do only one good thing every day, make it sitting down to enjoy a meal. If you can, sit down with your friends and family. When I was growing up, regardless of whether we had basketball or hockey practice or music class or wanted to hang out with friends, my family sat down together at 6:00 p.m. to share a meal. Those dinners were loud (there were six of us, all competing for air time—and seconds) and usually quick, but it was family time. Then I left home and started cooking in restaurants. I was always working at dinnertime and got used to fending for myself, and before I knew it, I'd been living that way for 10 years. Only in my 30s—by then divorced, living alone, and with few good friends—did I realize how much I had missed. I had cared about me and not really about anyone else. I needed to change, and I did. In a full-circle-sort-of-way, recently, when Alia and I were ready to eat and my three-year-old didn't want to sit down for dinner, I leaned down to him, asked him to look me in the eye, and said calmly, "Look, I need you to stop playing and get ready for dinner. Your mom, you, and I are family, and dinner is always family time. It's a very important time when we sit down together, share food, and make time for each other." He stood up immediately, and said, "Ok, Daddy." I was so proud of him—and of myself. Alia smiled. And then my son slowly sat down on the kitchen floor and scooted toward the bathroom on his bum. Oh, for fuck's sake . . .

I first discovered this dish when working at Le Sélect Bistro in Toronto, a restaurant well known for preparing traditional bistro dishes in a warm and welcoming environment. I was 19 years old and very susceptible to falling in love—and I did, with food, women, song, and drink. Every Sunday night after regular dinner service had finished, the staff would have their family meal together. Gathered around a table in the restaurant's long, narrow space on Queen Street, with jazz playing and Belgian ale flowing and the very last customers canoodling in quiet corners, we'd unwind over plates of duck confit, steak frites, and cassoulet. The best restaurants have this energy where staff members become like sisters and brothers, the owners can be parental at times, and we all welcome guests into our space for a couple of hours. When we're working, we take pride in doing our best for our "family," whether it's at the bar, in a section of the dining room, or in the kitchen. But after hours, eating together, sharing drinks, and talking brings us all closer together. Why not do that at home this weekend over a bowl of delicious cassoulet? This fantastic recipe was developed by Chef Anne and one of her lead cooks, Ted Aleck.

CASSOULET

Serves 8 to 10

PORK

3½ pounds skinless, boneless pork butt

3½ pounds pork belly, whole slab

2 quarts Sweet Pork Brine (page 377)

¼ cup rendered duck fat

4 cups finely diced onions

4 cups finely diced carrots

4 garlic cloves, chopped

1 herb sachet (8 parsley sprigs, 5 thyme sprigs, 1 bay leaf) (page 36)

2 cups white wine

Salt and pepper

BEANS

2 pounds dried navy beans

1 pound slab bacon

1 smoked ham hock, split in half (ask your butcher to do this on their band saw)

½ pound fresh pork skin

2 large onions, finely chopped

4 garlic cloves, crushed with the side of a knife

1 herb sachet (8 parsley sprigs, 5 thyme sprigs, 2 bay leaves, 2 whole cloves) (page 36)

2 Tbsp chopped thyme

1 Tbsp salt

ASSEMBLY

6 Toulouse sausages (page 290) or mild garlic sausages

6 legs Duck Confit (page 304)

½ cup rendered duck fat (divided)

1 loaf white sandwich bread (Pullman)

recipe continues

Evenly tie the pork butt so it resembles a small log. Place the pork butt and pork belly in a nonreactive container and pour the sweet brine over the top so the meat is submerged. Cover and refrigerate for 4 days, turning it once a day.

Remove the meat from the brine, transfer it to a plate, and refrigerate overnight, uncovered, allowing it to dry. Place the beans in a bowl, cover with water, and refrigerate overnight as well.

For the beans, drain the beans and place them in a large pot over medium heat. Add the bacon, ham hock, pork skin, onions, garlic, herb sachet, thyme, and salt, cover with about 2 inches of water, and bring to a boil, skimming off any foam that rises to the surface. Turn down the heat to a simmer and cook until the beans are tender, about 2 hours. Allow the beans to cool completely in the liquid before removing and discarding the herb sachet.

Transfer the bean mixture to a nonreactive container and refrigerate overnight to allow the flavors to develop.

Preheat the oven to 325°F. Remove the pork from the brine. Score the skin of the belly in a crosshatch pattern at ½-inch intervals.

Heat the duck fat in a large ovenproof frying pan over high heat. Sear the pork shoulder and belly on all sides until golden brown. Transfer the meat to a plate and set aside.

Turn down the heat to medium, add the onions, and sweat until translucent. Add the carrots and garlic, and sweat until fragrant and lightly caramelized. Add the herb sachet, then deglaze with the wine. Return the pork shoulder and belly to the pan, then place a small round sheet of parchment paper on top of the meat. Cover the pot with a lid and roast in the oven until the meat is tender, 2 to 2½ hours.

Remove the lid, and allow to cool in the pot at room temperature for 1 hour, then transfer the pork shoulder and belly, skin side up, to a plate and refrigerate, uncovered, overnight. Strain the pork roast liquid through a fine-mesh sieve into a clean bowl and reserve. Discard the solids.

On the day you plan to eat the cassoulet, preheat the oven to 450°F. Line a baking tray and a large ovenproof frying pan with parchment paper. Strain the beans through a fine-mesh sieve, reserving the liquid in a saucepan and discarding the herb sachet. Strip the meat from the ham hock, then discard the bone, skin, fat, and cartilage. Set aside the beans.

Bring the bean liquid, reserved pork roast liquid, and ham hock meat to a simmer over medium heat and reduce to about 2 quarts. Season with salt and pepper. Strain through a fine-mesh sieve, and add the ham hock meat and the chopped thyme to the cooked beans. Reserve the liquid.

To assemble the dish, arrange the sausages in a single layer on the baking tray and roast for 20 minutes, turning them at the 10-minute point. Remove from the oven and allow to cool completely. Slice into 2-inch rounds.

Place the duck legs, skin side down, on the parchment paper in the frying pan. If they don't all fit in one pan, divide them between two pans. Add a few tablespoons of the duck fat to the pan, then roast on the lower rack of the oven until the skin is golden brown, about 15 minutes. Remove from the oven and allow to cool on paper towel or a kitchen towel to drain off some of the fat.

Preheat the oven to 325°F. Cut the slab bacon into medium dice and mix with the cooked beans. Remove the string from the pork shoulder and cut into 1-inch-thick slices. Cut the pork belly into large dice.

Cut the crust away from the bread and cut the slices into small cubes. In a food processor, working in batches, pulse the bread cubes until they become bread crumbs. Set aside.

In a large casserole, spoon three-quarters of the bean, ham hock, and bacon mixture. Arrange the pork shoulder roast slices, the sausage, the belly cubes, and the duck confit legs around the casserole. Top with the rest of the bean mixture, then sprinkle with half of the bread crumbs. Ladle the bean liquid into the casserole until it reaches the top. Cover with the remaining bread crumbs. Drizzle with the rendered duck fat. Bake, uncovered, until the bread crumbs are golden brown and the beans are bubbling, about 1 hour.

To serve, allow to cool slightly, then serve to your family.

NOTE: Start this dish six days before you plan to eat it (or if you're in town, maybe stroll in to Le Sélect's beautiful new space on Wellington Avenue late on Sunday evening, to eat some cassoulet and say hi to the family).

Alia and I met in the modern conventional way: boy logs on, girl logs on, yadda, yadda, yadda. When we first met in person, I was blown away by her confidence, her humor, her beauty. She had her shit together; it took me a little longer to get there! Family is very important to Alia, and at first she was understandably hesitant to introduce me to hers. But I get along famously with her family now, not least because we share an enthusiasm for delicious food. Alia's parents are from Jamaica, and when they moved to Canada in the '70s they worked hard to create a positive, nurturing life for their two daughters. Much like my family, that included a lot of dinner-table conversations around a platter of tasty food, often dishes from their homeland.

Curried goat has to be one of the most famous of those dishes from Jamaica, and though I had been cooking for a long time when I met Alia, I had rarely encountered goat. So, here is my mother-in-law Karlene's recipe for curried goat. The spice mix—a blend of allspice, cumin, coriander, and other fragrant spices—is unique to Jamaica and used in many stews there. The spice infuses into the meat as it cooks slowly, and the result is a spicy, melt-in-your-mouth dish that's great at any time of year. Serve this curry with a side of steamed rice to soak up the curry sauce.

CURRIED GOAT

Serves 6 to 8

1 (3 pounds) bone-in goat shoulder, cut in 2-inch pieces with a band saw

3 garlic cloves, finely chopped

1 Tbsp minced ginger

3 green onions, sliced (divided)

2 onions, sliced

½ Scotch bonnet pepper, seeds removed and minced

5 Tbsp Jamaican curry powder (divided)

3 thyme sprigs

1 Tbsp salt

½ tsp pepper

½ tsp ground cloves

¼ cup vegetable oil

2 cups Chicken Stock (page 360)

2 cups water

2 medium potatoes, peeled and cut in medium dice

1 Tbsp butter

In a large bowl, toss the goat meat with the garlic, ginger, 2 of the green onions, cooking onions, Scotch bonnet, 4 Tbsp of the curry powder, the thyme, salt, pepper, and cloves. Allow to marinate at room temperature for 2 hours.

recipe continues

Heat the oil in a large pot over medium heat. Working in batches, brown the goat in the hot oil and set aside in a bowl. Don't wipe out the pot.

In a pot over medium heat, bring the stock and water to a simmer, then turn off the heat, set aside, and keep warm.

Add 2 cups of the hot stock to the pot you used to brown the goat meat and bring to a simmer, scraping the bottom of the pot with a wooden spoon. Return the goat to the pot, stir, and bring to a simmer. Cover and simmer until the meat is tender, 1½ to 2 hours.

While the goat is cooking, bring the remaining 2 cups of stock back up to a simmer over medium-high heat. Add the potatoes, simmer for 15 minutes, and set aside. Do not drain.

Once the goat has simmered for 1 hour, add the potatoes and stock mixture. Add the remaining 1 Tbsp of curry powder, then continue simmering until the goat is tender, about 15 minutes.

Once the goat is tender and the sauce has thickened, stir in the butter to emulsify the sauce. Add the remaining green onions and season with salt and pepper.

To serve, ladle the goat curry into a large serving bowl and dig in.

NOTE: When making curry, wear something that you don't mind getting stained, like an apron. Curry sauce stains are notoriously difficult to remove, but a trick I learned from Karlene is to set the soiled fabric outside in direct sunlight, with a touch of soap rubbed into the affected area. The sunshine will bleach the stain out.

BUYING AND COOKING GOAT

Goat has a similar flavor to lamb, but goats are a little older when they're butchered, so their meat is tougher and must be cooked for longer. It is also delicious and easily digestible. Goats are among the lowest-maintenance and most resilient of farm animals because they will chew anything and pasture almost anywhere. Although they are raised for meat in many parts of the world, they are not too popular in European and North American cultures, maybe because goat meat doesn't come in any loin or steak forms. You can get baby (kid) goat, which works beautifully on a spit, but most of the goats you see on the market are 50- to 70-pound carcasses, often sold frozen and already cut up for stews and curries. If you can get your hands on fresh goat, I recommend trying it. Goats are the perfect meat animal, and it's high time we got more farmers raising them and more chefs using their meat!

During my time at Mistura, I worked with several new Canadians and formed particularly good friendships with two men from Bangladesh, Khalil and Mizan. During Ramadan, they abstained from eating while the sun was up. Each morning when they came to work, Khalil, Mizan, and the other observant Muslims we worked with would bring large trays of delicious food that their wives had prepared for them to eat once the sun went down. They would reheat the dishes and share them with the rest of the staff and we feasted on pakoras, onion bhajis, delicious curries, and one of my favorites, lamb biryani, a festive dish that is aromatic, flavorful, and very popular for serving large groups of people. Serve with naan bread and a yogurt-cucumber salad.

LAMB BIRYANI

Serves 8 to 10

½ cup + 3 Tbsp clarified butter (divided, see note)

1 onion, sliced

1 (2½ pounds) lamb shoulder, bone-in, cut in medium dice

5 garlic cloves, puréed (use a microplane)

2 Tbsp puréed ginger (use a microplane)

2 Tbsp salt (divided)

1 Tbsp chopped green chilies (jalapeño works fine)

1 tsp chili flakes or chili powder

1 Tbsp chopped mint

1 Tbsp chopped cilantro

2 cups plain yogurt

Juice of 2 limes

2 cinnamon sticks

6 whole cloves

3 black cardamom pods

1 tsp black peppercorns

1½ cups basmati rice

1 cup milk

1 tsp saffron

In a large frying pan over medium heat, heat the 3 Tbsp of clarified butter. Add the onions and cook until slightly brown and translucent.

Place the lamb meat in a large bowl. Add the onions, garlic, ginger, 1 Tbsp of the salt, green chilies, chili flakes (or chili powder), mint, cilantro, yogurt, and lime juice. Stir well and set aside.

In a large pan over medium heat, toast the cinnamon sticks, cloves, cardamom pods, and peppercorns until fragrant. Remove from the heat, allow to cool, then place the spices on a piece of cheesecloth and tie it into a sachet (or place them in a large tea infuser ball). Add this spice sachet to the lamb mixture, cover, and allow to marinate at room temperature for 1 hour. (Alternatively, mix the spices directly into the lamb mixture, but if do you this, you'll have to warn your guests to watch for them.)

recipe continues

While the lamb is marinating, soak the rice in 6 cups of warm water for 1 hour.

Melt the ½ cup of clarified butter in a large pot over medium heat. Discard the spice sachet from the lamb mixture, add the meat to the pot, and bring it to a simmer. Cook until the lamb is tender, about 30 minutes.

Bring 3 quarts of water to a boil in a medium pot over high heat and add the remaining 1 Tbsp of salt. Drain the rice, add it to the boiling water, and cook for 5 minutes. (It will not be fully cooked.) Remove from the heat and drain well.

Preheat the oven to 350°F. Heat the milk in a small pot over medium heat, then add the saffron. Allow to infuse for at least 5 minutes.

Pour the lamb mixture into a casserole dish just large enough to hold everything without crowding. Spread the half-cooked rice evenly over the meat and drizzle the saffron milk over top. Cover with a tight lid or aluminum foil and bake until the rice is tender, 30 to 45 minutes.

To serve, place the casserole dish in the middle of the table and eat immediately.

NOTE: Clarified butter, or ghee, can be purchased or easily made at home. To make clarified butter, slowly melt 2 cups of butter in a small pot over medium heat. Skim off any impurities that rise to the surface, and after about 30 minutes you should be left with the clear butterfat without the milk solids. Clarified butter keeps, refrigerated, for up to 6 months.

I come from a bit of a mixed-up Northern European background: there's some German, French, Irish, and English. My surname, Sanagan, is a bastardized version of the French name "St. Étienne" but many people assume it's some kind of British name. It's not, but Atherton, the family name of my mother, Pat, certainly is. And being the proper English family that they were, I'm sure they ate a roast every Sunday, something like a brisket, or maybe a silverside, since they were pretty broke. But I bet you they were dreaming of a nice rib of beef.

"Prime" rib traditionally refers to a 7-bone roast cut from the 12th bone to the 6th bone of the rib section of beef. It has the lovely interior fat and marbling that melts while the roast cooks, keeping the inside super moist. The rib bones protect the interior of the rib muscle from drying out, plus you get to gnaw on the bone after everyone else has left for the evening. This tender cut is expensive, but I recommend really splurging and buying the best you can. If you're only eating it a couple of times a year, it really is worth it. Serve with Duck Fat–Roasted Potatoes (page 343) and some lightly buttered boiled green beans.

PRIME RIB ROAST

Serves 8 to 10

SEASONING SALT

1 bunch rosemary, leaves picked and chopped

1 bunch thyme, leaves picked and chopped

1 bunch sage, leaves picked and chopped

10 bay leaves, leaves sliced

⅓ cup salt (divided)

8 garlic cloves

¼ cup pepper

PRIME RIB

1 (7–8 pounds) prime rib, 3 bones, frenched and cut away from the muscle (see note)

¼ cup olive oil

RED WINE SAUCE

3 Tbsp butter, cold (divided)

3 Tbsp beef trim (ask your butcher) or ground beef

3 shallots, chopped

1 garlic clove, minced

1 Tbsp all-purpose flour

1 cup red wine + ¼ cup for finishing the sauce (divided)

6 thyme sprigs

3 bay leaves

4 cups Beef Stock (page 361)

Salt and pepper

To make the seasoning salt, blitz the rosemary, thyme, sage, and bay leaves in a food processor with 2 Tbsp of the salt. Add the garlic and pulse to chop. Add the remaining salt and the pepper and pulse until well combined. The salt should have a greenish hue.

recipe continues

Remove the roast from the fridge and rub it all over with the seasoning salt, including on the bones, and then the oil. Allow the roast to come to room temperature before cooking, about 1 hour for this size of roast. This step allows the meat to cook more evenly.

Preheat the oven to 500°F and adjust the racks so the roast can fit in the oven. Have a roasting pan with an elevated roasting rack and a roll of strong butcher's twine ready (see note).

Place the rib eye back onto the rib bones to recreate what the roast originally looked like. Using strong butcher's twine, tie the rib bones to the meat, with knots in between each bone. Place the beef on the roasting rack.

Place the roasting pan on the lower rack of the oven, close the oven door, and immediately turn down the heat to 300°F. Cook for about 20 minutes per pound for medium-rare, or 2 to 2½ hours for a 7 to 8 pound roast. To test for doneness, insert a thermometer in the thickest part of the meat. The roast is cooked when it reaches 130°F. Remove the roast from the pan and transfer it to a platter. Cover with aluminum foil, then a kitchen towel, and allow it to rest for about 30 minutes while you make the sauce.

To make the sauce, first skim off any excess fat left in the roasting pan. Set the roasting pan over medium heat and deglaze with the 1 cup of wine, scraping up any cooked bits from the bottom of the roasting pan and reduce the wine by half. Melt 1 Tbsp of the butter in a medium saucepan over medium heat. Add the beef trim and brown it all over. Add the shallots and caramelize, stirring constantly, then add the garlic and stir. Add 1 Tbsp of the butter and the flour and stir until the flour is nut-brown. Add the thyme and bay leaves. Pour in the reduced red wine from the roasting pan and stock, and bring to a simmer. Season with salt and pepper, then simmer the sauce until it coats the back of a spoon.

Strain the sauce through a fine-mesh sieve into a separate saucepan and whisk in the remaining 1 Tbsp of cold butter and ¼ cup of wine. Pour into a gravy boat.

To carve the roast, cut and discard the twine. Cut the rib bones into individual pieces and arrange them on a serving platter. Using a long slicing knife, slice the beef and arrange it beside the bones. Serve the gravy alongside.

NOTE: A whole 7-bone roast weighs around 18 pounds—enough beef for at least 25 people. You can order a roast by the pound, though. Each bone accounts for about 2¼ pounds of weight, so account for 35 ounces feeding 3 to 4 people. Ask for the shoulder end, also known as the second cut, which is the rib close to the shoulder. There is more fat in this end, as well as the rib cap muscle, which is one of the most flavorful muscles on a steer. The loin end, or first cut, is also delicious, and leaner, but lacks the cap muscle. Ask your butcher to remove the rib bones and give you enough twine to tie them back on after you've applied the rub. If they won't give you twine, offer to buy some then never go back to that jerk. Also ask your butcher to remove the bone "plate" for you; you'll be tying this bone plate back onto the muscle before seasoning and roasting.

Prime Rib Roast

Sunday Dinner Marrow-Stuffed Beef Shank Pot Roast

On Saturdays growing up, my siblings and I would spend the day outside learning how to pop wheelies on our bikes, returning pop bottles until we got enough nickels to score a popsicle, and rubbing buttercup flowers under our chins to see if we liked butter. At the end of the day, we'd run home, filthy and panting, exclaiming, "WHAT'S FOR DINNER?!!!" Sanagans are experts at eating quickly, with one forearm protecting our dish from a sibling's wandering fork. All week long we'd wolf down scrambled eggs, pan-fried hot dogs, tuna noodle casserole, etc., but Sunday was different. It was the day that we went to church and did our homework—it was also the day my mom would make something a little special for dinner. Something like a pot roast.

All afternoon the aroma would fill the house, and as the sun began to set we would come to the table. The pot roast would be served with carrots cooked in the roasting juices, a chopped salad with various salad dressings, and of course, Creamy Mashed Potatoes (page 342). This was treasured time to talk through issues and troubles, to laugh at inappropriate jokes, to cry and to fear, to eat and to drink, and to be happy. This is why I love feeding people. This is how I became who I am. A shared experience over a pot roast.

SUNDAY DINNER MARROW-STUFFED BEEF SHANK POT ROAST

Serves 8 to 10

1 (about 8 pounds) beef shank, whole (see note)	1 celery stalk, chopped
3 Tbsp minced garlic + 4 garlic cloves, chopped	6 thyme sprigs
3 Tbsp finely chopped rosemary + 4 rosemary sprigs	4 bay leaves
Salt and pepper	1 Tbsp tomato paste
5 Tbsp butter (divided)	2 cups red wine
2 onions, chopped	3 cups Beef Stock (page 361)
3 carrots, chopped	2 Tbsp all-purpose flour

Preheat the oven to 300°F.

Use a sharp boning knife to clean the butterflied shank meat of any excess fat and veins. The silverskin is ok here, as it will melt during the cooking process. Using a spoon, scrape the bone marrow out of the shank bone and put it in a small bowl. Add the minced garlic and chopped rosemary, and mix everything well. Add a little salt and up to 1 Tbsp pepper.

Set the butterflied shank, cut side up, flat on a work surface. Season the meat with salt and pepper, then sprinkle the marrow mixture all over it. Fold up the meat, tie it well with at least five knots (page 27), and season with salt and pepper.

Melt 2 Tbsp of the butter in a large heavy-bottomed ovenproof pot over medium-high heat. Brown the roast on all sides, remove it from the pot, set it aside, and turn down the heat to medium-low. Add 1 Tbsp of the butter to the pot.

Add the onions to the pot and sweat, stirring occasionally, until translucent and slightly golden. Stir in the chopped garlic, carrots, and celery, and cook for another 10 minutes. Add the thyme and rosemary sprigs, bay leaves, and tomato paste, and cook for another 5 minutes.

Deglaze the pot with the wine and simmer until reduced by half, about 10 minutes. Return the roast to the pot and add the stock. Bring to a simmer, cover, and braise in the oven until fork-tender, 3 to 4 hours.

Remove the pot from the oven and transfer the roast to a cutting board. Strain the braising liquid through a fine-mesh sieve into a saucepan, and skim away any fat. Bring the sauce to a simmer over medium heat.

In a small bowl, knead the remaining 2 Tbsp of butter into a small ball with the flour. Whisk the mixture into the sauce, a bit at a time, whisking constantly until the sauce has thickened to your liking. Simmer for another 5 minutes to cook out the flour, then season to taste. Pour the sauce into a gravy boat.

To serve, cut away and discard the twine from the pot roast, slice the meat, and arrange it on a serving platter. Pour some of the sauce over top the roast and serve the remaining sauce on the side.

NOTE: A whole beef shank is definitely a cut you'll have to pre-order from your butcher or grocer. When you get it, ask them to butterfly it open and remove the shank bone. Then, request that the shank bone be split lengthwise on the band saw, revealing the bone marrow. Take the entire shank, bones and all, home with you.

CARVING A ROAST 101

- Allow a roast to rest for at least 20 minutes before carving.

- Use a sharp knife with a long blade.

- Don't "saw" the roast, rather slice in long fluid motions.

- If the roast is bone in, first carve the meat away from the bones in large pieces. Use a carving fork, or any large fork, for this.

- When using a carving fork, stab the meat close to the bone, about 1 inch deep, to secure the roast before carving. As you carve, pull the meat away from the bone with the fork.

- Slice the pieces of meat in ½-inch intervals before fanning on a platter.

- When it makes sense, serve the bones on the side. People love eating meat off the bone—don't prevent their joy.

When I was a young boy, Christmas Day began when my three siblings and I descended on the living room at 6:00 a.m. The tree—decorated with multicolored lights, popcorn and cranberry garlands, and hanging tinsel—hovered over a modest offering of gifts, and we squealed with excitement as our eyes bulged at these boxes wrapped up in glittery paper. As he did for most things, my father tried to create order out of the chaos (especially when the cat ate a bunch of tinsel and barfed it up in a corner of the living room, or climbed up the tree and brought the whole thing down). One of us would play Santa, distributing all the presents until each person had a pile at their feet. Only then could we begin to unwrap our gifts, but each of us had to patiently wait our turn, opening one present and thanking the giver, before balling up the wrapping paper and placing it in a large garbage bag that my dad had ready. There had to be structure, you see.

It was a relaxing day for all of us but my mother, who disappeared into the kitchen from late morning through afternoon, getting dinner together. As the turkey roasted, the smells wafting from the oven intensified and by 4:00 p.m. we were all salivating, yearning for a bite of the big bird. The smell of roasted turkey still takes me back to those days when I felt safe, warm, and loved. These days, I only roast a whole turkey at Thanksgiving (Christmas is reserved for prime rib now), and since I only do it once a year, I want to make sure it's a hit. So here is your hit turkey recipe! Serve with Creamy Mashed Potatoes (page 342) and your favorite holiday side dishes.

ROAST TURKEY WITH STUFFING

Serves 8 to 10

ROAST TURKEY

3 quarts water

1 cup salt

1 cup granulated sugar

6 garlic cloves

8 thyme sprigs

4 bay leaves

1 quart ice cubes

1 (15 pounds) turkey

Vegetable oil for drizzling

COMPOUND BUTTER

2 cups unsalted butter

1 bunch sage, leaves picked and chopped

1 bunch thyme, leaves picked and chopped

1 bunch chives, chopped

1 Tbsp ground allspice

Salt and pepper

½ cup Madeira or port

recipe continues

STUFFING

1 cup butter

2 large onions, cut in small dice

2 bay leaves

4 garlic cloves, minced

Giblets from the turkey, finely chopped

Liver from the turkey, finely chopped

2 celery stalks, diced

1 carrot, grated

1 bunch sage, leaves picked and sliced

½ tsp grated nutmeg

½ tsp ground allspice

Salt and pepper

½ cup Madeira or port (optional)

1–2 cups turkey or Chicken Stock (page 360)

4 cups 1-inch-cubed stale bread (cube it the day before and leave it to dry out)

GRAVY

2 cups white wine (divided)

2 Tbsp butter

2 Tbsp cooking fat (from the turkey)

1 turkey neck (from the bird), roughly chopped into smaller chunks

2 shallots, finely diced

1 garlic clove, chopped

¼ cup all-purpose flour

4 thyme sprigs

4 sage sprigs

2 bay leaves

Salt and pepper

3 cups dark turkey or Chicken Stock (page 360)

In a stockpot large enough to hold the turkey (see note), bring the water to a boil with the salt, sugar, garlic, thyme, and bay leaves. When the salt and sugar are dissolved, turn off the heat and add the ice. Allow the brine to cool until you can stick your finger into it, pain-free.

Remove the giblets, liver, and neck from the turkey (usually these are in the neck cavity). Set them in a bowl, cover, and refrigerate. Place the turkey in the stockpot with the brine (or place it in the brining bag, add the brine, and then place it in a bowl). Refrigerate for at least 15 hours (allow 1 hour per pound).

To make the compound butter, cut the butter into slices and arrange them on a plate at room temperature to soften. In a small bowl, mix together the sage, thyme, chives, allspice, salt and pepper to taste, and Madeira. When the butter is soft, add it to the herb mixture and, using a spatula, fold them all together. Shape the butter into a rectangle on a layer of plastic wrap, roll up, and refrigerate overnight.

On the day of the celebration, remove the turkey from the brine and pat dry. Discard the brine and set the turkey aside at room temperature while you make the stuffing.

To make the stuffing, melt the butter in a large saucepan over medium-low heat. Add the onions and bay leaves, cover, and, stirring frequently, sweat until the onions start to change color slightly, about 15 minutes. Add the garlic and cook for another 5 minutes, stirring frequently. Add the giblets and liver, cook for another 5 minutes, and then add the celery, carrots, sage, nutmeg, allspice, salt, and pepper. Turn up the heat to medium and sauté, stirring frequently, until the celery starts to take on a bit of color.

Add the Madeira (or port), if using, and reduce by half. Add 1½ cups of the stock and bring to a simmer. Place the diced bread in a medium bowl and pour the stock mixture over top. Mix thoroughly. If you find the mixture too dry, add a little more stock, ¼ cup at a time, until the stuffing is moist. Add some salt and pepper if required. Set aside.

Preheat the oven to 325°F. Have a roasting pan with an elevated roasting rack ready.

To prepare the turkey, lift the skin at the front of each breast and use your fingers to make a pocket between the skin and the breast meat. Cut the compound butter into ½-inch slices and slide the slices under the skin so they cover the breast. Stuff the cavity of the bird with the bread stuffing. Place the turkey on the roasting rack. Season the bird with salt and pepper and drizzle enough oil over it to cover the skin.

Place the pan on the center rack in the oven and roast, basting every 30 minutes or so with the pan juices, until a thermometer plunged into the thigh of the turkey reads 180°F and the breast or stuffing reads 165°F, 4½ to 5 hours. Remove from the oven and transfer the turkey to a cutting board. Wrap the turkey in aluminum foil and then a towel to keep warm while it rests.

To make the gravy, tilt the roasting pan slightly and skim the fat off the top of the drippings, reserving 2 Tbsp. Place the roasting pan on the stove over medium-low heat and add 1 cup of the wine. As it simmers, scrape the bottom of the pan with a wooden spoon to lift up all of the bits of caramelized roasting juices. Turn off the heat and set aside.

In a separate saucepan over medium heat, melt the butter with the reserved fat. Add the turkey neck, cook until brown, add the shallots and garlic, and sauté until golden. Add the flour and stir vigorously to make an aromatic roux. Add the thyme, sage, bay leaves, and salt and pepper to taste, and then deglaze the pot with the remaining 1 cup wine. Turn down the heat and stir constantly for about 5 minutes to cook the alcohol from the sauce. Add the stock, whisking to incorporate, and then add all the drippings from the turkey pan, mixing well to combine. Simmer for 5 minutes to incorporate the flavors. Strain the gravy through a fine-mesh sieve into a gravy boat.

Use a spoon to remove the stuffing from the cavity and place some in a bowl and some on the turkey serving platter. Carve the turkey (page 26).

To serve, present the platter of turkey with the stuffing and gravy to your hungry (and happy) guests.

NOTE: If you don't have a stockpot large enough to hold the turkey, purchase a brining bag from your local butcher. Be sure to start this the day before the celebration.

Nothing is quite as impressive as a whole roasted pig at the table. Now some people will be weirded out at seeing the face of the animal they are going to eat. But I like what my three-year-old said when he saw the roasted pig's face and I asked him what he thought of it: "It looks delicious, Daddy." And it is. The meat from a young pig is tender, as the muscles haven't had time to toughen up, so no matter how you cook it, you will end up with a succulent roast. Serve suckling pig with Soy Ginger Vinaigrette (page 370) and Duck Fat Fried Rice (page 347).

Marinate the pig the day before you plan to serve it and make sure you have a large roll of aluminum foil on hand.

WHOLE ROASTED SUCKLING PIG

In a food processor, purée the green onions, garlic, ginger, soy sauce, vinegar, and oil until emulsified.

Have ready a roll of butcher's twine. Place the suckling pig on its back and remove and discard any kidneys or other offal that is still attached. Run a knife between the skin and the rib cage, exposing the ribs by about 2 inches. Score the underside of the pig's leg and shoulder in three or four straight lines to allow the marinade to get deeper into these joints. Using your hands, rub the marinade all over the inside of the carcass, over the skin, and into the cuts you made next to the ribs and the legs.

With the pig still on its back, tie a length of butcher's twine around the center of the pig and knot it. Fold the back legs forward, tucking the feet through the twine. Now tie the rest of the pig with about six or eight knots (page 27) to ensure the meat cooks evenly. Wrap the pig in plastic wrap and refrigerate overnight.

Preheat the oven to 450°F. To create a roasting pan large enough to fit under the pig, unwrap a large sheet of aluminum foil but don't cut it away from the rest of the roll. Place two regular baking trays side by side on top of the foil. Now continue unrolling the foil until the baking trays are completely covered. Wrap the baking trays with two more layers of foil until they're stable enough that they don't buckle and separate as soon as you pick them up. Line the baking trays with parchment paper.

Serves a party of at least 15 people

1 cup chopped green onions

3 Tbsp chopped garlic

3 Tbsp chopped ginger

1 cup soy sauce

½ cup cider vinegar

½ cup vegetable oil, plus extra for rubbing on the skin

1 (15 pounds) whole suckling pig (see note)

Salt and pepper

Place the pig on the baking trays, season with salt and pepper, and rub it all over with oil. Roast in the oven for 20 minutes. Turn down the oven to 350°F and cook until a thermometer inserted into the thickest part of the pig near the thigh reads 175°F, about 2½ hours.

Carefully remove the pig from the oven, preferably with a friend. Using a spatula, and the twine as a "handle," transfer the pig to a serving platter. Pour any cooking juices over the pig.

To serve, set the platter in the center of the table and pass around a pair of tongs so your guests can pull apart the meat and skin and serve themselves.

NOTE: A "suckling pig" refers to an animal that has only been feeding from its mother and is around 15 pounds hanging (carcass) weight. The pigs we get in the shop are a little older and around 20 pounds, a size that works well in most conventional ovens. The next size up are "barbecue pigs," and their average weight ranges from 25 pounds to 40 pounds. They're great cooked on a spit over a large charcoal grill, and their meat is still quite tender.

Side Dishes

WHILE THIS BOOK FOCUSES ON ALL THINGS MEAT, it's important to think about what you're going to serve with your protein. I love cooking vegetables, especially when they're at their peak of flavor in season. Nothing beats a simple tomato salad in the middle of August, dressed with just a little sherry vinegar and good olive oil. Similarly, rutabaga, diced and poached in chicken stock and butter, makes for an excellent soul-warming side dish in the depths of February. The following dishes all pair very well with any of the recipes in this book, and in some cases, replace the meat as a main course.

Also known as pommes purée, mashed potatoes don't get much more luxurious than this recipe. In my restaurant days, I used to make them every day, and though I don't make mashed potatoes as often now, when I do, this is my go-to recipe. Plain mashed potatoes with a knob of butter are really only awesome when the potatoes are so new they've never seen the dark of a cellar—and that's just a few weeks a year. If you want to up the luxury in this recipe, add more cream and butter and serve them with shaved truffle.

CREAMY MASHED POTATOES

Cut the potatoes in half so they're all the same size. Place the potatoes, garlic, and bay leaves in a large pot and just cover them with cold water. Season the water liberally with salt, so it is just less salty than seawater. Set the pot over medium heat, bring to a simmer, and cook through, about 30 minutes. The potatoes are done when a paring knife inserted in one of the potatoes goes in easily but slowly slides out at the speed of honey dripping down a spoon.

While the potatoes are cooking, bring the cream and butter to a simmer in a saucepan over medium-low heat. As soon as it reaches a simmer, remove from the heat.

Once the potatoes are cooked, drain them and allow them to steam dry for 10 minutes. Discard the bay leaves but leave the garlic in the pot. Using a food mill or a ricer, process the potatoes into a large bowl or another pot. (If you don't have either a food mill or a ricer, use a potato masher, but don't use a blender. The speed of those blades with turn your potatoes into glue.)

Using a rubber spatula, fold the warm cream mixture into the potatoes. Mix well until fully incorporated, then season to taste. Fold in the nutmeg, if using, and salt, if needed.

To serve, scoop the potatoes into a serving bowl. Eat immediately.

Serves 6

2 pounds Yukon Gold potatoes, peeled (see note)

6 garlic cloves, left whole

4 bay leaves (dried are fine)

2 cups heavy (35%) cream

1 cup unsalted butter

1 tsp freshly grated nutmeg (optional)

Salt

NOTE: I like a sweeter yellow variety of potato like Yukon Gold for this recipe. A friend once told me that in Chef Daniel Boulud's kitchen they use fingerlings. Imagine having the job of peeling 33 pounds of fingerling potatoes every day! But, like everything else in fine dining, I bet they are *delicious*.

Few foods go with a roast better than properly roasted potatoes that are fluffy on the inside and crispy and golden on the outside. The golden exterior provides a comforting mouthfeel and the interior flesh is the perfect vehicle for any gravy you have. If you have trouble finding duck fat, you can achieve similar results with olive or peanut oil.

DUCK FAT-ROASTED POTATOES

Preheat the oven to 450°F and place a large roasting pan on the center rack to get hot.

Cut the potatoes in quarters lengthwise, then cut each quarter in half or in thirds. Make sure all the pieces are about the same size. Place the potatoes in a large pot with the garlic and bay leaves and just cover them with cold water. Season the water liberally with salt, so it is just less salty than seawater. Bring to a boil over high heat, turn down the heat to a simmer, and cook until the outsides of the potatoes start to soften, about 2 minutes.

While the potatoes are simmering, place the duck fat in the hot roasting pan and leave the pan in the oven.

At the 2-minute point, drain the potatoes in a colander. Discard the garlic and bay leaves. Shake the potatoes around in the colander while you add the flour to coat them. The shaking will rough up the edges of the potatoes, which will be useful when you're frying them.

Open the oven and carefully slide the floured potatoes into the hot duck fat. Use a wooden spoon to evenly distribute the potatoes in the roasting pan and cook until golden on one side, about 8 minutes. Turn the potatoes over, and cook for another 8 minutes. Check for doneness, then remove from the oven and set on kitchen towels to absorb any excess fat.

Sprinkle with salt before serving.

Serves 6

2 pounds baking potatoes, peeled (see note)
2 garlic cloves, left whole
2 bay leaves
½ cup rendered duck fat
2 Tbsp all-purpose flour
Salt

NOTE: I like Russets, a.k.a. baking potatoes, best for roasting as they have a more robust flavor and crisp up nicely in the oven. Yukon Golds work well too, though.

These scalloped potatoes take a long time to make but they are creamy, cheesy, and indulgent—great for large family meals and holiday celebrations. I start the day before by caramelizing the onions and garlic, which can take up to 3 or 4 hours. Additionally, this recipe can be cut in half easily if you don't have the hordes I normally do at our gatherings.

GRATIN DAUPHINOIS

Melt the butter in a large pot over medium-low heat. Add the onions, cover, and cook gently until translucent. Add the garlic, cover, and continue cooking, stirring occasionally, until the onions are a deep golden brown and all the water they have released has evaporated, 3 or more hours. Remove from the heat and set aside.

Preheat the oven to 350°F. Line a 13- × 18-inch baking pan or casserole dish with parchment paper.

In a large bowl, whisk together the cream and eggs. Season the mixture with the nutmeg and salt and pepper to taste.

Using a mandoline, slice the potatoes about ¼ inch thick. You can do this by hand but it's much trickier and your results may be uneven. Add the sliced potatoes to the cream mixture.

Using a spoon, arrange a quarter of the potato slices in a thin layer over the bottom of the baking pan. Sprinkle with a handful of cheese, spoon one-third of the caramelized onions over the cheese, and pour one-third of the cream mixture over the onions. Repeat this layering, finishing with a layer of potatoes and a sprinkling of cheese.

Cover the gratin first with plastic wrap, then aluminum foil. Place on the middle rack in the oven and bake until a paring knife easily pierces the center of the potatoes, about 2 hours. Remove the foil and plastic wrap and continue baking until the top of the gratin is golden brown, about 20 minutes. Remove from the oven.

Give the gratin a few minutes to stop bubbling and set before serving hot.

Serves 10 to 12

2 Tbsp butter

3 Spanish onions, thinly sliced in half moons

6 garlic cloves, minced

2 cups heavy (35%) cream

2 eggs

1 tsp grated nutmeg

Salt and pepper

10 medium Yukon Gold potatoes, peeled

3 cups grated Gruyère cheese

I made this simple peasant potato dish from Switzerland 20 times a day in the first year I cooked professionally. In that country it is revered and commonly served on its own with smoked ham and melted Gruyère cheese on top. After 25 years, I still remember how to flip it, like a potato pancake of sorts. Serve with sour cream and chives.

RÖSTI

Set a metal or bamboo steamer basket over a pot of boiling water. Place the peeled potatoes in the steamer and cook for 15 minutes. Remove from the heat, drain, and allow to cool. (Or cook them in simmering water for 15 minutes. Either way, they should be hard in the center and soft on the outside.)

When the potatoes are cool enough to handle, use a box grater to grate them into a bowl. Season them liberally with salt and pepper.

Melt ¼ cup of the clarified butter in a large (preferably nonstick) pan over medium heat. When the butter is hot, place the grated potato in the pan and use a rubber spatula to shape it into a disk. Fry the potato for 2 minutes, drizzle another ¼ cup of the butter around the outside of the rösti, but not on top of it, and continue frying on the one side for another 5 minutes.

Using your rubber spatula, carefully lift one edge of the potato to see if the underside is golden brown. When it is, hold the pan handle tightly with both hands and, in a wave-like motion, flip the potato in the air and catch it back in the pan. If you're reluctant to flip the rösti this way (I don't blame you!), invert it onto a plate and then slide it off the plate back into the pan. Return it to the heat, then drizzle the remaining clarified butter around the outside of the rösti. Cook until the underside is golden brown, about another 8 minutes. When fully cooked, remove from the heat.

To serve, cut the rösti into 8 wedges and arrange on a serving platter.

Serves 8

6 large Yukon Gold potatoes, peeled
Salt and pepper
¾ cup clarified butter (you can use ghee), melted (divided)

Perhaps one of the easiest potato preparations, and deeply rooted in French bistro cuisine, sautéed potatoes are a great side dish for meat. This recipe is rich, but not any worse than fries—and way easier to make at home.

SAUTÉED POTATOES

Peel the potatoes and slice them into ½-inch rounds. Do not rinse them or soak them in water.

Melt the butter in a large frying pan over medium-low heat. When it starts to foam slightly, add the potatoes, stir to coat, and allow to cook, stirring every few minutes, until golden, 30 to 45 minutes. Tossing and stirring the potatoes helps them to brown evenly.

While the potatoes are cooking, mince the garlic and parsley together to form a paste. You can use a mortar and pestle to do this; otherwise chop the garlic and parsley together to combine.

When the potatoes are golden and cooked through, sprinkle the garlic paste over top, stir well, and season with salt and pepper.

To serve, scoop the potatoes into a serving bowl. Serve immediately.

Serves 4

6 medium potatoes, preferably a yellow-fleshed variety like Yukon Gold

¼ cup butter

1 Tbsp minced garlic

1 Tbsp Italian parsley, leaves picked and washed

Salt and pepper

This delicious side dish is made even more bangin' with the addition of chicharrón! It's like I always say—if you can add chicharrón to it, do it! If you have pork lard, you can use that instead of duck fat, but I think the flavor of the duck fat works pretty well here.

DUCK FAT FRIED RICE

Cook the rice as per the package instructions. Fluff up with a fork and set aside.

Melt the duck fat in a large saucepan over medium-high heat. Add the green onions and garlic and stir well until fragrant. Turn up the heat to medium-high, add the cooked rice, and stir well with a wooden spoon to coat the grains with the duck fat and prevent it from sticking to the pot. The rice may take some coaxing to separate, so be patient.

When the rice is fully coated, turn off the heat and add the crumbled chicharrón. Season with salt and pepper, and stir well to incorporate the chicharrón.

To serve, top the rice with a few whole pieces of the chicharrón. Serve immediately.

Serves 4 to 6

1 cup short-grain rice

2 Tbsp rendered duck fat

½ cup thinly sliced green onions

2 garlic cloves, minced

1 cup crumbled chicharrón + a few whole pieces for garnish (see note)

Salt and pepper

NOTE: Chicharrón goes by many names, including pork rinds, scrunchions, crackling, etc. You can make your own, but any of the ones you can buy at the grocery store work well here too.

A delicious side dish, especially for Jerk Chicken (page 76). This dish takes a bit of time to make, but it is so worth it. In Jamaica, beans are referred to as peas. Soak the beans overnight to soften them before cooking.

RICE AND PEAS

Place the kidney beans in a bowl and cover with cold water. Refrigerate overnight.

Bring the water, stock, and coconut milk to a boil in a medium pot over medium-high heat. Drain the beans and add them to the pot. Turn down the heat to a simmer, cover, and cook the beans until creamy, about 1½ hours.

Stir the rice, green onions, garlic, Scotch bonnet, thyme, allspice, and salt and pepper to taste to the pot of beans. There should be about 1 inch of liquid covering the ingredients in the pot. If not, add more stock. Bring to a boil over medium heat, then turn down the heat to a simmer, cover, and cook until the rice is tender and has absorbed the liquid, about 20 minutes.

To serve, spoon the rice and peas into a serving bowl and serve immediately.

Serves 8 or more

1 cup dried red kidney beans

4 cups water

2 cups Chicken Stock (page 360)

½ cup coconut milk

2¼ cups long-grain rice

4 green onions, finely sliced

2 garlic cloves, minced

¼ Scotch bonnet, left whole

2 tsp chopped thyme

½ tsp ground allspice

Salt and pepper

Risotto has a reputation for being difficult to make, with cooks sweating bullets while constantly stirring the rice and hoping it doesn't overcook. This herbed version has only a few ingredients, which makes it a fairly simple affair. Pair this dish with stewed or braised meats.

SIMPLE HERBED RISOTTO

Melt 2 Tbsp of the butter in a medium pot over medium heat. Add the onions and sweat until translucent, then add the bay leaf.

While the onions are cooking, bring the stock to a simmer in a saucepan over medium-low heat.

Add the rice to the onions and stir well with a wooden spoon to coat it with the butter. Add the wine and simmer until it has evaporated, stirring every 30 seconds or so.

Start adding the chicken stock to the rice, ladleful by ladleful, stirring as you go. Allow the rice to absorb each ladleful of stock before adding the next. The rice will absorb the liquid and release its starch, creating a thick, soupy rice. Continue adding the stock until the rice is tender when you taste it. Italians call this moment when the risotto is perfectly cooked *all'ondo*, which translates as "like a wave." When you slowly drag your wooden spoon through the cooked rice, the risotto should slowly fall back into itself (kind of like the Red Sea fell back onto itself after Moses finished parting it in in the *Ten Commandments* movie).

When the rice is cooked, remove the risotto from the heat and stir in the remaining 1 Tbsp of butter, the chives, parsley, chervil, and cheese. Stir vigorously, until the rice is creamy.

To serve, pour the risotto into a serving dish and serve immediately.

Serves 4

3 Tbsp butter (divided)

2 Tbsp finely diced onion

1 bay leaf

4 cups Chicken Stock (page 360)

1 cup arborio or carnaroli (risotto) rice

1 cup white wine

1 Tbsp finely chopped chives

1 Tbsp finely chopped Italian parsley

1 Tbsp finely chopped chervil (or tarragon or celery leaves)

1 Tbsp grated Parmigiano-Reggiano cheese

Salt and pepper

I spent years making risotto in Italian restaurants. My chefs would probably not condone this recipe, as it calls for orange cheddar cheese, a decidedly un-Italian ingredient. But I bet anyone who has an appreciation for guilty pleasures, like mac 'n' cheese, will be all over this dish.

ROASTED CAULIFLOWER AND CHEDDAR RISOTTO

Preheat the oven to 350°F. Line a baking sheet with parchment paper.

In a large bowl, toss the cauliflower with the oil and season with salt and pepper. Arrange the cauliflower in a single layer on the baking tray and roast in the oven until nicely browned, about 30 minutes. Remove from the oven and set aside.

While the cauliflower is roasting, start the risotto. Pour the stock into a pot and bring to a low simmer over medium heat.

In another pot, melt 1 Tbsp of the butter over medium heat. Add the onions and sweat for 5 minutes, or until translucent. Add the rice and stir with a wooden spoon to coat it with the butter. Add the wine and simmer until it has evaporated, stirring every 30 seconds or so.

Start adding the stock to the rice, ladleful by ladleful, stirring as you go. Allow the rice to absorb each ladleful of stock before adding the next. The rice will absorb the liquid and release its starch, creating a thick, soupy rice. Continue adding the stock until the rice is tender when you taste it. Italians call this moment when the risotto is perfectly cooked *all'ondo* (page 349).

When the rice is cooked, remove from the heat and stir in the roasted cauliflower. Add the remaining 1 Tbsp butter and the cheddar, and stir vigorously until the sauce is emulsified.

To serve, pour the risotto into a serving dish and drizzle with the balsamic, if using. Delish, if not legit! Serve immediately.

Serves 6 to 8

2 cups cauliflower florets

1 Tbsp vegetable oil

Salt and pepper

4 cups Chicken Stock (page 360)

2 Tbsp butter (divided)

½ cup finely diced onions

1 cup arborio or carnaroli (risotto) rice

½ cup white wine

1 cup grated medium orange cheddar

1 Tbsp aged balsamic vinegar (optional)

NOTE: This also makes a great entrée for 2 to 4 people.

This simple side pasta salad goes very well with flavorful dishes like Roasted Leg of Lamb with Tzatziki (page 159), and the leftovers are great to bring in to work for lunch the next day.

ORZO SALAD WITH PEAS, CHILI, MINT, AND FETA

Cook the orzo in plenty of boiling salted water according to the package directions, drain well, and place in a serving bowl. Stir in the oil and lemon zest and juice.

Fill a bowl with ice water. Bring a small pot of water to a boil, add the peas, and cook until tender, about 2 minutes. Drain and place immediately in the ice water to retain their color. Drain again and add to the orzo. Add the feta cheese, chilies, green onions, mint, watercress, parsley, and salt and pepper to taste.

Toss well before serving.

Serves 8 to 10

1 (1 pound) box orzo

¼ cup olive oil

Grated zest and juice of 4 lemons

1 pound frozen peas (look for the smallest variety)

2 cups crumbled feta cheese

2 peperoncino chilies, sliced into fine rounds (or Cubanelles if you prefer sweeter)

½ cup chopped green onions

1 cup chopped mint

1 cup chopped watercress

½ cup chopped Italian parsley

Salt and pepper

This is a delicious early summer side dish. Grilling the asparagus gives it a more robust flavor, which matches well with the more aggressive chili, olive, and anchovy flavors in this recipe. I like to serve this with Reverse-Seared Lamb Sirloin (page 168).

GRILLED ASPARAGUS WITH MEDITERRANEAN FLAVORS

Preheat your barbecue to medium-high.

Trim the woody ends of the asparagus by holding one end of the spear in each hand and gently bending it until it snaps. Discard the tough ends. Place the asparagus in a bowl, add 2 Tbsp of the oil and some salt and pepper, and toss well. Set aside.

Place the baguette in a medium bowl. Pour the remaining 2 Tbsp oil over top and toss until well coated. Set aside.

Bring a pot of water to a boil over high heat, add the eggs, turn down the heat to a simmer, and cook the eggs for 9 minutes. Drain the eggs, then fill the pot with cold water and allow them to cool slightly. Peel the eggs while they're still warm and set aside.

To make the tapenade, purée the olives, capers, parsley, garlic, gherkins, and oil in a food processor. Season to taste and set aside.

Place the asparagus on the barbecue and grill, turning once or twice, until slightly charred, about 3 minutes. Set aside on a plate. Grill the oiled baguette until well toasted, then set aside. Once cooled, tear the baguette into rough "croutons."

To assemble, arrange the asparagus on a serving plate. Cut the eggs into wedges and place around the asparagus. Dot the platter with the tapenade, chili sauce, and mayonnaise. Scatter the croutons over everything, then arrange the anchovies on top. Finally, toss the cheese and chives over everything and serve.

Serves 4

ASPARAGUS

1 bunch green asparagus

4 Tbsp olive oil (divided)

Salt and pepper

½ baguette, cut in 1½-inch-thick rounds

3 eggs

3 Tbsp bomba chili sauce (see note)

3 Tbsp mayonnaise

3 Tbsp white anchovies (see note)

3 Tbsp shaved Parmigiano-Reggiano cheese (use a vegetable peeler)

2 Tbsp finely chopped chives

TAPENADE

½ cup black olives, pitted

2 Tbsp capers

2 Tbsp finely chopped Italian parsley

1 Tbsp minced garlic

1 Tbsp gherkins

¼ cup olive oil

Salt and pepper

NOTE: White anchovies are pickled in vinegar and have a lovely brightness. If you can't get your hands on them, substitute 3 Tbsp canned tuna (packed in oil) that's been dressed with a sprinkling of white wine vinegar and salt (do not use salted anchovies).

Bomba chili sauce is an Italian condiment of chilies and pickled vegetables in oil that pairs well with roasted meats. Look for it in thet pickle and mustard section of the grocery store. If you can't find it, chop up some spicy marinated eggplant instead.

This side dish is traditionally served in the springtime, when fresh peas are in abundance. But let's be serious. Everyone—chefs included—uses frozen peas, which means you can serve this dish at any time of year. Take that, nature! Peas convert their sugar into starch fairly quickly after being picked, but quickly freezing peas after harvest captures their sweetness before that happens. Which is why, more often than not, frozen peas are sweeter than fresh ones in season. I like to serve this dish with Baked Ham with Ginger Beurre Blanc (page 102).

PEAS WITH PEARL ONIONS, LETTUCE, AND MINT

Fill a bowl with ice water. Bring a medium pot of water to boil over high heat. Add a healthy pinch of salt, followed by the peas. Boil until the peas are fully cooked, about 10 minutes for fresh peas and 2 minutes for frozen ones. Drain and cool immediately in the ice water to retain their color. When the peas are cold, drain and refrigerate them.

Fill another bowl with ice water and bring another pot of salted water to a boil over high heat. Using a paring knife, cut out and discard the dirty core of the pearl onions. Blanch the onions in the boiling water for 1 minute, drain, and transfer them to the ice water to cool. When cool enough to handle, use a paring knife to peel them.

Have ready a length of butcher's twine. Melt the butter in a large pot over medium heat. Add the pearl onions and stir until lightly golden on all sides. Tie the thyme and bay leaves together with the twine and add to the pot. Pour in the stock, bring to a simmer, and cook until the onions are translucent and fully cooked, about 8 minutes. Add the peas and warm through. Turn off the heat, then stir in the lettuce and mint to wilt them.

To serve, season the vegetables with salt and pepper, pour into a serving bowl, and serve immediately.

Serves 6

3 cups peas, fresh or frozen

Salt and pepper

1 cup pearl onions

2 Tbsp butter

4 thyme sprigs

2 bay leaves (dried are fine)

1 cup Chicken Stock (page 360)

1 head Bibb lettuce, leaves separated, washed, and torn in smaller pieces

½ cup mint leaves

I love making this dish in the early summer when the new baby carrots reach the market. The vinaigrette highlights their natural earthiness and sweetness. This goes very well with braised and poached meats.

CARROTS IN VINAIGRETTE

Bring a pot of lightly salted water to a simmer over medium heat. Peel the carrots and trim the stem, leaving about ¼ inch of the greens. Add them to the boiling water and cook until fork-tender.

While the carrots are cooking, in a medium bowl, mix together the chives, parsley, sugar, oil, vinegar, and salt and pepper to taste.

To serve, drain the carrots and place them in a serving bowl. Add the vinaigrette, toss to combine, and serve immediately.

Serves 4

1 bunch (8–12) small carrots, greens attached
1 Tbsp chopped chives
1 Tbsp chopped Italian parsley
1 tsp sugar
2 Tbsp olive oil
2 Tbsp white wine vinegar
Salt and pepper

Ok, I'm probably not reinventing anything here, but this recipe is like magic in your mouth. It goes well with any meat for an easy weekday side dish.

ROASTED BROCCOLI WITH SOY BUTTER

Preheat the oven to 400°F. Line a baking tray with parchment paper or aluminum foil.

In a bowl, toss the broccoli with the oil and season lightly with salt and pepper. Arrange the broccoli in a single layer on the baking tray and roast in the oven until golden, about 12 minutes, stirring once halfway through.

Using tongs, transfer the hot broccoli to a mixing bowl. Toss with the butter and soy sauce until the butter melts. Serve immediately.

Serves 4

2 cups broccoli florets
2 Tbsp vegetable oil
Salt and pepper
2 Tbsp butter
2 Tbsp Japanese soy sauce (shoyu)

Baked beans can be contentious. When I think about all the possible flavor variations, I almost expect to hear that famous cry from *Iron Chef America* "Whose beans reign supreme?" Well, if you're like me and you like your beans a little tangy, a little sweet, and a little spicy, this version is for you.

SWEET AND SOUR BAKED BEANS

Drain the soaked beans and place them in a pot. Fill the pot with water to just cover the beans, set over high heat, and bring to a boil. Immediately turn off the heat and allow the beans to soak in the hot liquid for an hour, uncovered. This step, while unnecessary, makes the beans creamy in less time than if you didn't boil them.

Preheat the oven to 325°F.

Place the onion and bacon in a large ovenproof saucepan over medium heat and cook, covered, until the onion is translucent and the bacon has rendered some of its fat, about 5 minutes. Add the garlic, celery, bell pepper, Scotch bonnet, and ginger and stir well. Sauté until the vegetables have softened, then add the tomato paste and molasses. Cook, stirring frequently, for another 5 minutes to combine the flavors. Season with salt and pepper.

Stir in the passata, vinegar, and sugar. Bring the mixture to a simmer and cook for about 5 minutes. Drain the beans, add them to the pot, and then pour in the stock. Bring to a simmer, cover, and cook in the oven until the beans are cooked through and creamy, about 2 hours.

To serve, transfer the beans to a serving bowl and allow to cool slightly. Better yet, refrigerate them overnight and serve the next day, once the flavors have had time to develop.

Makes about 3 quarts of cooked beans

2½ cups navy beans, soaked overnight in cold water

1 Spanish onion, cut in medium dice

8 rashers bacon, cut in small dice

3 garlic cloves, minced

½ cup minced celery

½ cup finely diced green bell pepper

½ tsp Scotch bonnet, or jalapeño for less heat

¼ tsp dried ginger

2 tsp tomato paste

1 tsp fancy molasses

Salt and pepper

1 cup passata (puréed tomatoes)

2 Tbsp cider vinegar

2 Tbsp brown sugar

1 quart Chicken Stock (page 360)

NOTE: Start this the night before you plan to eat it.

While roasting a whole head of cauliflower makes for a striking presentation when plated, you miss out on the best part: the dark golden-brown roasted bits. Roasting the florets separately means more cut surfaces and lots of crispy bits!

ROASTED CAULIFLOWER WITH HUMMUS AND HALLOUMI

Serves 8

ROASTED CAULIFLOWER

¼ cup olive oil

4 garlic cloves, minced

2 Tbsp white sesame seeds

2 Tbsp finely chopped thyme

1 Tbsp paprika

Salt and pepper

1 whole cauliflower, cut in bite-sized florets

HUMMUS

2 cups canned chickpeas, drained (but liquid reserved)

2 garlic cloves, minced

½ cup tahini

¼ cup lemon juice

Salt and pepper

½ cup olive oil

SALSA VERDE

1 cup sliced green onions

3 Tbsp capers

3 Tbsp chopped gherkins

2 cups chopped Italian parsley

1 cup mint leaves

1 cup basil leaves

1 tsp anchovy paste

¼ cup sherry vinegar

¼ cup olive oil

1 Tbsp Dijon mustard

Salt and pepper

ASSEMBLY

2 Tbsp olive oil

1 cup medium-diced halloumi cheese

1 cup pine nuts, toasted until golden brown

1 cup pomegranate arils

Preheat the oven to 425°F. Line a baking tray with parchment paper.

In a large bowl, mix the oil with the, garlic, sesame seeds, thyme, paprika, and salt and pepper to taste. Add the cauliflower, toss well to coat, arrange in a single layer on the baking tray, and roast in the center of the oven for 10 minutes. Turn the florets over and continue roasting until they're deep golden brown, about 15 minutes. Remove from the oven and keep warm.

To make the hummus, place the chickpeas, garlic, tahini, lemon juice, and salt and pepper to taste in a food processor and purée while you slowly drizzle in the oil. If the hummus is too thick, add some of the reserved chickpea liquid. Scoop the hummus into a bowl, season to taste, and set aside.

To make the salsa verde, place the green onions, capers, and gherkins in a blender. Add the parsley, mint, basil, and anchovy paste, followed by the vinegar, oil, mustard, and salt and pepper to taste, and purée. If the salsa is too dry, add a little extra olive oil. Season to taste again and set aside.

To bring it all together, heat the 2 Tbsp oil in a large frying pan over high heat. When hot, carefully add the halloumi and fry on all sides until golden, then set aside to cool slightly.

To serve, spread the hummus over the bottom of a serving platter. Place the cauliflower all over the hummus, then top the cauliflower with a drizzle of the salsa verde. Scatter the halloumi, pine nuts, and pomegranate over everything and serve.

Basic Pantry Items

T HESE ARE ALL SIMPLE RECIPES you should have a handle on. They are either important flavor bases, such as a chicken stock, or enhancers, like a vinaigrette. These recipes would be staple pantry items in a restaurant, but home cooks rarely need them at all times, so consider making them in larger batches whenever possible, then freezing them to have on hand when you need them.

BASIC STOCKS AND BROTHS You don't need to be a chef to make an excellent stock or broth. What you do need to know, though, is the difference between stock and broth. Stock is a neutral base of flavorful liquid to accommodate a lot of different recipes. Broth is a more assertively flavored liquid that may eventually become a soup. The main difference is salt. You must be judicious when using it—especially if a stock might be reduced. If the original is highly salted, the reduction will be gross. Science, right? Because a stock is made to be a lighter base, the flavors don't have to be aggressive.

SAUCES The sauces in this section are great to have in the freezer so you can add them to a roasting pan to make a delicious last-minute pan sauce. Many of these sauces build on a demi-glace, a time-consuming reduction of veal or beef stock, so once you have invested the time to make it, finishing the sauce is actually pretty easy.

SALSAS, VINAIGRETTES, AND PICKLES I consider salsas, vinaigrettes, and pickles to be finishing touches because they have a level of acidity that cuts the richness of some of the fattier meats and a freshness that sings in your mouth.

MARINADES These marinade recipes are tried and tested. I recommend keeping some of them on hand in your freezer, ready to rub onto a roast or chops to give them a little extra oomph. I usually marinate meats for at least 8 hours so the flavor has time to seep into the surface of the meat before cooking.

SPICES, RUBS, AND BRINES Spices, including salt, and rubs applied to the outside of meats, like pork ribs or roast chicken, add flavor. Brines penetrate below the surface of meats, like ham or pork belly, to season them and add moisture.

Chicken stock is one of the simplest and most versatile of all stocks, and I try to have it on hand at all times. Whether you're deglazing a pan for a sauce or poaching vegetables for a bit of added flavor, chicken stock has many uses.

CHICKEN STOCK   *Makes 5 quarts*

Preheat the oven to 400°F. Toss the chicken bones with the salt, arrange them in a single layer in a roasting pan, and roast until golden brown, about 30 minutes.

While the bones are roasting, heat a frying pan over medium-high heat. Add the onions, cut side down, and sear until they're dark brown. Remove them from the pan and chop.

Place the roasted bones and onions in a stockpot with the garlic, carrots, onions, celery, leeks, thyme, bay leaves, and peppercorns. Add just enough water to cover the bones and bring to a simmer, uncovered, over medium-high heat. Turn down the heat to low, use a spoon to skim off any scum that's risen to the top of the stock, and simmer for another 2 hours.

Remove the stock from the heat and allow to cool for 1 hour before straining through a fine-mesh sieve into a clean container, like a mason jar. Refrigerate for up to 1 week or freeze for up to 3 months.

5 pounds chicken bones, preferably carcass or back bones

5 tsp salt

3 onions, cut in half widthwise

5 garlic cloves

4 carrots, cut in half

3 celery stalks, cut in half

1 leek, cut in half

6 thyme sprigs

5 bay leaves

1 Tbsp whole black peppercorns

Beef stock is another great stock to have on hand. It's the best stock to use for pot roasts and other slowly braised dishes, as its rich flavor complements the meat to create a savory masterpiece.

BEEF STOCK   *Makes 5 quarts*

Preheat the oven to 400°F. Toss the beef bones with the salt, arrange them in a single layer in a roasting pan, and roast until lightly golden brown, about 30 minutes.

While the bones are roasting, heat a frying pan over medium-high heat. Add the onions, cut side down, and sear until they're dark brown. Remove them from the pan and chop. Add the garlic, carrots, celery, leeks, and tomato paste and toss to coat the vegetables.

At the 30-minute point, add the vegetables to the roasting pan and roast for another 30 minutes.

Transfer the roasted bones and vegetables to a stockpot and add the thyme, bay leaves, peppercorns, and just enough water to cover the bones and bring to a simmer over medium-high heat. Turn down the heat to low, use a spoon to skim off any scum that's risen to the top of the stock, and simmer, uncovered, for another 6 hours.

Remove the stock from the heat and allow to cool for 1 hour before straining through a fine-mesh sieve into a clean container, like a mason jar. Refrigerate for up to 1 week or freeze for up to 3 months.

5 pounds beef bones, preferably from the neck or knuckles

5 tsp salt

3 onions, cut in half widthwise

5 garlic cloves

4 carrots, chopped

3 celery stalks, chopped

1 leek, chopped

5 tsp tomato paste

6 thyme sprigs

5 bay leaves

1 Tbsp whole black peppercorns

Veal stock is one of the foundational stocks in modern European-style kitchens. It is used predominantly as a reduction for Demi-Glace (page 364), which is the base for many sauces in French, Italian, British, and German kitchens.

VEAL STOCK *Makes 5 quarts*

Preheat the oven to 400°F. Toss the veal bones with the salt, arrange them in a single layer in a roasting pan, and roast until lightly golden brown, about 30 minutes.

While the bones are roasting, heat a frying pan over medium-high heat. Add the onions, cut side down, and sear until they're dark brown. Remove from the pan and chop coarsely. Add the carrots, celery, leeks, and tomato paste and toss to coat the vegetables.

At the 30-minute point, add the vegetables to the roasting pan and roast for another 30 minutes.

Transfer the roasted bones and vegetables to a stockpot with the thyme, bay leaves, and peppercorns, add enough water to just cover the bones, and bring to a simmer over medium-high heat. Turn down the heat to low, use a spoon to skim off any scum that's risen to the top of the stock, and simmer, uncovered, for another 6 hours.

Remove the stock from the heat and allow to cool for 1 hour before straining through a fine-mesh sieve into a clean container, like a mason jar. Refrigerate for up to 1 week or freeze for up to 3 months.

5 pounds veal bones, preferably from the neck or knuckles

5 tsp salt

3 onions, cut in half widthwise

4 carrots, chopped

3 celery stalks, chopped

1 leek, chopped

5 tsp tomato paste

6 thyme sprigs

5 bay leaves

1 Tbsp whole black peppercorns

A broth is similar to a stock except it has more flavor, more oomph, more balls. It is perfect for adding sparingly when reheating a ragù to loosen the sauce. It is used in risotto because the intense aroma encapsulates every grain of that rice and hugs it in an embrace of flavorful deliciousness. It is the best base for soups, as a well-made broth needs only a garnish and perhaps a little more salt to be eaten as is. Broth gives strength where stock gives sustenance, which may sound like little difference, but a stock just isn't as hardcore as a broth. We make broth onsite at the shop, and sell it fresh by the quart as well as hot from an urn in coffee cups. Customers go nuts for bone broth during the colder months, and while we're happy to make it for them, it's quite easy to create at home.

BONE BROTH   *Makes 4 quarts*

Preheat the oven to 375°F. Arrange the chicken and beef bones in a single layer in a roasting pan and roast until golden brown, about 45 minutes. Remove the bones from the oven and place them in a large stockpot. Don't wipe out the roasting pan.

Place the onions, garlic, carrots, celery, parsnips, and tomato paste in the roasting pan, stir to pick up some of the fat from the bones, and roast, stirring once or twice, until the vegetables are golden brown, about 45 minutes. Remove the pan from the oven and scrape the vegetables into the stockpot.

Pour 1 cup of the water into the roasting pan, place it over medium heat, and bring to a simmer. Use a wooden spoon to scrape the browned bits from the bottom of the pan and add them to the stockpot.

Pour the remaining 4½ cups water over the bones and vegetables in the stockpot. If the bones aren't completely covered with the water, add just enough to cover them. Add the peppercorns, salt, thyme, and bay leaves, and place over medium heat. Bring the broth to a simmer, then turn down the heat to low so it is *just* bubbling, maybe a bubble or two every 10 seconds. Allow the broth to simmer, uncovered, at this temperature for at least 8 hours, carefully skimming off any scum from the surface with a spoon.

After 8 hours, strain the broth first through a large colander and then through a fine-mesh sieve into a clean container. (This extra step helps ensure a clearer broth.) Season to taste, adding more salt to your liking. Refrigerate for up to 1 week or freeze for up to 3 months.

2½ pounds chicken carcass bones

1 pound beef knuckle bones, cut in small pieces (ask your butcher)

1 pound beef marrow bones, cut in small pieces (ask your butcher)

2 Spanish onions, cut in quarters

2 garlic bulbs, cut in half widthwise

4 medium carrots, cut in half widthwise

4 celery stalks, cut in half widthwise

2 parsnips, cut in half widthwise

2 Tbsp tomato paste

5½ cups water, cold (divided)

2 Tbsp whole peppercorns

5 tsp salt

8 thyme sprigs

6 bay leaves

Demi-glace literally means "half glaze" and it is made by reducing a rich stock—usually veal or beef—to create a concentrated, highly flavorful liquid that can be swirled into or drizzled over other foods or used as a base for other sauces.

VEAL DEMI-GLACE *Makes 2 cups*

Place the veal stock in a saucepan, uncovered, over medium-low heat and reduce until the sauce coats the back of a spoon, up to 8 hours.

Remove from the heat, strain through a fine-mesh sieve, and allow to cool to room temperature. Use immediately, or pour into an airtight container and refrigerate for up to 3 weeks or freeze for up to 6 months.

1 batch Veal Stock (page 362)

This sauce builds on the flavors already developed by the straight-ahead demi-glace with the introduction of red wine. This is the perfect sauce to complement a beef roast.

RED WINE DEMI-GLACE *Makes enough for 6 to 8 servings*

Melt 1 Tbsp of the butter in a medium pot over medium heat. Add the beef trimmings (or ground beef) and cook until browned. Stir in the shallots, turn down the heat to medium-low, and sweat the shallots until translucent, about 5 minutes.

Drain the meat and shallots through a fine-mesh strainer and discard the rendered fat. Return the meat and the shallots to the pot over medium heat.

Add the wine, thyme, and bay leaves. Reduce the wine by half, then add the demi-glace. Bring to a simmer and reduce until the sauce coats the back of a spoon. Season to taste, then strain through a fine-mesh sieve into a clean pot.

Whisk in the remaining 1 Tbsp of butter until the sauce is emulsified. Serve immediately, or pour into an airtight container and refrigerate for up to 3 weeks or freeze for up to 6 months.

2 Tbsp butter, cold, cubed (divided)

½ pound beef trimmings (ask your butcher for some) or ground beef

½ cup minced shallots

1 cup red wine

4 thyme sprigs

2 bay leaves

½ cup Veal Demi-Glace (above)

How to Thicken Sauces

Knowing how to thicken a sauce can be very helpful. Here are a few techniques you can use at home.

REDUCTION: Simmering a liquid to evaporate the water (and in a meat-based liquid, to concentrate the natural collagen) not only thickens the sauce but also concentrates its flavor. A demi-glace (see facing page) uses this technique. It's best used with veal or beef stock because these stocks have the highest concentration of collagen; a reduced chicken stock will be much lighter. I find a neutral stock makes the best reduction because it can be seasoned afterward if needed; too flavorful a stock may become overwhelming when reduced.

CORNSTARCH SLURRY: Mixing equal parts cornstarch and a cold liquid (most commonly water) to form a slurry and adding it slowly to a sauce gives it body. This technique is best used when you want to thicken a liquid that is already very flavorful, because cornstarch doesn't add any flavor. I often use it to thicken a braising liquid and serve the thickened sauce or gravy alongside the roast that was cooked in it.

ROUX: Cooking equal parts flour and fat (most commonly butter) over medium heat until it has the consistency of toothpaste and then adding a hot liquid and whisking well to avoid lumps creates a thickener with a slightly nutty flavor. This method is great for thickening turkey and chicken gravies (and adding finely diced giblets or livers to the roux as you brown it gives the whole gravy more flavor).

BEURRE MANIÉ: Kneading equal parts flour and softened butter by hand to create a soft, malleable paste and whisking it into a sauce adds body and a soft sheen. It's best used as you would the cornstarch slurry, for sauces and braising liquids that you want to thicken without the glossy look that cornstarch can impart.

This sauce is great on a striploin or tenderloin steak. I like to cook the steak in a heavy-bottomed pan and then deglaze the pan with this sauce before pouring it all over the meat. Pickled peppercorns can be found in most grocery stores alongside the pickles, but if you can't find it, substitute 2 tablespoons of freshly cracked peppercorns.

BRANDY PEPPERCORN SAUCE *Makes enough for 6 to 8 servings*

Melt 1 Tbsp of the butter in a medium pot over medium heat. Add the beef trimmings (or ground beef) and pepper, and cook until the beef is browned. Stir in the shallots, turn down the heat to medium-low, and sweat the shallots until translucent, about 5 minutes.

Drain the meat and shallots through a fine-mesh strainer and discard the rendered fat. Return the meat and the shallots to the pot over medium heat.

Add the brandy, and then the bay leaves and thyme. Reduce the brandy by half, then add the demi-glace. Bring to a simmer and reduce until the sauce coats the back of a spoon. Add the cream and bring back to a simmer, then strain through a fine-mesh sieve into a clean pot.

Stir in the peppercorns, then whisk in the remaining 1 Tbsp butter until the sauce is emulsified. Season with salt and pepper, to taste. Serve immediately, or pour into an airtight container and refrigerate for up to 3 weeks or freeze for up to 6 months.

2 Tbsp butter, cold, cubed (divided)

½ pound beef trimmings (ask your butcher for some) or ground beef

1 Tbsp freshly cracked black pepper

½ cup minced shallots

½ cup brandy

2 bay leaves

4 thyme sprigs

½ cup Veal Demi-Glace (page 364)

¼ cup heavy (35%) cream

2 Tbsp pickled green peppercorns

Salt and pepper

A good tomato sauce is easy to make and way tastier than any versions you can buy in a jar. And it's incredibly versatile: toss it with pasta, use it as a base for a meat ragù, or pour it over a pan-seared chicken breast. Use the best-quality canned plum tomatoes you can find—San Marzano from Italy are great, but I've had delicious results from Californian tomatoes as well. Your kitchen will smell wonderful while the sauce is simmering, so invite some friends to sip wine with you while you prepare dinner.

BASIC TOMATO SAUCE   *Makes 2 quarts*

Place a large saucepan over medium-low heat and warm the oil. Add the onions, stir, and cover the pot. Allow the onions to sweat until translucent, about 5 minutes, then stir in the garlic. Cover and sweat until the onions and garlic are almost golden, about 10 minutes.

Add the tomatoes and their juice and season with salt and pepper. Bring the tomatoes to a simmer, and use a wooden spoon or a potato masher to break them up. Simmer, uncovered, until the sauce is slightly thickened, about 30 minutes.

Use a food mill to process the tomato sauce into a clean pot (see note), discarding any seeds or skin. Return the sauce to the stovetop to simmer and add the basil leaves. Allow the basil to infuse for about 5 minutes, then turn off the heat. Serve immediately, or pour into an airtight container and refrigerate for up to 2 weeks or freeze for up to 6 months.

6 Tbsp olive oil

½ Spanish onion, finely minced

3 garlic cloves, minced

2 (each 28 ounces) cans whole plum tomatoes

Salt and pepper

6 whole basil leaves

NOTE: For best results, use a food mill to separate out the seeds and skin, which can give the sauce a bitter flavor. If you don't have a food mill, use the potato masher to break up the sauce as much as possible and serve it a little chunky. Avoid using a blender, which will purée the seeds and could lead to a bitter tomato sauce.

Use this sauce to marinate thinly cut short ribs or as an ingredient in a stir-fry. Start the sauce the day before you plan to use it so the flavor has time to develop.

TERIYAKI SAUCE *Makes about 2 cups*

8 green onions, chopped

3 Tbsp chopped ginger

2½ Tbsp chopped shallots

1½ Tbsp chopped garlic

1½ cups soy sauce

¼ cup mirin

3 Tbsp honey

2½ Tbsp brown sugar

1 tsp sesame oil

1½ Tbsp cornstarch

1½ Tbsp cold water

In a saucepan over medium heat, mix together the green onions, ginger, shallots, and garlic into the soy sauce and bring to a boil. Turn off the heat, transfer to a nonreactive container, and refrigerate overnight.

Strain the soy mixture through a fine-mesh sieve into a clean saucepan and set over medium heat. Add the mirin, honey, and brown sugar, and bring to a boil. Turn down the heat to low and mix in the sesame oil.

In a small bowl, combine the cornstarch and water to make a slurry. Slowly add it to the sauce, stirring constantly, to thicken. Simmer until the sauce coats the back of a spoon, then allow to cool to room temperature. Serve immediately, or pour into an airtight container and refrigerate for up to 2 weeks or freeze for up to 6 months.

My dad has never made barbecue sauce, but he definitely uses it. And I thought it sounded cool to have his name in this recipe title. Now that I'm a father myself, I suppose this is *my* barbecue sauce, which I use for my Baked Saucy Ribs (page 130) or even as a burger topping.

DAD'S BBQ SAUCE   *Makes 1 quart*

1 Tbsp vegetable oil

1 cup diced white onions

2 tsp minced garlic

1 Tbsp tomato paste

½ cup packed dark brown sugar

1 tsp salt

Pinch chili flakes

1¼ cups ketchup

1 cup unseasoned rice wine vinegar

½ cup fancy molasses

¼ cup yellow mustard

1 Tbsp Frank's RedHot sauce

Heat the oil in a saucepan over medium heat. Add the onions and sauté until caramelized, 5 to 7 minutes. Add the garlic and sauté for another 3 minutes, then add the tomato paste and cook for 3 more minutes.

Add the sugar, salt, chili flakes, ketchup, vinegar, molasses, mustard, and hot sauce and simmer, uncovered, for 20 minutes.

Remove from the heat, allow to cool slightly, and purée with an immersion blender. Use immediately or pour into an airtight container and refrigerate for up to 2 weeks.

Use this mild fresh salsa as a side sauce for grilled meats, especially chicken breast and pork chops.

TOMATO SALSA   *Makes about 1½ cups*

6 plum tomatoes, seeds removed and finely diced

½ cup finely diced seedless cucumber

¼ cup finely diced red onions

Grated zest and juice of 1 lemon

2 Tbsp finely chopped chives

Salt and pepper

Place all the ingredients in a bowl, stir well to combine, and allow to marinate, covered, for 1 hour at room temperature before serving. Leftover salsa will keep refrigerated in an airtight container for 5 days but I don't recommend freezing it (you'll eat it before that need arises anyway).

Serve this vinaigrette in a bowl as a dipping sauce for Whole Roasted Suckling Pig (page 338) or Simple Poached Chicken (page 66).

SOY GINGER VINAIGRETTE   *Makes just about 1½ cups*

½ cup light Japanese soy sauce (shoyu)

½ cup sherry vinegar

2 Tbsp vegetable oil

½ cup sliced green onions

1 heaping Tbsp minced ginger (use a microplane)

In a bowl, whisk together all the ingredients and serve. Refrigerate leftover vinaigrette in an airtight container for up to 2 weeks.

Originally from Argentina, chimichurri is an herb pesto of sorts that is a traditional sauce for grilled steaks. It is also delicious on beef heart, pork, and chicken kebabs.

CHIMICHURRI   *Makes about 1 cup*

2 cups finely sliced Italian parsley	¼ cup finely diced shallots	1 tsp pepper
¼ cup finely sliced cilantro	2 Tbsp finely diced garlic	1 cup olive oil
¼ cup finely sliced oregano	1 Tbsp salt	⅔ cup red wine vinegar

Place all the ingredients in a food processor and purée until emulsified. Serve immediately, or store in an airtight container and refrigerate for up to 2 weeks or freeze for up to 3 months.

Use with butterflied chicken or lamb chops or as a side sauce for grilled meats. This is also delicious with poached fish.

HERB PESTO   *Makes about 1 cup*

1 cup Italian parsley leaves, picked and washed	½ cup chopped green onions	½ tsp chili flakes
1 cup basil leaves, picked and washed	1 tsp capers	Salt and pepper
2 Tbsp tarragon leaves, picked and washed	1 tsp Dijon mustard	½ cup olive oil
	Grated zest of 1 lemon	

Place parsley, basil, tarragon, green onions, capers, mustard, zest, chili flakes, and salt and pepper to taste in a blender or small food processor. With the motor running, slowly drizzle in the oil, puréeing until the pesto is smooth and creamy. Season with salt and pepper, if necessary. Serve immediately, or store in an airtight container and refrigerate for up to 2 weeks or freeze for up to 3 months.

Bulgogi is a Korean dish of thinly cut meat, usually beef short rib meat or pork belly, that is grilled right before serving. This is my version of the marinade that gives those cuts a depth of flavor. If your grocery store doesn't carry gochujang (a spicy pepper and fermented bean paste essential in Korean cooking), I recommend sourcing it online.

BULGOGI MARINADE *Makes 2 cups*

4 garlic cloves, minced

1 cup finely chopped green onions

½ cup diced Spanish onions

¼ cup diced pears

1 Tbsp finely diced ginger

2 Tbsp brown sugar

1 Tbsp pepper

½ cup gochujang

2 Tbsp unseasoned rice wine vinegar

1½ tsp Japanese soy sauce (shoyu)

1½ Tbsp sesame oil

In a food processor, purée the garlic, green and Spanish onions, pears, and ginger until smooth. Add the sugar, pepper, gochujang, vinegar, soy sauce, and sesame oil and purée until emulsified. Refrigerate in an airtight container for up to 2 weeks or freeze for up to 3 months.

This is a basic all-purpose wet marinade, excellent on beef kebabs, hanger steak, and chicken breast.

HERB AND GARLIC MARINADE *Makes 2 cups*

⅓ cup finely diced green onions

¼ cup finely diced white onions

2 Tbsp chopped garlic

¼ cup chopped Italian parsley

2 Tbsp chopped rosemary

2 Tbsp chopped thyme

1½ Tbsp grated lemon zest

1 Tbsp salt

1 tsp pepper

2½ Tbsp lemon juice

1 cup olive oil

Place the green and white onions, garlic, parsley, rosemary, thyme, zest, salt, and pepper in a food processor. Add the lemon juice and purée. With the motor running, slowly add the oil until the marinade is emulsified. Refrigerate in an airtight container for up to 2 weeks or freeze for up to 3 months.

Angelo, an electrician associate of the shop from Cuba, often talked to me about the best steak sauces having tons of lime juice and cilantro. I tinkered for a bit to develop this recipe, and now we sell tons of bavette and flank steak rubbed in this marinade. It's also excellent with skirt steak, pork shoulder chops, and chicken legs.

CUBAN MARINADE   *Makes 2 cups*

1 cup chopped cilantro

¾ cup chopped Italian parsley

2 Tbsp grated lemon zest

1½ Tbsp grated lime zest

½ cup finely diced red onion

¼ cup chopped green onions

3 Tbsp chopped garlic

¼ cup salt

2 Tbsp pepper

2 Tbsp Spanish paprika

¼ cup lemon juice

¼ cup lime juice

1 cup olive oil

In a medium bowl, mix together the cilantro, parsley, lemon and lime zests, red and green onions, garlic, salt, pepper, and paprika. Add the lemon and lime juices and oil, and mix to combine. Refrigerate in an airtight container for up to 2 weeks or freeze for up to 3 months.

Another great all-purpose marinade. Use it on pork tenderloins, chicken wings, chicken kebabs, and spatchcocked Cornish hens.

HONEY MUSTARD MARINADE   *Makes 2 cups*

1 cup Dijon mustard

½ cup grainy mustard

1 cup honey

3 Tbsp prepared horseradish

3 Tbsp finely chopped rosemary

In a medium bowl, whisk together all the ingredients until emulsified. Refrigerate in an airtight container for up to 2 weeks or freeze for up to 3 months.

I call this my Middle Eastern marinade because it contains the warm spices of coriander, cumin, and fennel, all popular in the cuisine of the Cradle of Civilization, and works especially well with lamb. Use this on lamb leg, lamb chops, bavette steak, and whole chicken.

MIDDLE EASTERN MARINADE *Makes 2 cups*

½ cup finely sliced green onions

½ cup chopped garlic

3 Tbsp grated lemon zest

2 Tbsp chopped thyme

1 cup olive oil

¼ cup lemon juice

4 tsp salt

1 Tbsp ground coriander

1 Tbsp ground fennel seeds

1 Tbsp ground cumin

2 tsp pepper

1½ tsp ground cinnamon

In a food processor, purée the green onions, garlic, lemon zest, thyme, oil, and lemon juice until the mixture has the consistency of pesto. Add the salt, coriander, fennel seeds, cumin, pepper, and cinnamon, and blend until emulsified. Refrigerate in an airtight container for up to 2 weeks or freeze for up to 3 months.

If shawarma were facing a run for its money by another other meaty street snack in Toronto, it would definitely be facing off against souvlaki. Commonly made with chicken or pork, skewered, then grilled, the addition of this marinade really pops the flavor profile.

SOUVLAKI MARINADE *Makes about 1½ cups*

¼ cup finely diced garlic

¼ cup salt

1½ Tbsp dried oregano

1 Tbsp pepper

2 tsp paprika

1 cup olive oil

6 Tbsp lemon juice

2 Tbsp hot mustard

In a food processor, purée all the ingredients until emulsified. Refrigerate in an airtight container for up to 2 weeks or freeze for up to 3 months.

The south of France is a glorious place and makes use of delicious ingredients such as olives, rosemary, and capers. This recipe was developed with these Provençal flavors in mind and is great on lamb leg cutlets, chicken legs, and lamb chops.

PROVENÇAL MARINADE *Makes 2 cups*

½ cup sun-dried tomatoes, rehydrated

1½ Tbsp minced garlic

1 Tbsp pitted black olives

2 tsp capers

1 tsp grated lemon zest

1 Tbsp chopped rosemary

1 Tbsp chopped thyme

1 tsp dried marjoram

1½ Tbsp salt

1 tsp pepper

½ cup olive oil

½ cup lemon juice

In a food processor, purée all of the ingredients. Refrigerate in an airtight container for up to 2 weeks or freeze for up to 3 months.

Shawarma is a dish of marinated and slowly roasted meats served with rice or in a pita, and it has to be one of the most popular street foods in the world. In Toronto, it seems like we have more shawarma shops than Starbucks! This marinade is great on chicken thighs and beef kebabs.

SHAWARMA MARINADE *Makes 2 cups*

¼ cup minced garlic

3 Tbsp finely diced red onions

¼ cup chopped Italian parsley

4 tsp salt

2 tsp pepper

2 tsp ground cumin

2 tsp paprika

1 tsp ground turmeric

1 tsp chili flakes

½ tsp ground cinnamon

1¼ cups olive oil

In a medium bowl, whisk together all the ingredients until well combined. Refrigerate in an airtight container for up to 2 weeks or freeze for up to 3 months.

Use on roast beef, roast pork, and whole chicken.

HERB SALT *Makes just over 2 cups*

4 bay leaves	1 Tbsp chopped thyme	1 Tbsp minced garlic
1 Tbsp chopped rosemary	1 tsp chopped sage	2 cups kosher salt

In a food processor, purée the bay leaves, rosemary, thyme, sage, and garlic at high speed until well combined. Add the salt and pulse until the mixture is slightly green. Refrigerate in an airtight container for up to 2 weeks.

Use on pork ribs, whole chicken, and chicken breast.

BBQ DRY RUB *Makes just over 3 cups*

2 cups kosher salt	3 Tbsp garlic powder	2 tsp rubbed dried thyme
1 cup sweet paprika	4 tsp dried rosemary	
3 Tbsp onion powder	1 Tbsp pepper	

Mix all the ingredients in a large bowl until well combined. Keep at room temperature in an airtight container for up to 2 months.

Use with ham, chicken, and pork loin. If you want to brine a large cut, like a whole turkey, multiply the recipe by 10.

ALL-PURPOSE BRINE   *Makes 2 cups*

3 juniper berries	1 garlic clove	1 Tbsp salt
1 star anise	1 rosemary sprig	2 tsp sugar
1 tsp peppercorns	2 cups water	1 bay leaf

Preheat the oven to 350°F.

Spread the juniper, star anise, and peppercorns on a baking tray and toast until fragrant, about 10 minutes. Remove from the oven and set aside.

With the side of a knife, smash the garlic clove with the rosemary.

Place the water in a small pot, add the toasted spices, garlic, rosemary, salt, sugar, and bay leaf and bring to a boil over high heat. Immediately turn off the heat and allow to cool completely before using. If you're using the brine immediately, leave the spices in. If not, strain out the spices after 8 hours. Refrigerate in an airtight container for up to 2 weeks.

Use with pork roast for cassoulet and pork chops for smoking.

SWEET PORK BRINE   *Makes 2 quarts*

1¼ cups salt	2 tsp mustard seeds	1 tsp coriander seeds
½ cup brown sugar	1 tsp whole peppercorns	½ tsp whole cloves
2 garlic cloves, cut in half	1 tsp whole allspice	1 bay leaf
1 cinnamon stick	1 tsp ground ginger	2 quarts water

Place all the ingredients in a medium saucepan over medium heat and bring to a simmer. Cook for 5 minutes, then turn off the heat and allow to cool. Refrigerate in an airtight container for up to 2 weeks.

ACKNOWLEDGMENTS

THIS BOOK WOULD NOT HAVE BEEN POSSIBLE without the help of many people. I would say there are too many to mention, but that's a cop-out. So . . .

Family

My delightful wife, Alia, has stood by my side from the first day I had the idea to open the butcher shop. She saw potential in me that sometimes I didn't see myself and pushed me to become a better business owner, chef, and butcher. She is my editor, confidante, consultant, recipe taste tester, best friend, and partner. I owe her so much and will continue to repay her with love, respect, and meat. Our son, Desmond, who lights up any room he enters and eats anything I put in front of him, has given me a reason to grow up and be a man he can look up to. I am at my best with him in my life.

My mother and father have been massive supporters of my career choices. Despite the fact that I didn't take the scholarly path they (probably) wanted me to, their belief in me has never wavered. My sisters, Kate and Mary, and brother, Chris, and their partners—Matt, Aaron, and Danielle respectively—have shown me continued love and support. Their children—Alice, Henry, Molly, Lucy, Harry, and Penny—are excellent young people who will someday make excellent Sanagan's employees. I love you all.

Alia's family have also been huge supporters and promoters of all that I do, and have enfolded me into their family and its traditions. Karlene and Andrew have welcomed me lovingly into their home as a son, sharing their love and letting me help with holiday feasts and other delicious meals. Dominique and Alan are wonderful new siblings for me, and their children, Henry and Josie, are Desmond's de facto siblings.

Work

In the food business, you spend more time with the people you work with than your family at home, so it pays to surround yourself with good people. My career has allowed me to create relationships that I cherish with some of the hardest-working and most talented people you could ever hope to meet. I want to thank Brian Knapp, the Chief Operating Officer of Sanagan's. Brian has been with me since Sanagan's barely had any fridge space. He has been integral in growing Sanagan's into what it is today, and what it will become. Claire Renouf, our faithful Store Manager in Kensington and longtime customer-favorite, is our rock. Our Head Butcher Jerry Kokorudz, a strong Sanagan's leader and a great butcher, helped me assemble many of the cuts seen here. Chef Anne Hynes, whose delicious recipes are scattered throughout this book, has been a tremendous asset to the Sanagan's family. And Scott Draper, our Charcutier, has a wealth of knowledge and his fantastic French-centric charcuterie menu allows Sanagan's to stand above the crowd. Quite a few people have come and gone (and come back again) to Sanagan's, and I would like to acknowledge every employee's contribution to the growth of the shop. Thanks to you all!

Mentors, Chefs, Farmers, and Friends

Thank you for guidance, direction, inspiration, and for teaching me to cook, butcher, farm, and laugh. In no particular order: Massimo Capra, Jason Bangerter, Sean MacMahon, Jay Schubert, Murray Thunberg, James and Ian Sculthorpe, Rob Pawley, Neil Vandendool, Jean-Jacques Quinsac, Shane and Brenda Forsyth, Mark Trealout, Dave Haman, Rajiv Surendra, and the Meat Club. Special thanks go to Scott McKowen and Christina Poddubiuk for creating the design vision for Sanagan's, much of which is woven throughout this book. Also, thank you to all the people who helped put together the old and new shops, friends who have supported and promoted us over the years and eaten our tested recipes, professional advisors, suppliers of fantastic Ontario products, and everyone else who has been involved in this journey.

Cookbook Team

Everyone at Appetite has been a pleasure to work with, and I thank them for their patience while working with a rookie. Thanks to Zoe Maslow for believing in me and giving this project the green light. Thanks to Lucy Kenward for taking a messy manuscript and forming it into a cohesive text, to Leah Springate for the most excellent book design, and to Lindsay Paterson for facilitating everything. An extra special thanks to Peter Chou for the beautiful photography and to Ruth Gangbar for making the recipes look (and taste) so good.

Customers

Finally, I wouldn't be anywhere without the loyal support of all of our customers, many of whom have been with us since day one, and those who continue to discover us every day. Toronto is the best city anywhere, and its people respect and support each other. The food in this city rivals anywhere else in the world, from fine dining to strip-mall takeout spots. I have been fortunate enough to travel all over the globe, and no matter where I go, I always end up missing this city, its people, and their food. I am so proud to be a part of the food industry in Toronto, and it's our amazing customers who continue to shop with us and support small, family farms and the quality meats we are lucky to purvey.

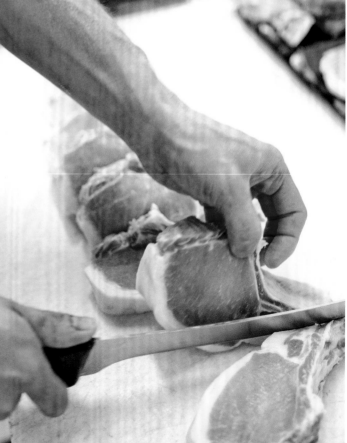

GENERAL INDEX

A

antibiotics, 12

B

beef
    breeds, 175–76
    buying, 176–77
    cooking methods, 34–35, 210–12
    cuts, 180–85, 188–93
    feet, 263
    grades, 11
    grain-fed, 12
    grass-fed, 10
    hamburgers, preparing, 221
    heart, 262
    kidney, 262
    liver, 262
    marrow bones, 263
    ordering roast, 330
    ordering shank, 333
    organic, 11
    oxtail, 263
    raising, 173–75, 178
    steak, about, 186
    steak, cooking methods, 210–12
    tongue, 263
beurre manié, 365
brains: veal, 264
braising, 36
breading cutlets, 122–23
brines, 359
broths, 359
butchers, 9
butchery techniques, 22–25

butter, clarified, 328
butter: beurre manié, 365
buying meat, 9–13

C

carving chicken, 26–27
cattle. *See* beef
caul fat, 164
charcuterie, 281–85
chicken
    breeds, 48–49
    buying, 49
    carving, 26–27
    cooking methods, 32
    cuts, 50–54
    deboning legs, 25
    free-range, free run, 11
    gizzard, 265
    heart, 265
    liver, 265
    pastured, 11
    plucking, 56–57
    raising, 47–48
    spatchcocking, 24
    ten-cut, 23
    trussing, 22
cornstarch slurry, 365
curing salt, 294

D

deboning chicken legs, 25
duck
    heart, 265
    liver, 265

E

ears: pork, 262

F

feet: beef, 263

G

game
    buying, 238–41
    regulations about, 237–38
    types, 238–41
ghee, 328
gizzard, chicken, 265
goat, 326
goose, 265
grilling, 37
ground meats, 13

H

halah meats, 12
hamburgers: preparation tips,
    221
harissa, 156
heart
    beef, 262
    chicken, 265
    duck, 265
    goose, 265
    pork, 261
hormones, 12–13

K

kidneys
    beef, 262

RECIPE INDEX